I'll Be Back
When Summer's
in the Meadow

A World War II Chronicle

Volume I
1942-1943

Compiled and Edited by
Melanie A. Ippolito

2020

First Author Edition

ISBN 9798612411505

This work was first designed, produced, and published in the United States of America by the Merriam Press in 2011.
merriam-press.com

Contents

The Editor

August 2011

Melanie Ippolito lives in upstate New York with her husband Len. Their two grown sons and many of their extended family live close-by, and she still has ties to her cousins in Northern Ireland. Melanie is a graduate of the University at Buffalo with a BA in Sociology. She has worked in a number of public libraries throughout the years. This is the first volume of a World War II trilogy.

Dedication

This book is dedicated in loving memory
to my mother and father
and to my sister
Colleen

Muriel and Ray
Colleen and Melanie
1951

Acknowledgments

I wish to thank my family members for their support.
I am grateful for the encouragement and counsel given me by
Carol Coburn, Sharon Gibson and Linda Quinn.
Katherine Patterson for "planting the seed."
And special thanks to my publisher,
Ray Merriam.

Introduction

I was thirteen when I saw them. We had recently moved and the letters, hundreds of them tied up into neat little bundles, were spilling out of two rather battered cardboard boxes in an upstairs closet. I knew immediately what they were as I had heard the story many times. My mother was a war bride from Belfast, Northern Ireland. My dad had been stationed at Musgrave Park with Harvard's 5th General Hospital in the spring of 1942.

My parents met at a dance at the Albert Whites Ballroom in Belfast. My mom explained, "After staring at me most of the night he had the cheek to ask me to dance at the very end of the very last dance of the evening, and then insisted on seeing me home." My dad told it differently; it took him most of the evening to get up his nerve to approach her.

It was an intense whirlwind of a courtship. They talked of marriage around the time the 5th General was shipping over to England. My mom was just 20 at that time and her parents would not give their permission for her to wed. My grandparents did not want to see their eldest daughter living so far from home. The problem was compounded by the fact that my dad was Roman Catholic and my mom's family was Methodist. My grandparents were convinced that nothing but unhappiness would follow their daughter; they knew of many 'mixed marriages' that had ended in heartache. They were fond of my father, but believed strongly that it could never work. That was a reality in Northern Ireland in the 1940s.

My parents were separated by war for close to three years and for another seven months after the war ended. Their letters written to each other almost daily tell their story. As a thirteen-year-old I respected their privacy and gently put the spilling bundles back into the boxes as best I could. My next encounter with the letters happened, sadly, shortly after my mother's death at just 65 years of age in the spring of 1988. My father, brother and sisters and I were sorting through Mom's belongings. Toward the back of her closet I came upon the letters. When my father saw me tucking some of the bundles back into the now seriously crumbling boxes, he told me he wanted to burn them. I

Albert Whites Ballroom, Belfast.

do not know if it was his grief that made him say that, but I pleaded that he should give himself time to think before destroying something that was obviously so precious to our mother. I told him there had to be a reason Mom kept the letters safe for so many years.

Ten years later, in March of 1998, my dad passed away just days before his 81st birthday.

Once again my sisters, brother and I had the sad task of going through a parent's belongings, the letters were still there...

My father had never spoken much about the war. Like many others of his generation he wanted to forget the horror he had seen.

One story my dad did tell us has stayed with me. Dad took my mother to eat at a hotel in New York City just after she arrived in America. Mom burst into tears when she saw all of the food. She was thinking of her family back in Ireland doing without. Many times, when I was a young child, I watched as my mother packed up boxes of food to send to her family in Ireland.

My mother was 16 years old when on September 3, 1939 the United Kingdom declared war on Germany. On October 25, 1940 the first sirens sounded in Belfast and again over twenty times more before the first bombs fell. In April and May of 1941 Belfast endured over ten hours of bombing by the German Luftwaffe. On Easter Tuesday alone at least 900 people in Belfast were killed during close to six hours of bombing. Belfast's shipyards and munitions factories made it an attractive target. My mom, caught away from home during one of the raids, spent long hours in an air raid shelter while her parents were frantic with worry.

Much of what they experienced I learned from the letters. The letters were self-censored by my parents and later read by army and civilian censors. In one of my father's early letters home he wrote, "All the things I would like to write about would be censored." Some of the letters did have words cut out of them by the civilian or army censors. These are indicated by the word *censored*.

I will start at the beginning. My parents saved most of the letters they wrote to one another. My grandmother kept some of the letters her son wrote to her, especially those written in 1942, but I have very few that she wrote to my father. Since they were in the boxes along with several from other relatives, I can only surmise that my mother had asked my grandmother if she could have them.

Many of the approximately 2,000 letters have been edited for content and space, and a few for privacy considerations. Some names have been changed for reasons of privacy. Nothing of historical or sociological significance has been omitted.

—Melanie A. Ippolito
August 2011

1942

MY father, Raymond, born in March of 1917, grew up in Lockport, a small town near Buffalo, New York. His parents were Benjamin and Jane Friscia. He had three sisters, Josephine, Rose and Dorothy. Dad was inducted into the army in April of 1941 and sent to Fort Bragg near Raleigh, North Carolina.

Fort Bragg
Monday, March 24, 1942

Dear Mother,

I've been sleeping all day catching up on the sleep I lost during the weekend. I had a wonderful time but it's a good thing I don't do it more often or I would be run ragged. The trip back was very rough but I didn't mind. In New York I had a three quarter hour layover. I met 2 other fellows flying up so we had a good time waiting for the plane. I got into camp about 2:30 a.m. so still had time for some sleep.

Fort Bragg. Ray Friscia third from right.

We start classes Friday so I'll be quite busy during the week, if you don't hear from me you'll know the reason. Those doctors expect you to know everything so I will be studying every night from now on. Well, I'll cut this letter short because I'm going to sleep—we have a big weekend ahead of us.

Thanks again for everything, I don't know how to express it but you know what I mean. It was really great to get home and see the family but it's so hard leaving. Tell Dad and the girls and Ben they're really wonderful and thank them for everything also.   —*Loving son, Raymond*

NORTHERN IRELAND

My dad was assigned to the Medical Corps and worked in a lab at the 5th General Army Hospital. He arrived in Northern Ireland on May 12, 1942.

> Wednesday (The rest of the date was censored.)
> I know now the date was May 13, 1942

Dear Mother,

We arrived in Ireland and all is safe and well. Northern Ireland is very beautiful, everything is in bloom. I have never seen so many beautiful flowers in all my life. Their trees are so old, the country is so green and well taken care of, everything is just so.

About our setup I can't say very much only that we have a lovely building for our hospital. It has a big outdated swimming pool, ten tennis courts and two golf courses nearby, so you can see we really have it very nice.

About the people, well, it seems you are in a different world—they are 100 years behind the times. The few cars they have they drive on the left side of the road, the steering wheel is on the right. You see more horse drawn carts and bicycles.

The homes are old and beautiful, especially the estates of the land-holders. I wish you were here to see it all, especially the flowers.

We got our mail today. I received one of your letters postmarked Feb. 18. Keep on sending the paper because they say we will get mail every two weeks. I wrote you a letter when we were on the boat, did you receive it? Did a certain girl write to you?

If you can send me canned food and fruits, all you can. You can't buy any food here, everything is rationed and nights before you go to bed you would like something to eat but can't get it.

Well, that's about all for now. Give regards to all, Dad, Rose, Ben, Jo, Dot, etc. and tell Tom Hanley there are lots of redheads just like him here. —*Loving son, Raymond*

May 22, 1942

Dear Mother,

You know by now that I'm in Northern Ireland. I have been wondering if you have received my letters. I haven't received any mail yet but hope to soon.

We are working in the hospital now and like it very much. The hospital itself is very nice considering everything. I am working in the lab and we are very busy right now. We have a wonderful lab setup and our major is very good to us. If you don't hear from me very often it's because I'll be busy and won't have time to write, so don't worry about me. We have a ---*censored*--- the hospital ----------*censored*-------- bowling green and golf courses. I think we are very lucky to be where we are. Tomorrow I'm going to Belfast to buy a tennis racket & shoes. I had a little trouble with the English money at first but I'm getting the knack of it fast.

The Irish people are very good to us, and the girls are not bad. They play all American music and are starting to dance the way we do. I went to Belfast the other night to a dance and had a very good time. You can't get all the food we got back home but get along very well. About the food I told you to send I want it mostly for night snacks. I would like some pineapple juice, if you send it, don't forget to send everything in cans. I don't need any money—we are getting about 58 dollars a month now and hope soon to get more.

We have a radio in the lab so we get all the news—keep sending the papers so I can read what's going on in town. I have been wondering about the car, I read you can have 3 gallons of gas a week—you can't go far on that. Maybe it's a good thing I'm not home—I wouldn't be able to do anything. I can do more in the army than most civilians and see more too. It's really not bad here. We will be able to go to Belfast more often and Belfast is a very lovely town.

Well, that's about all I can write about, all the things I would like to write would be censored so I'll try to write what I can.

Hope everyone is feeling fine and give my regards to all. Tell them I will write as soon as I find something to write about. Give love to all and hope to hear from you soon. —*Loving son, Raymond*

Sunday, June 7, 1942

Dear Mother,

I received your letter yesterday and was very pleased to hear from you. I wrote in my other letters what I wanted. I would like a little of the food I asked you about. We are getting enough food to eat, it's only at night the stores close early and you can't buy any.

Oh, about the paper, keep sending it because I receive it once or twice a month, and even though it's a little late it's really good to get a home paper.

Mother, when you write to me write on only one side of the paper because the censors cut out words on both sides of the page.

Give my regards to everyone and tell them I'll write as soon as possible. I hope Dad and the girls are fine, hoping to hear from you soon.   —*Loving son, Raymond*

Lockport, NY
June 17, 1942

Dear Son,

Yesterday I received your first letter and this morning your airmail letter and you can't believe how pleased I am to hear from you. I told all the neighbors about it.

As soon as I can I will send you the paper for your film and also the rolls. Tomorrow I will send you a box. I won't tell you what it contains but if you are pleased with it let me know and I will send more. We are supposed to send no more than 11 lbs. at one time. Please let me know when you receive the box so I can judge how long it takes for you to receive it. Ray, I hope you are receiving the papers because I have been sending them right along. It came over the radio today that they passed the law to raise the soldiers' pay starting the first of June. If you want anything else please let me know and I will be glad to send it to you. Grandmother and all the family are pleased that I heard from you. I'm closing my letter for the time being. Hope this letter will find you in the best of health. Good-bye, good luck and God bless you, my son. —*Your Mother*

July 26, 1942

Dear Mother,

I finally found some time to write a few lines, honest, you never have one minute to yourself, there is always something to do.

I received the box of film that you sent and also the one box of food. I received the box of food today and boy I could hardly wait to open it up. It was swell, just what I wanted, the cake arrived in good condition. I have everything under lock and key. If possible send the juice and fruit in small cans. We get enough food only our last meal is at 5 o'clock and about 10 o'clock you get a little hungry and boy, that's when it comes in handy. When you make up another box put a can of jam in, also some kind of meat, in small cans. The raisins and prunes are very good, I'll keep them for awhile.

I've been receiving your letters, today I received the one you wrote July 13th so it doesn't take that long.

About the King and Queen, I just missed seeing them by about 2 minutes. I went up to the road and they had just gone by, but maybe I'll get another chance later.

About the cablegram, it only takes 24 to 48 hours for a cablegram to reach here. This is the address to me if needed:

5th General Hospital
AMACUR CHARMING

Each letter stands for something, try to figure it out.

I will send some pictures soon—I have the negatives but can't get much paper here to print them.

It keeps very cool here and it is always raining. I go dancing as much as possible—the only thing is everything closes up at 11 o'clock. I have met a few really swell people and have been invited over to their houses.

Tell the girls it wouldn't kill them if they dropped me a line now and then.

With love I will close, and again, thanks for everything. —*Loving son, Raymond*

August 12, 1942

Dear Mother,

I hope you are not too worried about me not writing, but I just don't seem to find time.

I received two packages, the print paper, newspaper and film you sent airmail. About the pictures, I will send some home soon.

The food was very good. I enjoyed the gum also because we can only get one pack of gum a week. When you send another package I would like a few boxes of candy. I hope I'm not putting you through too much trouble asking for everything, but over here you can't just go into a store and buy anything like back home. Either they're always out of supply or you have to have coupons to buy them. We have no coupons.

I'm still receiving the paper and it feels good to read what's going on, it makes me feel as if I was home again.

About me, it's the same old story, still working hard and when I do get a little time off I get away from it all and try to enjoy myself. This country is beautiful but very dead. All there is to do is go to the show and dance. Everything closes about 10:30 and at 11:00 we have to get the last trolley back to camp because it takes a good hour to walk back. After you're back in the barracks the lights are out so to bed you go and that's the same every night. Blackout begins about 9:30 now and boy, it really gets black here.

Pat said something about Rose and Ben being engaged, I didn't know it was announced yet.

How is Dad, boy, I could use a little of his wine, his special brand. I hope he's not working too hard.

How is the dog? Tell the girls to write.

Hoping everyone is in good health. I will be waiting for my next letters. —*Loving son, Raymond*

August 23, 1942

Dear Mother,

I received your letter the other day (August 6th) also Dot's letter. I was very much surprised to hear from one of my brat sisters. Tell Dot I'm glad she wrote and I hope she was pleased with her birthday telegram.

Since the last time I wrote I received two more packages and boy it was OK. Most of the canned food I am saving in case someday we won't be able to get a full meal. We are getting all we want now so don't worry about me not eating. I would like some cookies—the ones you sent the last time were very good.

How is the dog? I ask about him but you never say anything about him, did something happen to him?

I went to a bathing beauty contest in Bangor and boy, was it fun. The fellow that took my picture for the "Stars & Stripes" was there and took pictures.

I'm still working hard and long hours. This afternoon I did three blood transfusions alone so you see I don't have much time to myself.

Tell everyone hello, I hope to get time to write. Regards to Dad and the "brats."

Thanks again for everything.   —*Loving son, Raymond*

Corp. Friscia
Ireland

Tech. Corp. Raymond Friscia, son of Mr. and Mrs. Benjamin Friscia, 255 East Ave., is featured in an illustrated layout in the Stars and Stripes, service newspaper, with other members of his hospital unit in Northern Ireland. The boys are shown going about their duties ministering to patients of the AEF. In service since April of last year, Corp. Friscia formerly worked at the Merritt plant.

September 2, 1942

Dear Mother,

I received the letters you sent August 11 & 18, I also received Dot's letter. I'm glad Dot enjoyed the cablegram I sent and hope I can be home for her next birthday.

About the food, as I've said before I've received everything so far except the box you mailed August 10th. I'm glad you sent the funny papers in the boxes because I really miss them.

Everything is going along OK here. I'm going out a little more now and seeing Ireland, etc.

Ray Friscia
Musgrave Park, 1942

Last night we had a dance in Belfast at one of the best dance halls in town. I haven't enjoyed myself so much since I've been here. I took my Irish girlfriend with me—in fact I had 5 girls with me, boy, you should hear them talk. One of the girls won second prize in the beauty contest a few weeks ago so you see I couldn't help but enjoy myself. You have a "wolf" in the family, Mother, that's what they all call me.

I'm glad to hear everyone is fine and well, I hope you are not worrying over me because I'm really OK and enjoying myself.

Regards to all and thanks a million for all you are doing for me.
—*Loving son, Raymond*

Thursday, September 10, 1942

Dear Mother,

Please don't send anymore Spam. I hate it and besides that's all they have here in Ireland, the way they feed it to us. —*Loving son, Raymond*

Thursday, September 17, 1942

Dear Mother,

Your mail didn't take that long, only 8 days for the last letter. I received the box you sent, that only took three weeks and boy it really was good.

How do you like the pictures I've sent of my girlfriend? Last night we had another dance and I had a really good time. —*Loving son, Raymond*

October 1, 1942

Dear Mother,

I received your letters of September 14th & 19th and was glad to hear from you. I sent you a telegram yesterday to see if you received the china I sent, you haven't mentioned it as yet.

I received the box you sent with the chicken three weeks ago. The cake and crackers were in excellent condition and really tasted good, in fact everything from home tasted good.

Well, about me there's nothing to say, just the same old thing, nothing new or exciting. The pictures here in Belfast are about a year or two old and I've seen most of them back home. It's very damp and raining everyday now so you just don't feel like going out. It also gets dark sooner and with the blackout it makes things even worse. I'm still working hard and still doing the same work.

Give my love to all, —*Loving son, Raymond*

Thursday, October 8, 1942

Dear Mother,

I'm glad you received the china in perfect condition, I was worried about that.

Please continue sending boxes because now and then the meals are not so hot. If possible I would like a can of Nestlé's hot chocolate.

I have two pictures here in front of me that you sent. Dad looks good but he's getting a few more gray hairs I see. Tell him to take it easy and not work so hard.

I have a slight cold but everyone in Ireland has one, even the Irish. I haven't taken any more pictures because the sun is rationed here also. When it does come out we can't waste it on pictures. They had their summer here a few weeks ago for one day. The sun came out and stayed out for about four hours, so you can see it's very lovely here.

Say hello to everyone for me. —*Love, Raymond*

October 25, 1942

Dear Mother,

I received another box last week, the one with candy, grape juice and cookies, etc. It was very good while it lasted. I hope they will let you continue sending them over, they were saying they might stop sending boxes, but I doubt it.

It's very gloomy here, it rains every day and now to make matters worse it's getting cold.

I've been working in the bacteriology department so have been working a little harder, also doing some studying at night.

Hope everyone is in fine health and spirit. —*Love, Raymond*

November 7, 1942

Dear Mother,

I received your letter a few days ago and it was good to hear from you. This is the first letter I've received in nearly a month. There was an article in the paper saying everything sent from September 5th through October 3rd was lost at sea. I also received your cable. It costs us about $1.50 to send one. —*Love, Raymond*

Monday, November 23, 1942

Dear Mother,

I received the letter you sent October 21st, it took exactly one month. I also received the three boxes, as I stated in my telegram. They were swell. It's good to get some good canned food once in a while.

I'm still OK and feeling fine. I'm seeing Ireland a lot more now and go out quite often. The Red Cross has a dance three times a week now so I go out and enjoy myself. The weather has been very nice lately, I hope it keeps up.

When Mrs. Roosevelt was here I talked with her for a few minutes, she was very nice.

I wish you would send me a picture of the Christmas tree. They don't have Christmas trees here so I guess I'm going to miss it this year. This will probably be the last letter you receive from me before

Christmas so give everyone my regards and wish them a Merry Christmas for me. Words can't express what's in my heart so please don't feel sad that I'm not there. I'll be thinking of you and Dad and the family every minute. I'm hoping to hear from you soon. To the most wonderful mother and father in the world—Merry Christmas and Happy New Year. —*Love, Raymond*

Muriel Mitchell

MY mother, Muriel, born in December of 1922, lived with her parents, A. Victor and Hannah Mitchell, two younger sisters, Olive and Audrey, and their dog named Scamp, on Posnett Street in Belfast, Northern Ireland. Her younger brother, Wilfred, had died years before at the age of 5. My mom was 6 at the time and survived the whooping cough that claimed her little brother.

Their brick row house was similar to its neighbors and located near the center of the city. There was a long narrow hall as you entered the front door. Immediately to the left was a door leading into a sitting room. This was the most formal room in the house and used mainly for company. My mother's piano was in this room. Continuing down the hall to the left was the entrance into the main living quarters. This consisted of a living and dining area, which led into a kitchen or scullery and on to the pantry. On the right side of the dining area there were storage cabinets and built-in shelves. These were under the staircase. Off the scullery was a door leading into a small walled-in concrete backyard. The walls were over 6 feet high and a backdoor led into an alley that connected all of the row houses on the block. The "outhouse" was located behind the scullery but one had to go into the yard and through a short corridor to reach it.

If you continued another few steps down the entrance hall a staircase led up to the second floor, which consisted of two bedrooms and a bathroom. There was a bathtub in the bathroom, a hand basin and a towel rack. They kept chamber pots under the beds. A second flight of stairs led to a third floor. There was a finished attic used as a guestroom with a room toward the back made over as an office for my grandfather. There were coal-burning fireplaces in each room on the first, second and third floor, with the exception of the bathroom. My mother shared a bedroom on the second floor with her two sisters, who were 10 and 12 years old.

My parents saw each other early on Christmas Eve 1942, to say goodbye. The 5th General Hospital was shipping over to England. Several months later my dad would return to Ireland on furlough.

My parents communicated by letter, telegram and telephone. My mother's family did not have a telephone or electricity in their home so my dad would call over to Inglis, the firm at which my mother was employed. She worked there Monday through Friday and Saturday mornings.

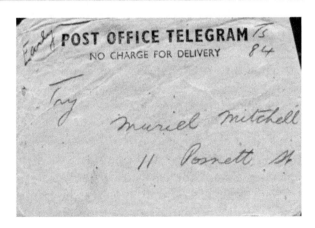

Friday, December 25th, 1942

Dearest Muriel,

It seems so funny that I am writing this letter to you. It's just about 6:00 now and I'm going to get dressed and meet you about 7:30—that's my feeling. Honest, Muriel, I miss you. I knew I loved you but didn't think I loved you as much as I do until I left you. I think about you every minute. I just can't realize I'm not seeing you tonight and other nights.

Christmas Eve we spent getting our hut ready. I went to bed about 11:00 p.m. Christmas Day I slept till 11:00, had dinner, a good one, went to sleep again until 5:00 and then to a beer party. I just got back, it's about 10:00 now. After this letter I'll go to bed. That's my Christmas, I hope you had a more pleasant one than I had.

The place here is really nice, Muriel, but gosh, I really love you. I sent you a telegram yesterday, did you receive it?

We're starting to get things setup. Tomorrow we'll have to start working and boy, there's a lot of it here too.

I haven't been to town yet, it's about two miles away. I hear there is not much down there.

Will write to you again tomorrow and hope to hear from you soon. Regards to all the family. *—All my love, Raymond*

Saturday, December 26th

Dearest Muriel,

Just a few lines to let you know that I'm OK. I received a lot of mail from home today, also three boxes of food and Christmas presents. I wish I was there so you could have some of it.

I wrote and told my mother about us, I'll let you know what she has to say as soon as I hear from her.

I sent you a telegram Christmas Eve, did you receive it?

The hospital here is very nice but I still wish I was back there with you. I haven't been out of camp yet so really don't know much about the place. They say it is very nice here but my heart is still in Belfast.

What did you do for Christmas, did you go to the Red Cross? Are you still having trouble with your mother?

When you see Dorothy and Laura say hello to them for me, if you don't mind send me Dorothy Clarke's address so I can write and thank her for the party Monday night.

I still can't get used to the idea that I'm not seeing you. If I were there now it would be about time to meet you for the dance at the Red Cross, I'm sure going to miss those dances too. *—Always thinking of and loving you, Raymond*

Monday, December 28th

Dearest Muriel,

I didn't write yesterday as I visited *---censored---* for the first time, the only thing to do there is visit the churches.

Do you still miss me as much as I miss you? I have you on my mind every minute of the day. I never really loved anyone until I loved you.

How is it at work, are they still kidding you? Did you go to the Red Cross on Christmas Day? *—Hoping to hear from you soon, Raymond*

Wednesday, December 30th

Dearest Muriel,

Another night of staying in and reading and writing. The boys wanted me to go out tonight but there's nothing of any interest for me here, everything I want is in Ireland.

The fellow you talked with at the Red Cross on Saturday told me you talked with him for a while and said you felt very sad and wondered why I left. As I told you before I tried to stay but they had my name on that list and there wasn't anything I could do about it.

I heard today that we can come to Ireland on furlough, I'm going to make sure and if so I'll get my furlough as soon as possible and come flying over. *—Loving you always, Raymond*

11 Posnett Street
Thursday, December 31st

Dearest Ray,

Your first two letters arrived today and I am answering them as I promised. You phoned me this morning and you'll never know how good it made me feel to hear your voice again. On Christmas Eve I phoned your number three times and even then couldn't realize that you had gone. I cried all that afternoon and on Christmas Day. Mommy and Daddy were both very nice to me. I expect they both realized I was missing you pretty badly.

On Christmas Eve night I went up to see Dorothy and Laura. They tried to make me laugh, but when I did try laughing tears came instead. They invited me up for tea on Christmas Day. Tex arrived with a friend named Walter. Walter danced with me at the Red Cross that night and wanted to take me home but I refused and walked home with Lily instead. On Sunday I went with the girls to the Red Cross again. An American named Oscar danced with me. He asked me if I would have a Coca-Cola with him, I told him no as I wanted to speak with a girlfriend. He came over again to dance with me and in the course of our conversation wanted to know if I would go with him to the New Year's Eve dance—again I refused. You remember Charlie the boy who wrote me a letter which I didn't answer, well, he came over while Oscar was talking to me and asked me to dance. He asked me if you were away yet. I told him yes, and then he said, "Oh, that's fine, what about coming out with me." You can guess how mad I was at him saying, "Oh, that's fine," but you'll never know how mad *he* was when I left him. Maybe I shouldn't write about all this, Ray, but I always told you everything and besides I want you to know that you can trust me. Maybe there wouldn't be any harm in going around with other boys while you're away, but I don't want to do that for in my opinion it isn't right. I love you, Ray, and miss you more than I can describe. You said you would be getting leave soon, can you give me any idea when? Write to me often and please let me know what day you receive this letter. I will write again tomorrow.

By the way, Mommy is just the same about us getting married. Sometime when I get Daddy by himself I'm going to have a quiet talk with him and tell him everything.

I must stop writing now and get ready for the New Year's Eve dance at the Red Cross. I probably won't enjoy myself, but then I never do unless you are with me. Your photograph is on the dressing table in my bedroom and I kiss it night and morning.   —*Yours as always,* Muriel

PS A Happy New Year & please be good.

Working in the Lab.

January 1943

Friday, January 1ˢᵗ

Dearest Muriel,

Last evening we had a little beer party and at about 8:00 they said there was a dance down at the Red Cross so we got in the trucks and were taken down. Well, to make a long story short, I never had such a miserable time in all my life, none of us even had a dance. We got back to camp at about 11:30—one of the boys had a quart and I had a few more. Every fellow was feeling the same way as I was and saying they wished they were back in Belfast. No other girl looks good to me Muriel, I have you on my mind every minute.

About the phone call, it was really wonderful to hear your voice again. I get so lonesome and depressed at times—so every time I do I'm going to call you up. Do you think it will be OK with the office? I hope so, just hearing your voice makes me feel a hundred times better.

Monday we start working in the lab, it's really a wonderful lab which will make things more pleasant.   —*Loving you always, Raymond*

Friday, January 1ˢᵗ

Dearest Ray,

At the moment Olive and Audrey are doing their best to annoy me. They are singing "You are my Sunshine" at the top of their voices and trying to take my attention off writing this letter. Everything is quiet now as I'm only after giving them a piece of my mind and it has taken some effect.

How are you getting along? Are you growing to like your new destination any better? Or do you still miss me as much as you said?

I just love those two letters you sent me and keep reading them over and over again.

You mention that you had written home to your mother telling her about us. I only hope she doesn't take the news as badly as my mother is doing. Every time I mention anything about us she just tells me how she feels about it and I'm not to mention anything more about it----------------------.

Daddy is working late tonight and I'm only after having a talk with Mommy. She did her best to make me break off with you. We talked for a while and then I started crying at some of the things she said. She then realized just how much I care for you and has just said, "Please yourself, marry Ray, and I hope you'll never rue the day you do so."

Ray, are you still as determined to marry me as you were? If not please write and tell me. I don't ever want to rue the day I marry you so I just want to make sure you'll always love me as I love you. If your mother strongly objects are you going to marry me against her will? I'm all confused. I love you and just hate hurting my mother. I could be very happy about all of this if only she was happy too.

Take care of yourself. I'm sorry now that I told you about Mommy but it's too late to start writing another letter.   —*Yours as always, Muriel*

Sunday, January 3rd

Dearest Ray,

It's 6:30 p.m. on Sunday and I'm just in the right mood for writing. I expect you'll wonder at me not being at the Red Cross but somehow I don't feel like going there so often since you have left. I received my membership card with my photograph on it last Wednesday, so now I can get in anytime without having to wait for an invitation card. I promised to tell you what I did all week and now I have a chance to do so. On Monday night Lily and I set out to go to a show. We decided to go to the Opera House to see the Savoy Players in a play named "Charlie's Aunt." It was quite good.

On Tuesday night Lily and I went to Albert Whites. I didn't feel like going but went anyhow. It was crowded as usual. The dance should have been quite good but I didn't enjoy myself at all. Wednesday night I stayed home and washed my hair and went to bed early.

Thursday night Lily, Dorothy, Laura and I went to the New Year's dance in the Red Cross. Everything went well until 12:00, then the lights were switched off for a few seconds and everyone started kissing his or her partner. I escaped from mine and had just reached the side when about six Americans caught hold of me. I struggled as best I could but two of them held me while another one kissed me. They were all pretty drunk and if it hadn't been for another boy who had danced with me earlier coming on the scene and telling them to leave me alone, I don't know how I would have got rid of them. Directly after I got my coat and Lily and I walked home together.

I still refuse to go out with anyone else, Ray. I go to the dances with the girls and enjoy myself as best I can without you, but all the time my mind keeps wandering back to the days when you were with me. —*Always yours, Muriel*

Monday, January 4th

Dearest Muriel,

Yesterday it was a beautiful day so about six of us started out for a walk and ended up in *censored* before we came to *censored*. We walked all around the city and country roads and took lots of pictures. At the end of the walk we reached *censored* and went in the Red Cross and had a few Cokes. By seven o'clock I could hardly walk anymore, we went to a show, then back to the Red Cross at ten for a few more Cokes. About eleven o'clock we started back to camp, honest, I thought I would never make it—I still have blisters on one foot.

Today we started to set up the lab. We were unpacking boxes all day. Tomorrow we have to wash all the floors and clean the windows so you can see they're really making a housemaid out of me.

We are going to get furlough soon and will be able to come over to Ireland. When can you get another week or maybe three days off work? If I know ahead of time I can ask for a certain date, so if possible let me know. How are Mother and Father, what have they to say? — *All my love, Raymond*

Tuesday, January 5th

Dearest Muriel,

I just received your first letter today and words can't express how happy I was to receive it. Muriel, you said something about not knowing if you should write and tell me about everything. Remember we had an understanding that we would so let's keep it that way.

I see your father and mother still don't approve but we can wait until you're 21 and then do as we please. Maybe in time they will change their minds, I hope so.

We have snow over here today. I thought the climate in Ireland was bad, England isn't any better, in fact it's not as good. —*Loving you always, Raymond*

Tuesday, January 5th

Dearest Ray,

Today I received two more letters from you. It took them over a week to reach me and since Thursday the 31st I've been watching for the postman. Already I have sent you three letters, two by air mail and one by ordinary post. Please let me know when you receive them. Someone told me that since the war letters going by air mail to where you are stationed didn't arrive any quicker than they did by boat.

Do you remember in my second letter I told you about having a talk with Mommy? She is just as much against me marrying you as ever. She likes you I know, but she says that on account of religion we couldn't stay happy together for long. Daddy had a long conversation with me. I just can't go into detail about all that he said but all I can do is leave it up to you to talk to him when you come over on leave. He definitely doesn't want me to turn and he says the marriage could never be happy and if he thought it would be under the circumstances, he wouldn't object in the least. Ray, I think if you could get talking to Daddy you could maybe make him change his mind and then he could talk Mommy round. I don't mean change his mind about me turning but make it clear to him we could be happy you staying your religion and me staying mine. I told him that but he said your mother would object at me not turning and your church would never rest until I did so. I know Daddy likes you and it is only on Mommy's account he is being so stubborn. Did you tell your mother I was a different religion? Do you think she will mind much? Surely people living in America can't be like here.

You asked if the girls at the office are still kidding me, well, they are and are always asking if I got anymore letters.

Did you find out what was wrong with Luke, is he writing to Marie or have they broken up?   —*All my love, Muriel*

Thursday, January 7th
Dearest Muriel,

Yesterday we had to clean up the lab as we were having a General in to inspect our place so all day we cleaned then had to do the same with the barracks.

I received a few more packages from home, also books and papers. I have enough here to read for awhile to help pass the time. I sent home for a radio and hope to receive it soon.

Tomorrow I may go to the Red Cross dance in town. I probably won't dance but I just have to get out of here at least once a week or I'll go nuts.

I wish I would get some of your letters because there's nothing to write about unless I do hear from you.   —*Loving you always, Raymond*

Friday, January 8th

Dearest Muriel,

Just received your letter written January 1st and was happy to hear from you.

Muriel, remember months ago I said I couldn't marry you because of the things that are coming up now. We talked over things we would have to go through and things we would both have to give up. Remember I told you we had to face a lot of obstacles but that after the war we can do as we please. That's why I didn't want to say anything to your parents before I left because I knew they wouldn't like it so please, Muriel, don't start anymore trouble. I told you we would have to start from scratch and other things which will make it hard for us. I just want you to realize what you'll be giving up and when you are sure you love me we'll get married. I'm not trying to talk you out of marrying me, Muriel, because I love you too much, but I don't want you to be unhappy after we are married. So please don't have any more trouble at home because I hate being over here thinking you're miserable over there. I want you to be as happy as can be expected and someday this mess will be over and we can be together again. What were the things your mother said that made you cry? Muriel, the best thing to do is forget everything until I come over on furlough and then we can talk to them, but for now don't cause any more trouble.

About me liking this place any better, I never can as long as I'm away from you but will have to make the best of it. —*Loving you always, Raymond*

Friday, January 8th

Dearest Ray,

Your letter dated the 30th arrived today and I was very pleased to receive it.

I haven't been out much this week either and I've stopped dancing except on Saturday nights. Next Monday I'm starting music again after my Christmas holiday and then I'll be studying so much for my examination, I won't have time to go out at all.

Mommy and Daddy haven't said anything to me about you since I had my talk with Daddy on Sunday night. No doubt they have discovered that all they say doesn't make me change my mind.

I think of you every minute of the day, too and keep wishing you were here. The little locket you gave me is one of my most treasured possessions.

Everybody here sends their regards and the girls in the office are still asking, "How's Ray, and what are you going to do if he stops writing?" Don't think they are being catty—they just love to tease me. — *All my love, Muriel*

Saturday, January 9th

Dearest Muriel,

Saturday night and staying in again. I received your letter written January 3rd today. I also haven't gone out with anyone because I feel the same way you do. Last night I went to the Red Cross dance, it wasn't bad but I couldn't enjoy myself. I had one dance all evening and about 11:30 we called a taxi and came back to camp. Luke was trying to take me out of my sour mood but soon I had him feeling the same way. Muriel, I don't know what to do or say, I really miss you more than I even thought I would.

How is everything at the office? Don't forget to let me know what you're doing and give my regards to the family. —*Loving you always, Raymond*

PS Mother wrote and said if you need any more powder or lipstick to let her know.

Ray Friscia and Luke Piccarreto in England.

Saturday, January 9th

Dearest Ray,

It's three p.m. on Saturday and once again I'm writing to you. Mommy and Daddy have gone to the Majestic and the children are out. After writing this letter I'm going to get dressed, have tea and then go to the Red Cross.

I wish with all my heart you were here to go with me for somehow I can't get used to going anyplace without you. I probably won't be out at all next week and will write to you every day.

When you are writing don't put names of places in your letters as one I received was censored. —*I'll love you always, Muriel*

Sunday, January 10th

Dearest Ray,

I haven't much to tell you except that Lily called around today and suggested going to the Red Cross. There isn't much to tell you about the dance except that the crowd seemed strange to me, but a few of them must have been there before and noticed us together for they asked me about you. I haven't been to the concerts since last we were there together so I can't tell you anything about them.

Even though I may not have much to write about I'm forwarding you a letter at every opportunity and hope you are doing the same. — *Yours as always, Muriel*

Tuesday, January 12th

Dearest Muriel,

Waited for a letter today but didn't receive one so hope there is one tomorrow.

I wrote a letter home yesterday and told Mother everything, first let me tell you about her letter. She told me she bought a new house, a two family home. She told me my sister Rose, who was married recently, was going to live in one apartment and the other was for me so I think she has a very good idea I'm going to marry you. I'm hoping I receive an answer to my letter quickly because I really want to know how she takes it. I don't think I'll have too much to worry about. — *Loving you always, Raymond*

Tuesday, January 12th

Dearest Ray,

Yesterday was one of the happiest days I've had in a long time. First you phoned me and then I arrived home at lunchtime to find three letters waiting. Your letters never come regularly. Sometimes I don't get any for a few days and then two or three arrive at once.

I laughed when I read about you walking so far on Sunday and taking a blister on your foot, you poor dear, did it hurt? I can just picture you on the return journey grumbling about being tired, in fact I bet you grumbled long before the journey back.

About your furlough, if I was to say when I want you to come over it would be right away. Hard as it is I'm trying to be sensible about this and keep telling myself if you were to come over now you would be away again and I might have a long, long time to wait before seeing you again. So instead if you want to wait awhile I can always have the pleasure of your coming to look forward to. Again, if you come soon, could you get another furlough later on in the year? Also, do you think it would be better to wait until you get an answer to the letter you sent your mother and see how she feels about us, then you will know better what to say if any difficulties arise as regards my mother and father? But please yourself, Ray. I'm leaving it to you to decide when you want to come over and don't forget to let me know beforehand. —*I'll always love you, Muriel*

Wednesday, January 13th

Dearest Ray,

When you get this letter I want you to count all the letters you have received from me and let me know how many there are. By the sound of your letters you don't seem to have received many of mine and I was wondering if they were reaching you safely.

As regards to phoning, Ray, I think it will be all right for you to phone me at the office. Anytime you do phone me I always ring through to Miss Collins afterwards and thank her for letting me speak to you. She probably understands, I don't think she will ever refuse.

Tonight I'm going with Lily to the opera house to see "Rebecca." The play must be good as it has been retained another week. Tomorrow night I'm not going out as I want to polish up my piano practice a little before starting in earnest Friday night.

You were telling me how the boys razzed you the first time you phoned me, well, I'm sure you weren't razzed any more than I was. Vi Balmer, the girl who works beside me, told Graham that when I was told I was wanted at the Time Office phone I made one wild race across the room and almost took stools, desks and office staff with me. Next time I must try hard to keep calm and collected and then they won't have any cause to make fun of me. —*Yours as ever, Muriel*

Thursday, January 14th

Dearest Muriel,

Waited for a letter today but did not receive one, this is the third day I haven't received a letter. Is it because you haven't been writing or is it just the mail set up?

Well, how are you and what are you doing with yourself? How are your piano lessons coming? I hope you are staying in like I am, I haven't been out since Sunday. They had a few pictures for us here with Jack Benny, Bob Hope and Bing Crosby. I forgot the names but they were very good.

As you know I expect to go to London this weekend. It will be my first time so I don't really know how it will be or if I'll like it.

The boys here are kidding me for staying in every night, saying you are going out with other Yanks, but I tell them not my little girl, she's true to me and I trust her. I only wish that I was out with you tonight, of course I wish that every night.

I hope to hear from you soon, please try not to have three days go by before I hear from you because I really look forward to your letters. Give regards to the family and write soon.   —*All my love, Raymond*

Thursday, January 14th

Dearest Ray,

Your two letters, one dated the 7th and the other the 8th arrived today and the one you wrote the 8th worries me. Surely you must know that I love you more than I thought I could possibly love anyone. Anything that has been said to me at home hasn't discouraged me in the least—in fact it has made me realize it more. I expect that letter worried and discouraged you a great deal and perhaps I shouldn't have written it, but I wanted to let you know just how my people feel about everything and have you prepared. I didn't want you coming back here thinking everything would be easy and then getting a shock.

You asked me what my mother said that made me cry, well, she told me if I thought anything of her I wouldn't go against her in any way.

I asked her was there any other reason besides religion to make her refuse, and she said, "No, I like Ray alright, but a mixed marriage is never a success and you have it in your power to write and break off gently with Ray." When she said that, Ray, I couldn't keep from crying. Please don't think badly of my mother, it would take you to have been born here to understand the reasons for her being like she is.

Don't worry about me, Ray, everything is peaceful here now. I haven't talked about you in ages and don't intend to start anymore rows. Mother and Father have both got sufficient warning of our intentions and until you come over I'll say nothing more regarding us.

I must stop writing now as I have to practice, wash my hair and get to bed early. —*Yours as always, Muriel*

Friday, January 15th

Dearest Muriel,

That phone call was really a hard one to get. I started at 10:00 and it wasn't until 11:45 that I talked to you, most of that time I was waiting to get your call and I almost gave up. It was really good to hear your voice again, I wish I could call you up every day. I'm glad to hear there is no more talk at home about us.

I'm getting my clothes pressed and cleaned up for tomorrow ---------
----
------------------------------ *paragraph censored* --
--- I don't know what we're going to do but there's -----------*censored*----------- going so we should have a good time, and I don't mean with the girls.

I'll write to you from London, Muriel, and let you know how I'm enjoying myself, if I can.

Well, dearest, I hope I receive a letter soon, I didn't receive one today but maybe Monday I'll have three or four. —*Always thinking of and loving you, Raymond*

Saturday, January 16th

Dearest Muriel,

I wanted to call you up from London today but I didn't arrive until 1:00. I suppose you want to know what I think of London, well, I think it's swell, there's a lot doing here. It's something like New York City. If you were here with me it would be perfect. No matter how hard I try to enjoy myself I just can't, I keep thinking of you every minute. I try to enjoy myself alone but can't and never will until I have you next to me for always.

After we arrived we had dinner, after dinner we took in a show. About 7:00 we went to a dance here at the Washington Club. The dance is over (10:30) it's about 11:00 now, so before I go to bed (my first chance to write) I'm writing you this letter. No, I didn't go out with any girls and don't expect to. I made you a promise and don't expect to break it.

Tomorrow we're going sightseeing in the morning, in the afternoon to a show and until about 8:00 in the evening we'll hang out at the Red Cross. We have to catch the 9:00 train back. London is swell as I said before but give me Belfast, that's the only place I was happy, I wonder why. —*All my love, Raymond*

Saturday, January 16th

Dearest Ray,

Before writing about anything else I must tell you how glad I was to have those two phone calls from you, especially the second one. About 15 minutes before I got talking to you Miss Collins told me there was a call coming through for me and I'd better go down to the Time Office. I went down and waited for about five minutes and then she told me whoever was calling me couldn't be found so I went upstairs again and waited impatiently, all the while being razzed by the girls. The phone rang again and this time I wasn't disappointed. The Time Office is rather small and Mr. Graham is the only person who works in it. He hears me talking to you and is always kidding me, so now you'll understand why I can't say all I'd like to say to you when you phone me up.

You'll see by the date that I started writing this letter on Saturday, but it is Sunday now and I'm trying to get it finished and posted to you. First I must tell you why I couldn't write on Friday. When I came home from the office I practiced until 7:15, went to music and then got a tram up to Dorothy's to see her about a skirt pattern. When I got home I was too tired to concentrate on writing. Now for an explanation for not posting this on Saturday. You will probably laugh at this but I will tell you nevertheless. About 2:30 p.m. Mommy and Daddy went to the pictures and left me with Audrey and Olive. Olive went to music and I told Audrey to stay in until I came back as I was going into town to see if I could buy some lace without coupons. I went into town and arrived home again about 4:30. I hadn't a key with me and rang the doorbell, quite certain that Audrey would be there to let me in, but instead hadn't she gone out with Olive who by this time had got back from music. Ray, I was furious, I didn't know what to do. To make matters worse, Mommy and Daddy were going from the pictures to Mr. & Mrs. Ellis for tea and wouldn't be back until about 8:30. I tried to find Audrey and called at several houses where I thought she might be, but to no avail. Then about 5 o'clock when I'd given up hope the two young rascals came walking up the street. I asked Audrey what she meant by leaving the house and closing me out but she understood I had a key. It wouldn't have been so bad if Auntie Vi had been in, then I could have gone into her house and written to you. Well, to cut a long story short, I had to climb over the yard wall. I thought I'd never make it but I finally did and even yet Audrey laughs at me. After tea the girls called for me to go to the Red Cross so I had to leave this letter and I'm finishing it now. The dance was much as usual, two boys wanted to walk me home but I refused and walked home with Lily. I didn't go to the dance or the concert today as I don't enjoy myself there since you have gone.

In one of your letters you mentioned that your mother had written and wanted to know if I needed any powder, etc. Well, I still have plenty of powder and lipstick but maybe it would be imposing of me to have you ask her to send me some Max Factor Foundation and Cleansing Lotion as I have been in every shop in town trying to purchase it. I don't like asking her to do this but if you would let me know of anything she would like from Ireland, I'll forward it to her in return for her generosity.   —*Yours as always, Muriel*

Monday, January 18th

Dearest Muriel,

Back at camp after the weekend in London and boy, I'm really tired. It was swell in London until the last night as we started for the train station. It was just about 7:30 and I was all set to write you a letter because we weren't going to leave until 8:30, when the sirens sounded. Well, at first nothing happened, just people talking and us wondering if we should make a try to catch the 9:20 train. We finally decided to try so we went up and packed. We just got out of the Washington Club and boy, it started. We decided to walk to the Piccadilly Circus Subway (about six blocks) and all the way over there was a hell of a racket. Guns going off and the sky full of flashes and tracer bullets and little bundles from Germany, it really wasn't nice. When we got to the subway it was jammed with people, we couldn't get in so we had to stay out and watch the fireworks. Finally, at about 9:00 we got in the subway and down in the tubes, it was jammed up and warm and after an hour it was over. Our 9:20 train had gone so we went to the train station to see when the next train was leaving. It was 10:30 and the next train was 1:20 so we waited three hours and to top it off the train was packed. We reached camp at about 5:00. I found three letters on my bed—two dated the 9th, the other the 11th of January. I read the letters by flashlight and then went to bed. Yes, I still say, "I'm tired," especially today. It seems the more I sleep the more I want. The fellow you were speaking to at the Red Cross was Howard Merkel, the one you met in Lido's.

All the boys are over now so I guess you won't be seeing any of them.

Muriel, about my furlough, I wish you would say when you want me to come over so I can put in for it. The orders are I have to put in for it a month ahead of time so let me know. —*Loving you always, Raymond*

Monday, January 18th

Dearest Ray,

Another of your letters arrived today and I was very glad to receive it. It was the one you wrote on the 12th telling me about your mother buying a house with two apartments. I'm awfully glad and I don't think your mother will be against you getting married.

I never listen to the news, Ray, but right now I couldn't help hearing that there was a raid over London last night and now I'm worrying about you, and wondering if you are safe back at camp. You didn't tell me if your weekend pass ended on Sunday night or Monday morning, but anyway, I hope you weren't anywhere near the bombed area. I'll not be content until I get word from you and know that you are safe. Give my regards to Luke and write. —*Loving you always, Muriel*

Tuesday, January 19th

Dearest Muriel,

I hope you don't doubt that I love you because I do. When you wrote and told me you were having trouble with your parents it made me kind of mad. If I was there it would be different but you taking it alone, I don't like. I'm not mad against your parents, it's only human for them to feel the way they do, they want to make sure you're happy when you do get married and I don't blame them, but it's just the idea I'm not there with you. Don't think I dislike your mother and father because I think a lot of them, it's only natural for them to be the way they are so don't say anything to them for now, when I come over I'm sure we can straighten it out.

Tomorrow we start working in the lab but aside from that nothing new. —*All my love, Raymond*

Tuesday, January 19th

Dearest Ray,

Before I start telling you what I have in mind I must let you know I'm feeling pretty mad. I received a very nice letter from you when I arrived home at dinnertime, but the one I received tonight when I got home from the office made me feel far from happy. For instance just after you told me about getting your clothes pressed and cleaned there was a huge piece censored and after the censored part you have the words....I don't know what we're going to do but there's.....and then the next word is cut out, and after that you have.....going so we should have a good time but I don't mean with the girls. *What girls* ?? You may think me unreasonable, but after all, I wouldn't mind so much only that one word which isn't between there's and going leaves me with a doubt in my mind. I've tried to figure out what it could be and if it's what I think it is, it means that girls are going along with you. I shouldn't mind but somehow I know what girls can be like. You're no longer a wolf, or are you?

Please forgive me if this letter seems sour, as you put it, but I hate to receive letters censored so much as this one has been. Maybe I shouldn't jump to conclusions like I have, but you know me and know if I didn't love you I wouldn't be like this. I trust you so please forget about the first part of this letter or try to explain it and ease my mind a little.

I'm glad you said what you did to the boys when they razzed you about me going out with other "Yanks." I haven't been out with a boy since you left and don't intend to. I see no point in either a boy or girl going out with anyone else. Maybe I have old-fashioned ideas but I'll always stick to them. The girls in the office keep telling me that they're sure you aren't keeping true to me, but I never listen to them, they just like teasing me.

Well, I think I've written enough or perhaps too much tonight. I'll write you again tomorrow so cheerio for now. —*All my love, Muriel*

PS I'm not mad any longer. I just love you.

Wednesday, January 20th

Dearest Muriel,

There is nothing new here only as I said before we started to work in the lab today. Muriel, I packed a little box for you today. There are some things for the kids, and Mother and Father, cigarettes unless you want them, but you should have some left, I hope. Please don't get mad because I really have all the candy, etc. I want. I also put some books in for you that you can pass on to the kids, seeing you're staying in more you'll have more time to read. *—All my love, Raymond*

Wednesday, January 20th

Dearest Ray,

Just a hurried scribble to let you know that I'm fine. It's dinner hour and I want to write this now as Lily asked me to go to the Majestic tonight and I'll have to practice before I go. I'm still waiting to hear how you got along in London. Don't forget to write and tell me all about it and please don't think too much about the letter I wrote yesterday, I wasn't in good form when I sent it. I'm staying in tomorrow night and Friday night too, so you see I'm not going out much.

Look after yourself and think of me sometimes. *—Yours always, Muriel*

PS I hate the censors.

Thursday, January 21st

Dearest Muriel,

No letter again today, probably tomorrow I'll get 3 or 4 all at once. I just got back from town—it is about 10:30 now. We went to the Red Cross and drank Cokes and listened to music. We took the truck back—they have transportation for us now.

Luke called his girl up again tonight. I wish you had a phone at home so I could call you up every night.

I read in the paper where Belfast is going to have a big time celebrating the first arrival of "Yanks" January 26th, are you going to the Red Cross dance they are going to have, I hope not.

Well, Muriel dear, I hope everything is OK with you, give my regards to all. *—Loving you always, Raymond*

Thursday, January 21st

Dearest Ray,

Today it's just exactly a month since my birthday party and yet it seems like a year. Maybe it's because such a lot has happened since then that makes the time seem so long.

How did you get along in London on Sunday? I sincerely hope you weren't near the blitzed area. It worried me when I first heard of the blitz, but then London is such a big town it's unlikely you were in the danger zone.

After writing this I've got to practice scales for about two hours, wash my hair, do some sewing and get to bed early so you see I'm not lost for something to do. I believe if I stayed in every night I would still be busy. —*Loving you always, Muriel*

Friday, January 22nd

Dearest Muriel,

After I called you up this morning, about an hour later, I received two letters both postmarked the 13th. It took them 9 days to reach me. I see from your letters that you are still having your little talks with the family.

As regards to dates, I'm glad to hear you are not going out with anyone as I am doing the same.

About my furlough, as I said today, I'm going to have it sometime in April if possible, but may have to take it before. I will let you know.

I'm glad to hear it's OK to call you up at the office, I didn't know how they would take it. Tell Miss Collins thanks for putting the calls through.

Tonight if I have enough ambition and don't fall asleep as I usually do I'll go to the Red Cross dance with the boys. I don't know why I go because I don't dance, but they have an American band and I get more enjoyment just listening to them. If I were with you it would be different. —*Loving you always, Raymond*

Friday, January 22nd

Dearest Ray,

Thanks a million for that phone call today, you've no idea how good it made me feel to hear your voice again and I was so relieved to know you got safely back from London.

About your furlough, the way I feel I would like you to come right away, but as I said before, wouldn't it be better to wait for a reply from your mother. We have got to talk to Mommy and Daddy and if you can make Mommy change her mind about us you will have done something I can't do.

I have to go for my music lesson now so will stop writing. —*Yours as always, Muriel*

Saturday, January 23rd

Dearest Muriel,

I'm having a lot of luck lately, today I received two more letters and boy, was I glad. I'm glad you enjoyed the phone calls. I would like to call you up more often but now that I'm working I haven't time. You see, Muriel, it takes about an hour or two to get my call through and sometimes I have to wait half an hour but I'll arrange to call you up at least once a week.

What happened Saturday really "takes the cake" climbing over walls, did anything rip when you were going over? I wish I was there to see you, I'd probably laugh with Audrey.

Muriel, please don't ever think you're imposing on me when you ask for powder, etc. I told you my mother is only too glad to send it, but as things are now an article came out saying our parents can't send any more packages to us. It's to save shipping space so for now even I can't receive packages from home and boy, I'm really going to miss them. I'll try to get you powder from the PX here, if they have it.

Muriel, about your writing, I do enjoy your letters more than anything else and look forward to a letter every day, in fact if I could, I would like 10 a day. But I don't want you staying in every night for me, I'm not that selfish. If you have a chance to go out with the girls, go ahead, and you can skip a night now and then, but not too many.

Tonight, Saturday, I'm in charge of quarters so I'm staying in again. I have to go around every hour until 12:00 and see if the blackout curtains are drawn and make sure no light is shining through. I'm writing this letter in between the hours I'm checking up. Well, dearest, I better stop now as I have to make my last round, it's about 11:00 so I will say goodnight. —*Loving you always, Raymond*

Saturday, January 23rd

Dearest Ray,

It's 2:30 and I'm sitting, waiting for the postman to bring me a letter from you. I didn't get one yesterday and if you wrote on Monday there should have been one today. I don't blame you, I blame the censors, but they have their duty to do and I shouldn't grumble.

At the moment I feel rather miserable and I don't know whether to go to the Red Cross or to the pictures by myself. I would stay home only that would make the weekend seem long.

Did you go to the dance Friday night, you mentioned something about going when we were talking over the phone. How are you getting along? Do you still miss me as much as I miss you? The days when you were here were the happiest days of my life and it is only since you have gone that I have realized that.

The girls in the office still kid me about you and can't believe that I haven't gone out with anyone since you went away. One day after working hours, I started to smoke one of your cigarettes and immediately all the girls start accusing me of going out with another "Yank." I told them I wasn't and then they wanted to know where I got the American cigarettes.

At the moment I can't think of anything more to tell you so I'll stop writing. —*Loving you always, Muriel*

Saturday, January 23rd

Dearest Ray,

I've just arrived home and the time is 11:15. After a lot of thinking I went to the Red Cross and arrived there about 8:30.

Ray, I'm going to tell you something I'd rather not, but somehow I must tell you everything and though this may smooth out all right I feel like confiding in you. Lily played a mean trick on me. One night we had arranged to see each other and when I called at her house she wasn't in, in fact there wasn't anyone in. I was pretty mad at Lily, after her making arrangements with me. If she had left a message or called round and told me, but she didn't and I was very disappointed. Next time I was in the company of Dot, Laura and Lily, Lily didn't even trouble to explain or apologize and I didn't bother to speak to her because she didn't speak to me. Because I didn't do this Laura almost bit my nose off. She told me she had called Lily and asked her to go out.

I didn't see any of them since, until tonight, and would have said hello to Laura and even Lily but they ignored me completely. It may all seem silly to you but somehow I'll never like Laura as I once did. Now I'm home and wishing I had you to talk to. I just want you to know that no matter how Laura has changed lately, I'll always be grateful for the nice way she and Dot treated us when you were here. —*All my love, Muriel*

Sunday, January 24th

Dearest Muriel,

There's nothing new today but I thought I'd write a few lines anyway. I stayed around camp until 6 o'clock and then rode the truck into town to see a picture, went to the Red Cross for a Coke and then came back to camp. It's 10:30 now, at eleven the lights go out. Not very exciting or eventful, but that's every day. I'll write again tomorrow. —*Always yours my love, Raymond*

Monday, January 25th

Dearest Muriel,

Well, it sure was a blue Monday, today it rained all day long. I guess it rains as much here as in Ireland.

Muriel, I asked about the cleaning cream you wanted and found out they haven't any just now but maybe later they will and if so I will get it for you. I have a small bottle and will send it in the package I'm sending you.

How are you getting along? With me it's still the same, nothing new. I hope April comes around fast. —*Loving you always, Raymond*

Monday, January 25th

Dearest Ray,

The letter you wrote on Tuesday the 19th arrived today, but I still have not received the one you wrote on the 18th telling me about your weekend in London. Right now I haven't anything new to tell you. After I write this letter I'm going to the pictures with Audrey. She wants to come with me and Mommy has given her permission to. Yesterday I stayed home all day. I did some practice and after tea sat before the sitting room fire and read "Gone with the Wind."   —*Loving you always, Muriel*

Tuesday, January 26th

Dearest Ray,

Today your letters written the 18th and 20th arrived and I was delighted to receive them. I expected the one telling me about your weekend in London would be censored but it wasn't and I was very glad. Isn't it queer that on the weekend you decided to go to London there had to be an air raid.

Thanks for Marie's address, I'll phone tomorrow and see how she is getting along.

Ray, you said you had packed some things for the family and books for me. I hate to think that you're sending us candies, etc. which are meant for you and besides you may be leaving yourself short.

I phoned the Red Cross at lunchtime and Miss Anderson informed me there is a dance from 8 to 11 tonight. When I finish writing this I've got to go round for a music lesson at 7:25 and after I may go to the dance and leave early to get a tram. I won't be going out again until the end of the week so please don't think I'm going back on my promise of staying in. —*Yours as always, Muriel*

Wednesday, January 27th

Dearest Muriel,

I was lucky again today, I received two more letters from you dated the 21st and 22nd.

Muriel, about Ma and Pa, I'm not worried too much about it. If we can't make them change their minds, well, you'll be 21 this year so they won't be able to stop us, unless you want them to. I'm sure when I get there and explain everything to them they will be more than willing to let us go ahead with our plans.

It seems to be getting harder every time I call you up. I have quite a time getting through to you and when I do it's hard to hear you. Muriel, ask Miss Collins why I can't hear you so well. Maybe the connections there are weak, but whatever it is try and find out what is wrong.

I sent you a box today and in it had a bottle of face cream you wanted, I found it in my bags. I don't know when I'll be able to get any more for you, Muriel, but will do my best. There is something for everyone in the family but don't forget to take some for yourself. — *Loving you always, Raymond*

Wednesday, January 27th

Dearest Ray,

Another two letters arrived today and wasn't I pleased to receive them. I don't know what I'd do without these letters coming.

Ray, you said something about hoping I didn't go to the dance in the Red Cross Tuesday night. Well, after my music lesson I was feeling pretty fed up so decided I would go, if only for a chat with Dot. Lily didn't speak to me—I suppose she was mad because I didn't call round to see her.

Peter Smith, the fellow who went out with Molly (you remember the blond girl who works in Inglis and was at Albert Whites when I first met you) danced with me. He's no good, I can't go into details of my conversation with him but he started to talk in a way I didn't think nice. I stood up, told him I didn't want to hear anymore and walked away. Ray, you needn't ever worry about me going to the Red Cross now and then. I go to dance and if any of the fellows try to tag onto me I always get rid of them, somehow. The more I meet other boys the more I think of you. —*Loving you always, Muriel*

Thursday, January 28th

Dearest Muriel,

Tonight they're opening a new PX here at the camp, they're having a party for us and I hear we can have all the beer we can drink. If I like the beer I'll probably get feeling good, but if not, I'll just eat. It's going to have a restaurant so I guess I'll spend a lot of time there.

There's nothing else to do. If I do get, shall we say mellow, all they'll have to do is roll me into bed and I'll be done for the night. I could go out, maybe if I wanted to, but we both made an agreement and I expect to keep my part of it as you are doing, so don't ever worry about me. —*All my love, Raymond*

PS I think your letters are wonderful and without them I'd be lost.

Thursday, January 28th

Dearest Ray,

It's Thursday once again and I'm staying home to practice, it's raining very hard or I would go to a show.

I phoned Marie at lunchtime and had a very nice chat with her. She was glad at me phoning and said she had been thinking of asking Luke to ask you for my address. We have arranged to meet at 3:30 p.m. Saturday afternoon, go into town and have tea someplace.

I started writing this letter in the kitchen but had to come in the sitting room as Mommy started giving off to me again and put me in bad form. Cheerio —*Loving you always, Muriel*

Friday, January 29th

Dearest Muriel,

I really don't know what to think of the phone call we had today. When I first heard your voice I knew something was wrong, please, Muriel, let me know what it is. I told you if it's your Ma and Pa not to worry and let things alone until I get there.

What's this about Lily, Dot and Laura? Everything happens when I'm away. —*Loving you always, Raymond*

Friday, January 29th

Dearest Ray,

This is just a short note to thank you for the phone call. Please don't worry too much about what I told you. I have been very miserable last night and today, but I'm trying not to worry either. Last night Daddy talked to me again and tried to point out the disadvantages of us marrying. I cried in front of him and went to bed crying (felt awful today) so now you'll understand why I told you what I did over the phone.

I love you, Ray, so please don't think I'll ever stop loving you because I know I won't.

I'm going to the Majestic tonight as I have been staying home these past two nights. One of the girls at the office would have gone with me but I want to go alone as I don't feel like talking to anyone.

Once again, Ray, I want you to know I'm sorry about talking the way I did over the phone today, I should have known it would worry you and I don't want to have you worrying over there. *—Always yours, Muriel*

PS Audrey is only after asking me to take her with me to the Majestic, so I think I will.

Saturday, January 30th

Dearest Muriel,

I haven't received word from home for two weeks now and it has me kind of worried. Not that I'm worried about what my mother has to say about us so much, but I always think something is wrong at home when I don't receive one. It's probably due to the mail being held up somewhere.

By the time you receive this letter you should have received the package I sent you. I hope you like it. If there is anything more you want please let me know and I will try my best to get it for you.

That's about all I have to say for now and anyway, the boys won't let me continue this letter because they want me to play cards. *— Loving you always, Raymond*

Saturday, January 30th

Dearest Ray,

Last night when I came home from the Majestic I started coughing and have coughed ever since. Billy McKoewn, who works in our office, got tired of listening to me this morning and told me if I kept on the way I was doing, you would be carrying flowers to my grave when you come over on leave. He was kidding me something awful. I laugh now when I think of all that was said but I wasn't laughing much this morning.

Since Thursday night Mommy and Daddy have said nothing more about us.

You remember I told you I was seeing Marie today, well, we changed our plans, instead we are meeting tomorrow, Sunday at 4:30. We're having tea at Whitehall and will probably sit there for an hour or so, talking. *—All my love, Muriel*

Sunday, January 31st

Dearest Muriel,

Another Sunday gone by and nothing new to talk about, --------------
----
-- *large par-*
agraph censored --

--- we had a movie here then went to our PX and had a few beers, it's now about 10:00.

I'm still waiting for a letter from home but so far haven't had any luck. I'm glad to hear that you and Marie are going out together. I told Luke and he was pleased.

When I come over on furlough I have a big surprise, until then I can't say.   —*Loving you always, Raymond*

Sunday, January 31st

Dearest Ray,

It's Sunday, 8 p.m. and I've just arrived home after having been out with Marie. We went down to Whitehall and sat talking for a long time. I won't tell you what we talked about, but we did have a very interesting conversation about old times and all that.

All is quiet at home but I know Mommy is worrying a lot though she has said nothing since Thursday.

Give my regards to Luke and tell him I was out with Marie. — *Yours as always, Muriel*

February 1943

Dearest Muriel,

I'm writing this letter only after calling you up. I'm really glad to hear you're not too worried about the girls. I received your letter telling me about them and all I can say is to forget them, especially Laura and Lily.

About the boys you met stationed where I was before, I got a big kick out of hearing what you said. I bet they worked in the lab because there were two or three of them that said they were going to get a date with you after I left and I told them they would never have a chance.

Muriel, about the furlough, I'll come over March 3rd, you see March 9th is my birthday so I want to be with you, is that OK? What did your mother say to you last Thursday?

The two letters I just received I'll answer tomorrow, if I keep writing I'll miss my "chow" but most of all I want to have something to read and write tomorrow.   —*Loving you always, Raymond*

Monday, February 1st

Dearest Ray,

It's Monday night and I've just arrived home from the office. Your telephone call today was quite unexpected and I was very glad to get talking to you again. Ray, I don't know what has come over me lately I get so depressed. I don't know why, but this morning I got extra work to do and I felt like crying. Mr. Johnston, our boss, must have noticed me because he sent Norman over to help. The girls in the office tell me I'm not like myself, they say I used to laugh and make fun all the time and now all I do is sit and think of Raysie-Waysie, that's what they call you, do you mind? At night I don't care whether I go out or stay home, when I go out I feel you should be with me and when I stay home I sit wondering what is going to happen in the future. I don't know how you are feeling about coming over on furlough, are you feeling brave enough to talk to Mommy and Daddy? If all this was cleared up, Ray, I wouldn't feel half so bad. If Mommy and Daddy would give their consent I'd be the happiest girl in the world.

53

I feel better now I've written to you. Please be good and look after yourself. —*Yours always, Muriel*

Tuesday, February 2nd

Dearest Muriel,

I just got back from the show we had here at camp, the "Pied Piper," did you see it, if not you want to if it comes to Belfast. Honest, I really liked it—it was one of the best shows I've seen in a long time.

The reason I didn't want you to go to the Red Cross dance Tuesday was because I thought maybe it would be like New Year's Eve, not that I don't trust you, Muriel. But I was afraid the same thing would happen with all the boys drinking. Now that you did go and everything was OK I feel much better.

About me saying, "I feel tired," I still say it. There's nothing wrong with me, I just like to sleep.

Luke was very glad to hear you were going out with Marie, let me know how you're coming along as Luke wants to know also. —*Loving you always, Raymond*

Tuesday, February 2nd

Dearest Ray,

Before I write telling you about myself I must thank you very much for the package which arrived today. Mommy, Daddy and the children also say I have to thank you on their behalf. When you wrote and said you were sending a package I never told the family as I wanted it to be a surprise to them. When I arrived home at lunchtime the package was in the sitting room. I opened it and gave Daddy the cigarettes and Mommy the prunes and soap. The children were delighted with the comics and candies and I think they just about love you. The cream you sent is just what I needed and as I can't thank you on paper the way I like thanking you, I'll have to wait until I see you.

This afternoon I didn't go back to work but went to see the doctor as I haven't felt too well lately. He examined me thoroughly, told me I was run down, gave me a tonic and said I was to come back and see him in two weeks time. Mommy doesn't want me to go into the office until my cold is cured but I'm too busy and besides I want to try and take a few days off when you come on leave. Right now Mommy is coaxing me to hurry and get to bed so I think I'd better make this letter short and do what she says. —*Always yours, Muriel*

Wednesday, February 3rd

Dearest Muriel,

From your letter you wrote on January 28th I see it is still raining in Belfast, well, I guess I can't say anything about Belfast because it rains just as much here if not more. We do get a little more sunshine, I think.

I just got back from the show in town, it's about 10:30 now. Luke and I went to see "This Above All." Did you see it? It was really good.

Nothing more to say, if I had you with me I would have a lot to talk about but even though I haven't got you with me now, I can say and really mean it, I never loved anyone the way I love you. —*Loving you always, Raymond*

Wednesday, February 3rd

Dearest Ray,

How's everything with you, Ray, have you decided when you are going to come on leave?

I didn't go into the office this morning but got so fed up I went in the afternoon. The girls all gathered around me and wanted to know what the doctor said. Vera sat beside me all afternoon giving me advice such as get to bed early, cut out the dancing and so on. I haven't been dancing since Saturday week last and I don't think I'll bother going to the Red Cross unless you and I go together when you come on leave.

By the way, you asked me if I had my photograph taken yet, well, I haven't, but don't worry, I'll get one soon and send it to you. I must stop writing as tea is ready and after that I have to hurry to the Majestic.   —*Yours as always, Muriel*

Thursday, February 4th

Dearest Muriel,

In your letter you wrote Saturday, thanks for the paper clippings. I see they had quite a time, did you see any part of the parade?

You better take care of that cough—maybe it's too many cigarettes. You really shouldn't smoke so much.

Muriel, I wish you wouldn't get so depressed. Please be happy and have fun like you did before. I know it's hard to do but try anyway. I feel the same way as you do about going out but make the best of it. Don't worry about me coming over, I'm brave enough and nothing is going to stop me from seeing you and having a talk with your parents. —*Always loving you, Raymond*

PS My furlough is March 3rd. I'll give you more information later.

Thursday, February 4th

Dearest Ray,

It's Thursday night and I'm staying home. I've been practicing and after this I have lots to do. What's this about telling me of something which is going to be a big surprise? Why can't you tell me before you come over on leave, I'm bursting with curiosity. I'm hoping you phone tomorrow morning.

That tonic the doctor gave me is marvelous, I feel lots better already. Cheerio. —*Loving you always, Muriel*

Friday, February 5th

Dearest Muriel,

It's eleven o'clock now, I just got back from the dance at the Red Cross, I went down with the boys. These dances are nothing like they had at the Red Cross in Belfast. They had an English band and you know how I like them. Well, I'm beginning to be "a wolf," I had two dances can you imagine that. Really, Muriel, I don't know why I go, maybe it's just to get away from camp but I just can't seem to enjoy myself.

Luke just came in to say goodnight, we talked about the day you and Marie went out and wonder what you had to say about us. I bet you took us over the coals but don't worry, Luke and I talk about you and Marie so I guess we're even. —*To the one I love, Raymond*

Friday, February 5th

Dearest Ray,

This is just a few lines as there is nothing new to tell you. I went to music tonight and for the last two hours have been practicing. I wasn't going to write until tomorrow but somehow I must tell you again that I love you and I'm thinking of you every minute. You've no idea how I'm longing to see you and the thought of you coming over soon has me feeling pretty good.

Please write and tell me the big surprise, I can't wait until you come over. *Please!*

Cheerio. —*All my love, Muriel*

Saturday, February 6th

Dearest Muriel,

I didn't receive any letters today so there is not much to say. I may go into town tonight, if I don't feel like sleeping, and see a show.

Muriel, have you told your parents I'm coming over March 3rd, if so what did they have to say, if anything?   —*Loving you always, Raymond*

Saturday, February 6th

Dearest Ray,

Your letter dated the 1st of February arrived and boy it made me feel good. I've read it three times already and know that you love me.

About 5:30 I'm taking Olive to the Majestic to see "The Fleets In." Mommy and Daddy went yesterday to see it and they say it's very good, have you seen it?

About your furlough, you say you aren't coming until the 3rd of March, that suits lovely.

You asked what Mommy said to me on Thursday night, well, she only said what she always says, you know, about religion. Since then everything has been all right.

Take care of yourself and give my regards to Luke.   —*Yours always, Muriel*

Sunday, February 7th

Dearest Muriel,

Sunday, the day of rest and that's just what I've been doing. Three of the boys and I went into town to see a show and after the show to the Red Cross for a few Cokes. You know, Muriel, it seems I can't even enjoy myself at the show. I keep wishing you were sitting beside me, that I keep offering you cigarettes and after the show we run for the tram and miss it and wait for the next one in the rain. Finally after half an hour, it seemed that long, a tram finally comes along and we have to pack into it. We reach the square and walk home, go to our little love nest and kiss good night. That's what I miss more than ever, Muriel, and I'll never forget those days as long as I live.   —*Loving you always, Raymond*

Sunday, February 7th

Dearest Ray,

It's just about 9 o'clock and I'm taking the opportunity, the first today, to write to you. Greta called at 2 o'clock and we went for a short walk and called in the Lido for some coffee. She has gone now and I'm sitting here alone worrying about Daddy. He has been ill these last few days and hasn't gone into work. Right now he's very sick and honestly, Ray, I got frightened when I looked at him for he's as pale as can be. The doctor gave him some powder to take but it hasn't helped and if he isn't any better when I have finished writing this I'm going out to fetch the doctor again.

Please excuse this short letter, Ray, but I just can't concentrate to write. —*Yours always, Muriel*

Monday, February 8th

Dearest Muriel,

Another blue Monday and nothing much to say. It's been rather cold here the past few days, today especially. In another twenty-three days I'll be over to see you, isn't that swell. I hope the days keep going fast until I arrive to see you. As I sit here writing to you I keep looking up at the boys and laughing. Tonight, which is very seldom, all the boys are in writing letters because it's kind of cold out. I'm usually here alone nights when I write to you, but tonight I really have no cause to feel lonesome. —*Love forever, Raymond*

Monday, February 8th

Dearest Ray,

This is just a short scribble to tell you once again, I love and miss you more than anyone else in the world. I went to the Majestic myself tonight and just got back.

In my letter yesterday I told you Daddy is ill. He is a good deal better now but Mommy is making him stay home from work another week.

Have you had any word from your mother yet? I received your letter written on the 2nd of February today and if you wrote on the 3rd I'll get another one tomorrow. Cheerio. —*All my love, Muriel*

Tuesday, February 9th

Dearest Muriel,

Just received two letters dated February 3rd and 4th. I'm glad to hear you received the package and everyone was happy. The soap was for you but if you gave it to your mother it's OK. Muriel, I don't like the news about you going to the doctor, I hope it is nothing serious, please take care of yourself. —*All my love, Raymond*

Tuesday, February 9th

Dearest Ray,

I went to music tonight and when I got back washed my hair and here I am, close up to the fire writing this letter and drying my hair at the same time. Mommy and Daddy have company tonight so it is my turn to put Olive and Audrey to bed. They coaxed me to let them stay up a little longer so I guess I won't put them to bed until I finish writing this.

No, I didn't see the movie "This Above All," but Yvonne did, I must ask her about it. —*Yours as always, Muriel*

PS What is it you have to tell me that will be a big surprise? Please tell me!

Wednesday, February 10th

Dearest Muriel,

In our phone conversation today about the secret, well, I gave you a hint but I'm not telling you anymore until I get there. I want it to be a surprise.

Muriel, you said something over the phone about not going to the Red Cross because someone was following you home one night. Please tell me all about it, when did it happen? I'm glad to hear that you're not going anymore, I really didn't want you to go in the first place but I didn't want you to stay home because I said to.

Tonight the fellows and I are going into town to see "My Girl Sal." I heard it was very good. Did you see it? —*All my love, Raymond*

Wednesday, February 10th

Dearest Ray,

It's about 11:15 p.m. and I've just got back after spending the evening with Yvonne. She didn't come in the office today as her brother got married and tonight she called unexpectedly at our house and asked me to go to a show with her. We went to the Classic to see a picture named "Mrs. Hadley." It was a jolly good picture so if you haven't seen it, go see it if it shows over there. After the show we went in the Lido for supper and Mrs. Forte (you remember the woman who owns it) came over to me and asked me where you were. She said, "You know I used to see you come in here very often with an American, has he been moved?" I said you were away, Ray, but gave her no information as to where. (You know how careless talk cost lives.) Quite a number of people I know only slightly have been asking me the same question. Sometimes I get mad and wonder why people don't mind their own business.

I'm very glad that you phoned today, Ray, and boy, am I delighted to know what the big surprise is. The girls wanted to know what you had said to make me look so happy but they'll never know, not until I walk into the office someday with the ring on my finger. —*Yours as always, Muriel*

Thursday, February 11th

Dearest Muriel,

I really have been very lucky today, I received three of your letters and from home I received 5 packages of candy, juice, coffee and other things. I could hardly carry the packages to my room. I'm saving some of the candy for you and when I come over I'll bring them.

Muriel, I wish I could call you up every day but I can't. I'm working more and haven't got time. If you had a phone at home I would call you up every night.

I'm glad to hear the tonic the doctor gave you is making you feel better.

Don't forget to get a few days off because if you don't I'm not letting you go to work anyway. —*Love always, Raymond*

PS Tell Yvonne I said hello and send my regards.

Friday, February 12th

Dearest Muriel,

I received your letter of February 7th. So Greta is calling around now, how did she ever make it, you know what I mean.

I'm sorry to hear that your daddy is sick, please don't worry, he'll be alright soon. I wish there were something I could do to help.

Muriel, Luke is in the hospital with a very bad cold. Don't say anything to Marie as yet. I will let you know how he is coming along, if you do tell her she will worry about him.

It's about 11 o'clock now. I just got back from the Red Cross, they had an American band and it was swell. That's really the only enjoyment I get now that I'm away from you. When I come over I'm going to be next to you every second I can because they're too precious to waste. It will be about 3 in the morning before I leave so you better get lots of sleep now because when I get there you're not going to have much time to sleep. Is it OK with you? —*Loving you always, Raymond*

Friday, February 12th

Dearest Ray,

I'm sorry I didn't write yesterday but after practicing I went in next door to talk to Auntie Vi for what I intended to be only a few minutes. She is going over to England tonight to spend a month there and last night I helped her to pack her cases. We then sat and talked for ages about everything and then I told her about us and about you coming over on March 3rd to speak to Mommy and Daddy. Auntie Vi is on my side and she advises me to go ahead and marry you. She has an aunt who married a boy with a different religion and their marriage has been a success even though they both kept their own religion. They have a family and some of them went her way and some went his. Anyhow, when I came back in the house it was too late to write and I went to bed with a guilty conscience.

Tonight I stayed home and Mommy and Daddy went to visit. I practiced, then put Audrey and Olive to bed and now I'm writing you.
—*All my love, Muriel*

Saturday, February 13th

Dearest Muriel,

I went to the hospital where Luke is, it's about a mile away. I went this afternoon and he is coming along fine. Muriel, please don't say anything to Marie, he doesn't want her to know because she will worry. Luke will tell her all about it when he's out. I left about five o'clock and met the fellows at the Red Cross, we had our supper, or what you call tea, and then went to a show. It's now about 10:30, I just got back and that's what I did today.

I can hardly wait until March 3rd, don't expect to be away from me for a second. —*Yours always my love, Raymond*

Saturday, February 13th

Dearest Ray,

Once again it's Saturday and once again I've received a letter from you, the one dated the 8th of February. Mommy and Daddy have gone to a show and Olive is at music. I'm sitting here listening to the wireless and writing at the same time. You say the weather is cold over there, well, here it is cold and windy and now and then there is a shower of rain. I bet Auntie Vi and her two children, Ray and Betty, had a rough crossing to England last night, but they won't mind, they're used to traveling in rough weather.

Olive has just come from music and believe it or not she is insisting on writing you a little note which she will not let me read. She says she is thanking you for the books even though I told her I have thanked you already.

I'll end now, Ray, as I have to go to the library and get a book for Daddy. —*Yours as always, Muriel*

Dear Ray,

I want to know if there are any good-looking girls over there.

Muriel is taking me to the pictures tonight, who are you taking? Do not tell Muriel what I have written in this note as I told her I was thanking you for the comics, it was very kind of you to send them. When you come over I *might* give you a kiss, but do not tell Muriel. She is finishing her letter. —*Yours truly, Olive*

PS Thanks for the sweets too, and excuse bad writing.

Sunday, February 14th

Dearest Muriel,

It's St. Valentine's Day and I must apologize for not sending a card or something. All I can do now is wish you had a happy Valentine's Day with all my love. Being in the army you forget all about holidays and birthdays.

I received your letter today from February 8th. I'm glad to hear your daddy is much better, I was a little worried for awhile. How is your cold coming along? I hope it's OK, are you still taking the tonic the doctor gave you? Don't forget to go back and see him.

About myself, well, I slept most of the day. Tonight I went to a show here at camp and saw "Magnificent Days," it was really funny. After the show I went to the PX and had a Coke. It's now about 8:30 and here I am writing to you. You see I'm leading a very quiet life but will make up for it when I come over to see you. I guess there's not much more to say, there really is a lot I want to say but will wait until I come over. —*Love, Raymond*

Sunday, February 14th

Dearest Ray,

Another week ended and now only seventeen more days to wait and then you'll be over here. About me getting off work for a week, well, I'll ask the boss and maybe he'll let someone else do my work while I am off. If he refuses to do this I'll take a day or two off anyhow.

It has rained all day and I haven't been out at all. I just sat around, sometimes practicing, sometimes reading, so you can tell by that I'm leading a very quiet life. —*Always yours, Muriel*

Monday, February 15th

Dearest Muriel,

Received your letter today dated February 9th. I'm glad to hear you are still going to your music lessons, don't forget when I come over I want to hear you play some songs.

While I'm writing this letter I'm drinking some coffee I've just made. My mother sent it over and boy is it good. So as not to have any arguments when we get hitched you can make tea for yourself and I'll make my coffee.

Better stop now, the boys want lights out, so until tomorrow. — *All my love, Raymond*

Monday, February 15th

Dearest Ray,

Two more letters arrived today and I was delighted to receive them. In the one you wrote on Wednesday after phoning me you said you had given me a hint as to what the big surprise is. Have you lost your memory or was I hearing things? Don't mind me, Ray, I'm just in a good mood after receiving your two letters and not only that, I've had good fun in the office. This morning when I arrived there I noticed that over the "Staff Only" sign on the office door someone had hung a large sign with the words "Local Gestapo" printed on it. The boss was furious and is still trying to find the guilty person. No one in the office knows who did it, but we all think it is someone of the other workers who has a grudge against our boss.

Yvonne is coming down tonight to help me with some sewing. At any moment she may come to the door so I want to have this letter written before she does come.

Ray, about the Yank who followed me home from the Red Cross, well, I'll tell you all about that when you come over on leave. It would take too long to tell you in writing. *—Yours only, Muriel*

Tuesday, February 16th

Dearest Muriel,

I received your letter today dated February 10th. I try to keep a secret and you always get it out of me before I can surprise you, you're a little brat, but a sweet one. You can be the third engaged girl in the office but don't say anything yet until I come over. I want you to come with me when we pick out the ring so you can have your choice. I have been wondering what Mommy and Daddy will say when they hear about it.

Luke is getting out of the hospital tomorrow and should be back to work soon.

I just got back from a show here at camp, "Holiday Inn" with Bing Crosby. It's about 9:00 now and I better get to bed as I have to get up early and go to work.   —*Always yours, Raymond*

Tuesday, February 16th

Dearest Ray,

Received your letter dated the 11th of February today and I don't need to tell you how glad I was to receive it.

When I arrived home from the office I had tea and then went up to see the doctor and would you believe it, Ray, I've gained 2½ lbs. inside two weeks. The tonic he gave me must have been good or his scales are out of order, which Daddy says is most unlikely.

Anyhow, the doctor gave me a prescription for another tonic and I haven't to go back as he says I am fit and well, isn't that marvelous? After I left the doctor's house I didn't feel like going home so instead I suddenly made up my mind to go to the Majestic and see a picture named "Bedtime Story." As it is drawing near the time I told you I'd be sleeping I think I'll end and not break my promise. Take care of yourself.   —*Forever yours, Muriel*

Wednesday, February 17th

Dearest Ray,

Once again I'm writing to you and this time to answer your letter dated 12th February which arrived today. Daddy is feeling alright now and is back at work again, it is only now and then he has a bad attack.

I'm very sorry to hear that Luke is in the hospital and promise you I won't say a word about it to Marie. Give him my regards and I hope he recovers soon.

About staying with me until 3:00 in the mornings, that's certainly OK with me, that is if Mommy and Daddy don't object and under the circumstances I wouldn't be surprised if they do.

How about your mother? Haven't you heard from her yet? As supper is ready I think I'll end.   —*Loving you always, Muriel*

Thursday, February 18th

Dearest Muriel,

Received two more letters from you today. In one of the letters was Olive's little note. Tell Olive it was very sweet of her and I will answer all her questions when I come over. Most of all tell her not to forget her promise, she told me to make sure I didn't let you know what she wrote so I can't say a word.

I received a telegram from home today wanting to know if I'm OK and why I haven't written. It's funny, I have been writing home quite often but it seems they haven't received my letters. --------------------------Censored------------------------ the boys wanted me to go out dancing but I refused, I would rather stay in and write to you.

Well, Muriel, that's about all for tonight, we have to start going to bed about 10:00 now because starting Monday we have to get up at 5:30. I'll be seeing you soon, only 13 more days to go. —*All my love, Raymond*

Friday, February 19th

Dearest Ray,

In your letter, which arrived today dated the 14th, you apologized for not having sent me a card on St. Valentine's Day but it really doesn't matter. I didn't know it was St. Valentine's Day until someone told me, so that accounts for me not having sent you one.

You're a darling for phoning me today. I heard you quite clearly the first part of the call but after that there was such a noise that I couldn't make out what you were saying. Between you and me I think Miss Collins must listen to our conversations because when I was speaking to her later she remarked that the connections were bad. I won't say anything because if I do she'd probably stop you from speaking to me. None of the other girls are allowed phone calls and they often wonder that she lets me speak to you.

Ray, you've no idea how much I'm longing for the 3rd of March to come. About me getting off work, I'll do my best. I'm kept very busy and today I had a row with the boss and got so mad I haven't spoken to him since. Pretending that I'm sick won't work because one of the girls got to know you were coming and told the others, and as news spreads fast in Inglis the boss would be sure to hear about it. But don't give up hope, Ray, I'll do all that's in my power to get off and be with you as much as possible. —*Forever yours, Muriel*

Friday, February 19th

Dearest Muriel,

Just writing this letter after our phone conversation, it was really good to hear your voice again. At the end the phone went dead and I couldn't even say cheerio—I hope you don't think I hung up. I tried to call you back but didn't succeed.

Tonight if I do go out it will be to a show or the Red Cross, our 5th General band is playing so I may drop in for awhile.

It's about time for chow so I better stop, only 12 days to go. *—All my love, Raymond*

Saturday, February 20th

Dearest Ray,

Once again it is Saturday and as usual I am home alone. Mommy, Daddy and Audrey are at the pictures and Olive is at Music. I have only been out one night this week so I have made up my mind to go to the Red Cross tonight. Please don't worry about me, Ray, because I'll leave early and get a tram home, and you know I won't bother with other boys beyond dancing with them if they ask me. In eleven more days you'll be here and I'll be happy again. Cheerio. *—Always loving you, Muriel*

Saturday, February 20th

Dearest Muriel,

It's Saturday afternoon and Luke has been here, don't tell Marie, but Luke is going to give her a ring also.

Muriel, I have received the letter we have been waiting for. My mother said it was OK for me to marry you, in fact she was expecting it so it was no surprise to her.

Last night I went to the dance, as I told you the 5th General Hospital band played. After the dance I helped to pack the instruments into the truck and then came back to camp.

It's only 11 more days my love and boy, I can hardly wait. *—All my love, Raymond*

Monday, February 22nd

Dearest Ray,

I must tell you the good news. Today I plucked up the courage and asked the boss if he would let me off from the 3rd until the 10th of March and very much to my surprise he said yes, but only on the condition that I only take a week's holiday instead of a fortnight, in the summer time. I'm only after telling Mommy and boy, is she mad. She is still as much against me marrying you as ever and she doesn't even want to talk to you about it when you come over. Ray, I wish with all my heart that this was all straightened out and believe me it's going to take a lot of straightening.

As it's about 7 o'clock and about time I was leaving for the pictures I must end now. Please don't worry, everything may come all right. —*Yours as always, Muriel*

Tuesday, February 23rd

Dearest Muriel,

I think this will be the last letter for now, until I come over. This should reach you Saturday or Monday and I will be there Wednesday or Thursday. We should stop for now and what we have to say we can say when I come over.

I have to start packing and have my clothes cleaned and pressed. Until I hold you in my arms, God bless you, Muriel, only seven more days. —*Yours always, Raymond*

Tuesday, February 23rd

Dearest Ray,

So you have to get up at 5:30 in the mornings, that's terrific but you shouldn't be tired if you go to bed at 9 o'clock the night before, "if!" Pardon me, Ray, I couldn't help the "if," I just had to write it. How do the rest of the boys like the idea, are they as much against it as you are or do they like the early morning air, it's very refreshing I have heard.

Isn't it marvelous, Ray, only eight more days and then we'll be together again, I can hardly realize it. —*Yours as always, Muriel*

PS Daddy didn't say a word last night, I thought he was going to lecture me.

Wednesday, February 24th

Dearest Ray,

As most likely this letter won't reach you until Tuesday the 2nd of March, I'll stop writing until after your leave because if I do write this week again you won't receive my letters in time. Ray, you've no idea how happy I am when I think of seeing you in only another week. I can hardly realize it and the fact that I've managed a week off work has made me even more happy. I can hardly wait until I see you—I have so much to talk about. —*Always my love, Muriel*

Barracks. Bottom photo shows Ray's friend, Luke.

Mail Call.

Mail Call.

Relaxing in the Barracks.

March 1943

Friday, March 12th

Dearest Ray,

It seems so queer me writing to you again when only yesterday we were together but I suppose I'll just have to get used to you being away. At the present moment I'm feeling pretty awful. I arrived home last night wearing your ring, I also wore it all day today and believe it or not neither Mommy nor Daddy noticed it until tonight when I was just leaving to go to music. I was warming my hands at the fire when Daddy said, "Let me see your ring." Immediately as he said that Mommy almost had a fit and so had I because I can't understand how she missed seeing it at dinner hour. She said she understood I wasn't to become engaged until I am 21 years and was hoping and praying that I would change my mind before then. Daddy isn't taking it so badly and when Mommy said she would never let me go to America, he said he didn't care if I went to Hong Kong. This isn't a pleasant letter for you to receive but perhaps the one I write tomorrow will have better news. Since we parted yesterday I feel dazed—the week we spent together seems more like a dream. I only wish Mommy would understand that I'd never be happy without you.   —*Yours as always, Muriel*

PS I hope you got safely back to camp.

Saturday, March 13th

Dearest Ray,

It's Saturday once again and as I sit here I can't help thinking of how happy I was last week when you were here with me. Just about this time we were in town looking around the shops for an engagement ring. Now I have the ring but I haven't you. I'm missing you more than I can describe but as neither of us can help that I am going to try and be cheerful.

Last night, just when I was going to bed, Aunt Vi came in and I think she must have talked to Mommy and Daddy about us for they haven't said a word to me about you since. I must get talking to her and find out if Mommy is going to give in and if she is I won't feel as badly as I do. Your phone call today made me happy, as I said before don't worry about me, I'm only in love and there are millions like me.
—*Yours always, Muriel*

Sunday, March 14th

Dearest Muriel,

This afternoon at about two o'clock Luke and I went for a walk. We went miles out in the country and took some swell pictures. We found a haystack and in one of the poses I almost fell asleep, I was so comfortable. When I have them developed I will send them over to you, I hope they come out good. We came back about five and had, as you call it, tea. Then we went to a picture here at camp named "My Heart Belongs to Daddy," did you see it? It was kind of silly but made me laugh, and that was the first time since the day I left you. After the show we went up to the lab and sat around talking and now here I am writing this letter. I really don't know what I'm going to do with myself, I miss you so much. Luke is coming over at the end of the month to see Marie. Instead of him cheering me up, listening to him I get all the sadder. I wish I was coming over with him but as you know that's impossible. I'm quite sure I can come in three or four months from now so let's keep our hopes up that the time will go quickly. I'm still waiting for the picture of you that you promised me. I hope you send one to me soon and remember, one with a smile. —*All my love, Raymond*

Sunday, March 14th

Dearest Ray,

It's 5 o'clock. Mommy and Daddy and the children have gone walking and I'm taking this opportunity to write to you.

Last night I went to the Red Cross dance and honestly, Ray, the place was packed so much there was little room for dancing. Dot and Laura were there with their boyfriends and they said hello and later on in the night Dot came over to me. She said she noticed I was wearing an engagement ring and wanted to see it. She also said she was sorry she didn't see you when you were over but wishes to be remembered and sends her congratulations.

At 10:40 I got a tram home alone. I was speaking to Kathleen Bailey in the cloakroom and she sends her congratulations too, and wishes us the best of luck.

When I arrived home last night I called in to see Aunt Vi. She said she spoke to Mommy and advised her to let me go ahead and marry you. Daddy said he knew I would marry you anyhow and Mommy might as well get used to the fact and not spoil our chance at happiness. I've felt a great deal better after hearing that and now I'm looking forward to your next furlough and my 21st birthday. —*Always loving and missing you, Muriel*

Monday, March 15th

Dearest Muriel,

Today we really started working, I was busy all day. Wednesday is my day off so I can call you up—we have one day a week off now.

Luke got a letter from Marie today and in it she told him how much she liked your ring. I guess she wants one also. Give her my regards and tell her Luke will be over soon.

Tonight there's another show at camp and after the show we have some Glenn Miller records they're going to play for us. —*I love you, Raymond*

Monday, March 15th

Dearest Ray,

Today has been rather miserable for me. At lunchtime when I was about to rush into town to buy some shamrock for you, Mommy started crying. I asked her what was wrong and she told me she hadn't been able to sleep these last few nights for thinking of having to part with me after the war. I understand just how she feels and had a quiet talk with her and told her I loved you so much I could never be happy without you. Ray, I'm between the devil and the deep blue sea and I'll be like that until Mommy stops worrying like she is. Usually every mother worries over losing a son or daughter but they all get over it and I told Mommy she would too. Please don't let this annoy you, everything should come all right. —*Yours as always, Muriel*

Tuesday, March 16th

Dearest Muriel,

I'm writing this letter in the lab tonight. I'm working or on duty as I was in Belfast. This week I have it twice, tonight and Saturday. I don't mind as I have nothing else to do so I'd just as soon work.

Luke just got through calling up Marie, I wish you had a phone at home but I'll call you up tomorrow at the office.

About myself, there is nothing new, the same thing every day. This getting up at 5:30 is killing me, I hope I get accustomed to it soon. —*Love, Raymond*

Tuesday, March 16th

Dearest Ray,

At lunchtime today when I was coming home with some of the girls out of the office one of them told me I needn't get any shamrock to send to you. She had got some to send to her boyfriend and though she tried three Post Offices, none of them would accept it. They informed her that owing to a new rule shamrock wasn't allowed to be posted overseas. I can't understand why, but expect they have their own reasons.

I wish I was seeing you soon instead of having to wait months, and all the time I'll keep hoping you don't start inquiring about Scamp.

Well, as it is time I was going to my music lesson I'll end now. Cheerio. —*Always loving you, Muriel*

Wednesday, March 17th

Dearest Muriel,

I received your first two letters today. I expected your mother to go into a fit but as I said before please don't start any arguments. Tell Aunt Vi to keep talking to them and please don't worry as I'm sure everything will turn out all right.

Today I was going to call you up but I had to work this morning. I was going to call you up this afternoon but just happened to think of Shamrock Day and remembered you wouldn't be working so I'll have to try later on during the week. Please forgive me but in this army you never can tell what's going to happen.   —*I love you, Raymond*

PS I'll be expecting the shamrock you promised me. Have you gotten the pin yet?

Wednesday, March 17th

Dearest Ray,

Today as you know is St. Patrick's Day and I got off work for the half-day. Victor asked me to go with him to the Midnight Matinee in the Ritz tonight but I said no because I didn't want to go, and not only that, I wouldn't satisfy the people who gossip in Inglis. They tell me I'm crazy to refuse other "dates" and yet if I didn't refuse them, how they would talk. One of the girls saw Dorothy the other day with an American officer, she sure goes around but then she isn't in love and can't be blamed.

Next Thursday the 25th I'm playing at a concert so I'm going to be kept rather busy practicing until then and won't have much time to go anywhere.   —*Yours as always, Muriel*

Thursday, March 18th

Dearest Muriel,

I just got back from the show here at camp. The name of the picture was "Pride of the Yankees" with Gary Cooper. It was really a good picture but I don't know if you would like it because it's about baseball. After the show I went back to the lab to finish up a little work I had left. It's now about 10:30.

Muriel, I was talking to an Air Corps officer today, I feel like joining the Air Corps. He gave me the papers to fill out and told me what to do if I wanted to join. I really don't know what to do because I have you to think about, also, if I join it would break up all our plans and I hate to do that because I love you too much. My mother wouldn't like it, but I have my life to live and should do what I think is best for me.

If I weren't engaged to you I would join but seeing things the way they are I think I better forget the whole thing. Please don't worry about what I have said here, I just wanted you to know how I felt about everything.

Luke is coming over shortly, when he does I'll let you know and maybe you can all get together for an evening. He wants to see your ring. He may want to get Marie one something like yours.

I received a few more birthday cards from home, they had been damaged by seawater but I was still able to read them. It's the first time I ever received mail in that condition. —*Yours Forever, Raymond*

Friday, March 19th

Dearest Muriel,

I really have reason to be happy today because I received three letters. Tell Dot and Kathleen thanks for their kind words, it's a wonder they went out of their way to speak to you.

I really don't want you to go to the dances, but once in awhile I don't think will hurt you. I'm very jealous but I have to overlook some things because I can't expect you to sit home every evening. As long as you don't have any dates after the dance I won't mind too much.

Tell Auntie Vi I thank her very much for being on our side and think she'll make a swell aunt. I'm glad your mother is changing, as time goes on she'll get used to it and won't take it so hard so please don't worry.

About the shamrock, don't worry about it too much because I can always get some when I come over. Rules are rules and we have to follow them. —*All my love, Raymond*

Saturday, March 20th

Dearest Muriel,

Saturday night and I just finished working. I finally got around to writing you a few lines. Luke is here writing to Marie. In one of her letters she said you hadn't called her up and made any arrangements to go out, if it's so you better call her up soon.

Muriel, you said something about you not wanting to write and tell me what happens at home because it annoys me. It's funny, with any other person I don't want to hear about their troubles, but with you I want to hear everything you have to say. —*All my love, Raymond*

Saturday, March 20th

Dearest Ray,

I haven't written to you since Wednesday mainly because I haven't received any of your letters yet and can't think of what is wrong. On Thursday night I started to write to you but owing to the mood I was in I decided not to and went to bed feeling rather miserable.

Last night I went for my music lesson and afterwards to a girl's house to practice. Kay is her name, she is singing four songs at a concert on Thursday night and I have to accompany her at the piano.

On Wednesday night Auntie Vi and I went to the Ulster Hall. Believe me, Ray, it would have been better if I'd gone to the Red Cross or else stayed home. An American from the 10th station was there and everywhere I went he followed me and kept asking me to dance. I made all kinds of excuses to get away from him but it didn't do any good for he came and sat next to me. He paid me the loveliest compliments imaginable, told me he'd love to call me his girl and kept coaxing me to go out with him. He knew I was engaged but told me I was silly to refuse him because as he put it, "Your boyfriend is going out with other girls, you can be sure of that." If I was to tell you all the things he said, you'd probably get mad so I'd better not. To cut a long story short, I ran and left him, got my coat and left early with Auntie Vi. By the way, the dance was from 9 until 2 a.m. and at about 11 p.m. Dot and Laura, along with a crowd from the Red Cross, arrived to spend the rest of the evening.

As it is time for tea I must end now.   —*Yours as always, Muriel*

PS I trust you and love you and hate that other American for the things he tried to make me believe.

Sunday, March 21st

Dearest Muriel,

Today is the first day of spring and it really was a wonderful spring day. I would have enjoyed it more if I hadn't been sick, about the same as when I was over on leave. If I don't feel better tomorrow I'm going to turn in a sick call.

Muriel, about other "dates," I know it's hard for you to stay home and not go out but I'm doing the same only because I love you so much, so I expect the same from you. So please don't ever have a date with anyone, unless you don't love me, then you can but if I ever hear about it that will mean you don't love me and be the end for us. I know I shouldn't write this, Muriel, but I'm going crazy. I was wishing your parents would let us get married before you're 21 because it's going to be a long and lonesome 9 months. Don't ever think I'll stop loving you, I have not gone out with any other girl since I left you on Christmas Eve and don't expect to.

I hope you're not too nervous next Thursday when you play in the concert.

I guess I better end now as I have an awful headache. I'm going to take a few of your headache tablets and go to bed. —*Always yours, Raymond*

Sunday, March 21ˢᵗ

Dearest Ray,

It's 4:30 Sunday afternoon. Last night after having tea I decided to go to the Red Cross Dance. The dance was unusually crowded and Dot, Laura and Lily were there. Dot and Lily were with boyfriends and Laura was alone so I expect that was why she came over to sit beside me when I arrived. She was more like her old self toward me and even went so far as to ask me to see her this afternoon, but I refused because I just can't forgive her so readily for her cold and distant behavior lately. I know if Lily had been free to sit with her she wouldn't have bothered to talk to me.

Later in the night one of the boys I danced with offered to leave me home, but I left him and rushed to the cloakroom hoping to get the last tram home. When I was waiting for my coat I got talking to a girl who was wearing an engagement ring and had a little badge just like the one you gave me on her coat. She asked me if I was engaged to the boy she used to see me with and told me she is engaged to a boy named Bamette and he is in the 5ᵗʰ General Hospital. She also said she didn't receive a letter from him this week and was almost sure the hospital had moved to you know where. —*Loving you always, Muriel*

PS I hope you're looking after yourself. Have you found out when you can have another furlough?

Monday, March 22ⁿᵈ

Dearest Muriel,

I was really glad to hear your voice again today but for some reason I think you have something on your mind besides being lonesome and missing me. If you are having trouble at home or the office, please, Muriel, I would like to know what it's all about. Maybe I could help you out and I wouldn't worry so much so please don't let me down— tell me what the trouble is.

About myself, today I felt a little better but tonight after I had my (tea as you call it) I laid on the bed for a few minutes to rest. I had some washing to do, but when I woke up it was 10:00. I could have kicked myself. It's now about 10:30 so after I'm through with this letter it's back to bed again.   —*Yours as always, Raymond*

Monday, March 22nd

Dearest Ray,

Today, after not hearing from you for a whole week I was very glad to receive your first letter and a phone call besides. You've no idea how happy I was to get talking to you again and my only regret is that I couldn't say all the things I wanted to say owing to the fact that there were others besides myself in the Time Office at the time. Honestly, Ray, I can't explain the way I felt when I heard you telling me that you love me and want to marry me before I'm 21. I would marry you anytime soon if Mommy and Daddy would only give their consent.

Mommy is always saying to me, "Why don't you go out and enjoy yourself instead of being content to sit at home nights like an old maid," but I just make it clear to her that I have no desire to go out. I think Mommy is still hoping that I meet some boy from my own town and forget about you. I try to please her in most things but to forget you would just be as impossible to me as reaching to the moon.

Tonight Yvonne and Isabel wanted me to go to the Floral Hall with them but as I wanted to write this letter, practice and wash my hair, I had to refuse.

Today I received an invitation card for a dance in the Red Cross Wednesday night. It is the First Annual Dance of District Hqt., U.S. Army and there will be dining, dancing and entertainment—at least so the card says. I haven't decided to go yet, but if I do decide to go, I don't want you to worry. You know you can trust me and besides the dance ends at 11:00 and I can leave early and get a tram home.   —*All my love, Muriel*

Tuesday, March 23rd

Dearest Muriel,

I just got back from the show they had here at camp, it's about 8:30 and I'm all alone, all the boys are out. After I'm through writing I'm going to bed and get a good night sleep.

Well, my love, how have you been? I would still like to know what the trouble is back home. Are they still kidding you at the office? —*All my love, Raymond*

Tuesday, March 23rd

Dearest Ray,

I haven't very much to tell you except that when I write this short letter I may, if I have time, go and phone Marie. I have to go for my music lesson earlier than usual tonight and after that to Kay's house.

Since I started writing this Mommy has said a few little things which I would like to tell you but it would take too long now. —*I love you, Muriel*

PS I don't know what's going to happen but Mommy is worrying herself to death, all because you're a different religion. She says she wouldn't care if you were my religion. Also that she wouldn't mind so much me going away if it was with someone of the same religion. What am I going to do, Ray? I'll go crazy if Mommy keeps on talking the way she is doing. She even says Daddy's worried about me too, and I think he is. Why did we ever have to meet? (Now I've given you an idea of what Mommy said.)

Wednesday, March 24th

Dearest Muriel,

I received your letter you wrote Saturday, March 20th and I'm very disappointed in you. Muriel, when two people love each other they trust and have faith in each other, but from your letter it seems to me you are doubtful. I was never so mad in all my life when I read your letter. Muriel, now get this straight, I love you and only you. I haven't been out with any girl since I left you Christmas Eve. If you don't believe me there is nothing I can do about it, if you're going to be that way there is no use of us being engaged. Another thing, I have written every day and just because you didn't receive any mail from me you didn't write to me. Do you give up that easy, what's wrong with you? When you love someone you never stop, just because you didn't receive my letters you get miserable and don't write, sometimes I wonder if you do love me.

Another thing, from now on *no more dances*, Red Cross, Ulster Hall or any other dance hall. If I ever hear that you go to any dance hall that means our engagement is broken. If you love me you will stay home, the same as I am doing. Every time you go to a dance something happens. So no more dances if you love me, if not, then you can go.

About that American from the 10th station, I want to know his name and where he works. I think, if I am not mistaken, he works in the lab. He told me he was going to try and get a date with you but I thought he was kidding. If I ever get my hands on him I'll break his neck. When a fellow makes a pest of himself can't you tell him to go and not make any excuses? Just don't speak to him or dance with him and tell him to go away or you'll call the M.P. Do something! But seeing you're not going to the dances anymore you won't have that trouble. Where was Aunt Vi all this time? Muriel, I made it clear to you before we got engaged why we shouldn't. I knew things like this would happen but I thought you understood what we both had to go through, that it would be very hard for you, very dull with no good times, etc.

I know this is a nasty letter but I just couldn't help it. Please don't give up so easily!

So now that's the way it is, no dances and no dates. If you don't want to keep to these terms I want my ring back. If you think you will be happier being like Dot and Laura please don't let me stand in your way. I'll have a broken heart but you won't see me or know how much I'll suffer.

I think I have said enough for tonight, in fact I said too much. Please, Muriel, don't get mad or cry, I love you and I know you love me. I'm going crazy here being away from you but I cheer myself up by thinking of the day we will get married and what a wonderful time we will have then, so please don't let me down.

I better stop now as it's 10:00 and the boys want the lights out, so until tomorrow. *—All my love, Raymond*

Wednesday, March 24th

Dearest Ray,

It's about 3:30 p.m. and believe it or not, I'm writing this letter in the office. The boss is out at the moment but I'll have to be very careful he doesn't come back suddenly and catch me writing a letter instead of attending to my work. Perhaps you'll wonder why I'm writing this now instead of waiting until I get home. The reason is that it annoys Mommy when she sees me writing every night and I don't want her to start talking to me the way she did last night

I still haven't made up my mind to go to the dance tonight, but if I do I'll write and tell you about it. There are lots of other little things I would like to say now but I haven't time. I'll write a longer letter next time so until then, cheerio. *—Yours as always, Muriel*

Thursday, March 25th

Dearest Muriel,

Tonight I'm on emergency duty and as I sit here writing I keep looking at the phone wishing there was some way of you calling me up as you did in Belfast. I guess those happy days are over and here I am all alone and lonesome and you are there feeling the same way. Muriel, yesterday, as you probably know by now, I wrote you a nasty letter. I'm really sorry now that I wrote it but I was so mad when I read your letter, especially what that fellow said. The letter also gave me the impression that you didn't trust me and thought I was going out with other girls and telling you lies. That's why I got so mad and wrote what I did.

Muriel, remember I told you I didn't think it was fair for you not to have a good time while you were young and be stuck with me and stay in and not be able to go out with other fellows, etc? But you wanted it that way and said it was worth it and you would wait for me if it were 6 months or 6 years. I know I'm mean and should let you go out but I told you before we got serious I wouldn't allow it and you agreed to it. In yesterday's letter I said that I didn't want you to go to the Red Cross or any other dance and I still feel the same. Maybe later on I'll change my mind but for now if you love me as much as you say, you won't go.

I love you more than words can express and will always be true to you. Keep your chin up and someday soon we'll be together for good and then we will laugh at all this. *—I love you. Raymond*

Friday, March 26th

Dearest Muriel,

There's nothing new here only that Luke will be over next week. I gave him the phone number so he probably will call you up sometime during the week.

Tonight I may go to the Red Cross, if so it will be the first time I've been out all week. If I don't feel much better than I do right at the moment I'll go to bed. Please take care of yourself, everything will be OK. *—I love you, Raymond*

Friday, March 26th

Dearest Ray,

Please forgive me for not writing yesterday but I didn't have a minute to spare. Kay called for me at 6 p.m. and we had to run over the pieces then leave for the concert and when I got back home again it was too late. I'm really sorry, Ray, and the fact that I received two letters from you yesterday makes me feel all the worse. When we arrived at the concert we found that hers was the first item on the programme. She sang very well and I was congratulated for the way I accompanied her. She had several encores and though I was a little nervous at first I soon overcame that and could have played all night.

About the dance Wednesday night, I went to it and would have enjoyed it if I hadn't been thinking of you. Most of the night I danced with a boy whom I knew, who used to dance with me sometimes long ago when you were here. He always tells me I'm the best dancer in the room and has christened me Sad, Mad and in Blue. (The cheeky little squirt.) There were some girls that I knew there so as they were leaving early I left too and came home with them.

As I haven't been to the pictures since you were here I'm going to the Majestic to see Dorothy Lamour in "Beyond the Blue Horizon," have you seen it?

About joining the Air Corps, Ray, even if it wasn't spoiling our plans I wouldn't want you to join. I agree with your mother, it's really too dangerous and I want you to remain alive. Of course, I know there's a war on but the work you do is most essential so please be a good boy and stick to it, most likely you wouldn't be happy in the Air Corps either.

It's about time I was leaving for the pictures so I'll end now.   —*Yours as always, Muriel*

PS All's quiet at home. There were no letters today. Don't worry, I have the pin, you don't trust me and I'm mad.

Saturday, March 27th

Dearest Muriel,

The phone call was short today and I didn't quite get what you told me so if you will write and tell me what you tried to say I can give you an answer. About the letter I wrote Wednesday, I hope you didn't take it too seriously because at the time I was quite mad. I told you I didn't want you to go to the Red Cross dances any more, well, I don't, but if you want to go once every 3 or 4 weeks and no more, it's OK, but no more.

My mother has been sending me telegrams, wondering why she hasn't heard from me. I can't understand it as I have been writing every week. Today I received two letters from home—one took only six days to reach me, the other thirty, so you see it's all mixed up.

Muriel, if you think there is a possible chance of us getting married before your 21st birthday let me know. I have to send papers over there to be signed by your father and mother, then from the date they sign, two month have to elapse before we can get married. If you think it's a good idea let me know.

Luke is on emergency tonight so we are both writing to Ireland. When Luke does see you he'll have something to give you from me. Please don't worry and take care of yourself. *—I love you, Raymond*

Saturday, March 27th

Dearest Ray,

Why had you to say the things you said on the phone today? This morning I had three lovely letters. Then you phoned me and called me a naughty girl and said that I don't trust you. I love you and trust you so please remember that. I guess the letter I wrote did make you mad. Ray, I know I shouldn't write telling you about other boys asking me out so in future I'll only tell you if, and when, I do go out. I love you too much to go out with any other boys I happen to meet so please trust me and don't ever worry. As regards to Ulster Hall, I'm not going back there even if you wanted me to. *—Yours as always, Muriel*

Sunday, March 28th

Dearest Muriel,

You better not let the boss catch you writing letters to me during office hours, he may get mad.

Muriel, about the dances again, I really don't know what to say. I really don't want you to go but then I wonder if it's fair to make you stay in. I'm always afraid you will meet someone else and go out with him, not that I don't trust you, I do with all my heart but I think engaged girls should stay away from dance halls. I stay in every night so I think you should. You knew when you got engaged you wouldn't be able to go out as you did before so please stay away from the dance halls as much as possible. I'm only out once a week, so if I can do it, I think you should too.

Muriel, you go to work and dances and other places and you never say anything about what happens. I wish you would describe more fully what you do during the day. Maybe you think I'm nuts but I just like to know what you do in more detail. *—Always loving you, Raymond*

Sunday, March 28th

Dearest Ray,

It's Sunday once again and no place to go except church. At 9 o'clock last night I went down to the Red Cross and had a few dances. Dot and Laura were there with Dot's boyfriend Al, and I was talking to them for quite awhile. About 10:25 p.m. I left the dance, got a tram home and phoned Marie to have a chat with her. When I was coming up home after phoning Marie I met Auntie Vi and Mrs. Lewis. They were coming from the Opera House and invited me in to have supper with them. Auntie Vi was kidding me about getting married, that she was going to be Matron of Honor and wear a suit of dusky pink and a nice big fox fur. Would you like to see me in a nice shade of pastel blue, that's what I've figured on wearing. I'm going through with everything when I'm 21 so please don't worry. —*Always yours, Muriel*

Monday, March 29th

Dearest Muriel,

About you not writing Thursday it's quite all right. I'm glad the concert went so well and that you were congratulated, that's why I want you to continue your lessons. You're a wonderful player and I love to hear you play the piano.

About joining the Air Corps, please don't worry, I'm not, it was just a brainstorm idea I had. If I could get back to Ireland I would join almost anything. As far as being happy, I'll never be until the day we are married.

I'm glad you got the pin, it's not that I don't trust you it's just that I'm so jealous. —*I love you, Raymond*

Monday, March 29th

Dearest Ray,

How are you getting along, are you still mad at me?

I expect Luke will be over here by the time you get this letter and I'm sure you miss him as I think he is the closest friend you have in the army. If I see him it will probably remind me of old times and make me wish more than ever that you were here again.

Ray, I would like to hear from your people, should I write to your mother or wait until I hear from her? I don't quite know what to do, please tell me and I'll do as you say. —*Forever yours, Muriel*

Dearest Muriel,

With me there is nothing new except I still have that cold hanging on and I can't shake it.

It's about 8 o'clock now and I was just thinking if I were with you now we'd either be home sitting next to the fireplace or at a show. Since I've been here I feel best during the day, it's not so bad while I'm working but after I'm through work and come back to the barracks I really start to feel lonesome. I guess that's something we can't help.

Please keep me posted on family affairs. —*All my love, Raymond*

Tuesday, March 30th

Dearest Ray,

I don't know quite how to begin this letter, today your letter dated March 24th arrived and it upset me very much. Believe me, Ray, I didn't do anything to deserve such a telling off. When I wrote that letter to you and told you about that other American it wasn't to make you jealous, it was only because you asked me to tell you everything that happened while you were away. Now, Ray, let *me* get this straight. If I were going out and having a good time as you call it, do you think I would write and tell you about the different boys I meet? In the first place, I'm not like Dot or Laura and don't want to be. When a boy whom I have just met compliments, flatters or should I say hands me a line, I immediately dislike him. You need never be afraid that I'll meet someone I'll care for more than you. Every minute you are away I'm missing and thinking about you and when I go to a dance, it isn't because I want to meet other boys but because I like dancing. You wrote and told me I wasn't to go to any more, so I won't. Seeing that you worry and don't quite trust me in going to dances nothing on earth will make me go again until I'm with you. I'm not wanting a good time and the only reason I went to Ulster Hall that night was because everybody who can dance goes to a dance on St. Patrick's night, even engaged and married people. The dancing was non-stop and I couldn't get talking to Auntie Vi as she was dancing with a friend of her young brother who is in the navy, but I want you to know that we came home alone. If I thought you thought I was going out with anyone I'd never forgive you. The way I love you I don't want to hurt your feelings in any way so from now onwards I'll go to a show when I feel like it and stay home other nights. I've changed, Ray, there was a time when I used to say I'd never let any boy dictate to me—that was before I met you and fell in love. You want to know what that American's name is, well, I don't know. All I can remember is that he is very tall and doesn't work in the lab. He was what you call a 'jerk,' and there are people like him everywhere. I said enough to him without you saying anything more. Please forget the whole thing, Ray, you'll only make me unhappy if you mention it again.   —*Yours as always, Muriel*

Wednesday, March 31st

Dearest Muriel,

It's about 10:00 and I just got back from the show, the name of the picture was "White Cargo," it wasn't bad but I had expected it to be much better.

Muriel, on the phone today you didn't sound very happy, I got the impression that something was on your mind, maybe I'm wrong but if not I would really like to know what it is.

I told you about Marie, she's gone to Dublin with her mother. Luke doesn't know how long they will be but just as soon as he hears I will let you know.   —*Yours as always, Raymond*

Wednesday, March 31st

Dearest Ray,

Today you phoned me and I was very glad to get talking to you again. That was three letters and a phone call in one day and because of that I'm feeling pretty happy. You said you had a cold and your voice sounded like it so please look after yourself. If your cold doesn't go away please let me know and I'll send you some Syrup of Irish Moss, it will cure it if nothing else will.

I'm sorry to hear about Marie's mother (being ill) and Luke's leave being canceled, I hope everything turns out right for him.   —*Always loving and missing you, Muriel*

April 1943

Dearest Muriel,

I'm sorry about the phone call Saturday, if I made you unhappy I didn't mean it. I guess being away from each other has made us very touchy. I never did doubt you loving me so please forgive me. I see you were at a Red Cross dance again, what did Dot and Laura have to say?

Muriel, please don't worry about me. I still have a little cold but it doesn't bother me now.

I just got back from a show at camp, the Glenn Miller Band was in it and boy was it good. —*Yours forever, Raymond*

Thursday, April 1st

Dearest Ray,

Everything is very quiet and dull here at present and the weather is just awful.

Yesterday when you phoned me you asked me to ask Mommy and Daddy if they would consent to us getting married before I'm 21 yrs. So far I haven't asked them as they have been pretty quiet lately and I'm afraid they'll go off the deep end again if I do. Another thing, Ray, are you sure you won't be sent to Africa? I hope not. If you ever inquire about Scamp I'll go nuts. At the moment he is in the best of health and I'm sure he'll be that way for the duration. —*Yours always, Muriel*

Friday, April 2nd

Dearest Muriel,

It's about 11:00 and we just got back from town and the Red Cross. At about 9:30 a fire started a block away (all us fellows dashed over) it burned for almost two hours and the whole town was lit up. It's a good thing there weren't any German planes around. We helped the firemen with the fire hoses and got our hands and pants dirty but it was fun. At 10:30 we left because they had it under control, went back to the Red Cross and washed up. Luke was there but he didn't dirty his hands. First real excitement since I've been here.   *—Loving and missing you, Raymond*

Friday, April 2ⁿᵈ

Dearest Ray,

Daddy bought a plot of ground a few weeks ago and at the moment he, along with Mommy and the two children have gone to the plot to plant seeds. As vegetables are very scarce now we have decided to grow our own.

At lunchtime today Mommy and I got talking and I told her you wanted to marry me before I'm 21 yrs. She nearly had another fit, Ray, and told me she will never give consent to me marrying at all, never mind before I'm 21 yrs. She says she's praying that something happens so we can't get married, but I told her I was marrying you when I came of age and the conversation ended at that. I guess we'll just have to wait, Ray, because it's hopeless trying to get permission.   *—Yours always, Muriel*

Saturday, April 3ʳᵈ

Dearest Ray,

Today is one of the most beautiful days I've seen in a long time. It's actually very warm and sunny. I'm here alone thinking of old times when we used to meet and go to Bellevue, do you remember the long climb up the hill and the lovely view there was?

In the office this morning Adeline and I arranged to meet tonight at 5:45 and go to a show. At the moment I haven't much news to tell you except that Greta called at lunchtime today to tell me she had found another job.

It's about 4:45 now so I think I'll have something to eat and go into town to meet Adeline. *—I love you, Muriel*

Sunday, April 4ᵗʰ

Dearest Muriel,

Let me explain why I didn't write yesterday. Yesterday I worked all day and after work I started to get sick like I was when I was over on leave. I went up to the doctor, got some medicine and went to bed. This morning I felt 100% better.

This afternoon I had off and it really was a beautiful day. Luke and I went for a walk and at 5:30 we went to the Red Cross and had supper. After supper we came back to camp and it's now about 7:30 and I'm writing to you.

Muriel, I'm really sorry, honest, I can see how wrong I was in writing that letter on the 24th. Please forgive me, I do trust you. I told you that you couldn't go to the Red Cross dances anymore. I'm sorry, Muriel, if you want to go it's OK, but not too often.   —*All my love, Raymond*

Sunday, April 4th

Dearest Ray,

Greta called this afternoon and we went for a short walk. She has gone now as she has to meet her boyfriend. Last night Adeline and I got in the Ritz after standing an hour in a line. After the show we had a hurried supper in the Lido as we had to get the last tram home. To-day has been another beautiful one and I'm wishing more than ever that you were here so we could go to Bellevue like we used to. —*Yours always, Muriel*

Monday, April 5th

Dearest Muriel,

Another letter arrived today dated April 1st, you said the weather there was awful, well, here it has been wonderful, warm and lots of sunshine.

About Scamp, I don't think you'll have to worry about him as far as I know, so hope and pray he'll be OK.

Tonight I'm working on emergency and trying to write this letter is like pulling teeth as I have to stop every few minutes.

Last night Luke called up Marie, she's home now. Luke may come over next week—if he does I'll let you know.   —*Loving you always, Raymond*

Monday, April 5th

Dearest Ray,

Two more letters arrived today and I was very glad and happy to get them. Somehow when I receive your letters I feel in great form and I must look happy for the girls in the office can always tell. Other days when I don't receive a letter and look not so bright they call me love-sick and tell me to cheer up, I'll soon be dead. Isabel is getting married in three weeks time and she is kidding me more than anyone else. She wants me to go to a show with her on Thursday night, so I think I will. —*Always yours, Muriel*

Tuesday, April 6th

Dearest Muriel,

I'm just about done writing all of my Easter cards for home. I was just thinking it would be swell if I could spend Easter with you this year but as things are it's almost impossible.

Tonight I was thinking of going to the show but instead I'm going to bed. I may go tomorrow night, Clark Gable and Lana Turner are playing together in "Somewhere I'll Find You," or something like that and they say it's very good.   —*Always yours, Raymond*

Tuesday, April 6th

Dearest Ray,

If by some miracle I could be all set for going over to marry you tomorrow I'd be the happiest girl in the world. As everything is now I can't help worrying. I'd give anything on earth to have Mommy and Daddy give their consent and not feel bad about it. The sooner they realize we do intend getting married the better so please send the papers across. Sometime when I find the courage and get Daddy by himself I'll show them to him and tell him straight that if he doesn't consent we are going to get married when I'm 21 yrs. Only there's one thing you must know. I can't make it harder for them to bear by getting married in chapel—it will have to be in a Registry Office or in my church. A marriage in either of these is a marriage in the eyes of the law no matter whether your church recognizes it or not. A Roman Catholic girl told me a wedding in a Protestant Church wasn't in the eyes of God, well, I think that was an awful thing for her to say because in any church that teaches about God a wedding is a wedding in His eyes. Ray, please let me know where it's to be and if you still don't want to get married in my church then we can get married in a Registry Office and that will settle everything. Try and understand my point of view, Ray, and send me your answer as soon as you get this. —*Always loving and missing you, Muriel*

Wednesday, April 7th

Dearest Muriel,

Receiving two letters today and having talked to you also, I feel very happy tonight. In your letter of Friday the 2nd I see you are taking a turn at farming. I think it's a swell idea, I wish I was there to help. Where is the plot of ground—is it far from the house?

I'm glad to see you're going to have your picture taken Saturday. My mother wants a few more of my picture to give to friends, etc.

She's been asking for others every time she writes. Can you see if they can make six more of the one you have and if they will let me know and I will send you the money. —*Always yours, Raymond*

Wednesday, April 7th

Dearest Ray,

Today I received another two letters from you, they were dated the 1st and 2nd of April. I'm very glad you phoned today, Ray, and I'm glad you're going to try to phone me again on Saturday morning.

The concert I played in was held in a hall connected with a church on University Road, if you know where that is. You asked if I have my dress yet, do you mean my wedding dress? If so, I haven't, but I have twenty coupons which I'm going to save and add more to, which I intend to beg, borrow or steal, and when I have enough I'll buy my trousseau. Did you tell your mother that my mother is against us getting married? —*I love you. Muriel*

Thursday, April 8th

Dearest Muriel,

Today I didn't receive any letters from you so I really haven't much to say. As you know Luke is coming over next week to see Marie, I wish I was coming with him.

I wrote a few more Easter cards to people back home so I hope I didn't leave anyone out, my aunts and uncles always expect a card.

Give regards to the family and take care of yourself. —*Always yours, Raymond*

Thursday, April 8th

Dearest Ray,

Tonight Isabel and I are going to the pictures, it will be a change to have someone with me but I'm not really caring as I've got accustomed to going by myself. How are you getting along, I only wish you were coming over with Luke next week because I know that seeing him will only make me miss you more than ever.

About leaving the Red Cross dance to put that fire out, I would have loved to have been there to see you. I bet it caused a lot of excitement in such a little town.

I must stop writing, Ray, Isabel is calling for me. —*Yours always, Muriel*

Lockport, NY, April 8ᵗʰ

Dear Ray,

I was very happy to get your nice long letter even if I did have to wait months for it. I had your mother send a package of things, when it was possible to send them, but she either forgot to say they were from me or you forgot to mention it. At any rate we are all well and busy as bees. There is no such thing as people sitting or hanging around anymore, everybody that is able is working.

No doubt your mother has told you all about the house she is fixing up. I talked her into buying it so it would give her a chance to think of something else besides you. Inasmuch as her worrying does you no good, I could not see the sense of it. I was afraid it was affecting her mind so I did more than my best to talk her into buying it. She is of course very tired but looks much better. She is kept so busy worrying about the painter, the paperhanger and etc, that it gives her a chance to forget My Boy...My Boy, for a few hours.

Edmond, as you may know is in Africa, he does not seem to like it even a little bit. He says he would like to get hold of the fellow that wrote the wonderful tales about Africa that he read in his school books. He says he is sure the fellow never made it his business to see the darn place otherwise he could not have possibly had the heart to write all the baloney. I see by the paper that his commanding officer has been put in charge of all ground forces. His name is Patton.

Things here are not bad at all, we still get plenty to eat...not the steaks we were used to but nevertheless the meat is not too bad, tho a bit tough. Since I have good teeth I do not mind it too much. As for canned goods, Grandmother never did like stuff out of cans so it really does not affect us much. Prices are a bit high, but not beyond our reach so that all in all we are not suffering a bit. The cut in gas to 1½ gallons a week goes a bit hard on us but if that is all we are called upon to do we will not mind. Too, people are so busy working and on all kinds of shifts that very few have much time for pleasure.

Your mother has the lower apartment done and it's a beauty. There is still quite a bit to be done on the upper where your sister is going to live. My place in Lowertown is coming along now, it will look very nice too when I am through with it.

I was going to send you an Easter card but thought that you might enjoy this more. Be good and take care of yourself. —*Love from all of us, Aunt Rose*

PS Your mother told me you got the cards. The fish must have a lot of fun reading some of these letters, Ah!

Friday, April 9th

Dearest Muriel,

Tonight I can't make up my mind if I should go to the show, the Red Cross dance or stay in and go to bed. Whatever I do it won't stop me from missing and thinking about you. It's funny—the boys here tell me I'm lovesick also. *—I love you, Raymond*

Friday, April 9th

Dearest Ray,

Your letters are coming all topsy-turvy, today I received two more, one dated March 31st and one dated April 4th. I was very glad to get them, especially the one with the photographs. Have you any more of the family, if so I'd love you to send them to me. The one of you, Dot and me is quite good and certainly brought memories. Can you remember where we were going that night?

I stayed in tonight and practiced. It's supper time now, Ray, so I better stop writing. *—Yours always, Muriel*

Saturday, April 10th
Dearest Muriel,

It's just about 10 o'clock now I just got back from town with Luke. We went to a dance hall, if you can call it that. Luke and I left after about an hour and went to the Red Cross. The boys wanted to know why I looked so sad and didn't dance. They don't know why but you and I do. I wanted to call you up this morning but was too busy. Tomorrow I have to work all day and at night pull emergency. *—I love you, Raymond*

Saturday, April 10th

Dearest Ray,

This afternoon I went into town and had my photograph taken as I promised. I hope they turn out good but I don't think so because I didn't feel like smiling and had to force myself to do so. It's 6:30 now and Mommy, Daddy and the children are at the plot.

I was very disappointed today when you didn't phone me, but I understand how difficult it is for you to get through and you were probably working and hadn't time.

I had a letter from the Red Cross and it says, "If for any reason you do not intend to use your pass, will you kindly return it for cancellation so we may make a place for someone on our waiting list." Ray, what should I do, should I return my pass or should I keep it so that we can go there next time you come on leave? I don't like going to the Red Cross when I know you don't like me to but as I received a letter from you telling me that you trust me and I can go once in awhile, I don't think you'll mind so much if I go tonight.

It's too late for a show and when I sit home on a night like Saturday night it only makes me get depressed. I promise you I'll leave early and get a tram home. —*Always loving and missing you, Muriel*

Sunday, April 11th

Dearest Muriel,

Before I start I want to say how happy I am today because I received three letters.

About the chapel, I'm not sure if I do have to marry you in chapel to make it recognized by my church but I'll find out and let you know. If we have to get married in a chapel it will be in a chapel. What we can do is get married in your church and then when we go home we will get married in my church. I think that is what most people do—I'll find out and let you know. About what that Catholic girl said, not being in the eyes of God, please, Muriel, don't pay any attention to talk like that. It really burns me up to see people in 1943 being so narrow-minded. There's nothing wrong in you getting married in a Catholic Church or me getting married in your church, so please don't worry about it too much.

About your wedding dress, I'll see if I can help you get some coupons. I really don't know much about getting married, what to do, etc.

Tonight I'm on emergency—Luke is here with me, writing.   —*I love you, Raymond*

Sunday, April 11th

Dearest Ray,

Auntie Vi is back in England again. She had a telegram to say her mother is very ill and had to leave on Friday night. I missed her today because I usually have her company on a Sunday.

Last night I went to the Red Cross dance about 9 o'clock and left it again at 10:15. Dot was there with her boyfriend Al, and she called me over to ask me how I was keeping and how you were getting along. Lily was there with an American from the 10th station. She's supposed to be engaged to her boyfriend who is in Africa and yet she is going out with another boy here. It's a wonder she promised to wait for the one who is away.

Everything is pretty quiet here except that Mommy keeps telling me to go out more instead of sitting in the house. Daddy has bought another plot and he along with Mommy, Audrey and Olive go to it nearly every night in the week. They would like me to go with them but I don't want to. They say Dr. Cooke and his wife have a plot next to ours and some nights he, along with his wife, is there. (Dr. Cooke is my doctor.)

As I want to practice I'll stop writing now.   —*I love you, Muriel*

PS I must phone Marie tomorrow and find out how her mother is. I hope Luke doesn't have to cancel his leave again.

Monday, April 12th

Dearest Muriel,

Last night I didn't sleep much. I was dreaming of you all night long and wishing you were with me. They say if you dream a wish long enough your dream will come true, I hope so.

I was just thinking, if you marry me against your parent's wishes they may not even come to the wedding or help you in getting set for the wedding. But, if say they did agree, what do you plan on having, a quiet wedding, or is it going to be a big affair? Let me have some idea so I can make plans as to what I should do.   —*I love you, Raymond*

Monday, April 12th

Dearest Ray,

Today I am feeling rather miserable, Mommy told me this morning that she can't sleep at night worrying about me and says she hopes I get some sense and break off with you. I'm absolutely fed up listening to Mommy talk that way. I know I'll never love anyone else the way I love you and yet Mommy tells me it's only calf love and I'll soon get over it. It isn't calf love, I'm positive of it but there's no use trying to make Mommy believe that, she just won't listen and that's what maddens me. About sending the papers over, I guess it would be hopeless. Mommy will never consent so I'll just have to wait until I'm 21 then go ahead without consent. Lots of girls have had to do that so I won't be the first one.

It's about time to go to the Majestic now so I'll stop writing. —*Yours as always, Muriel*

Tuesday, April 13th

Dearest Ray,

I haven't to go for my music lesson tonight owing to the fact that my music teacher has the flu. I'm staying home anyway as I have some mending to do and I want to wash my hair. Last night I went to the Majestic and saw "All Through the Night," it was quite good, have you seen it? As it was only 10:15 when I reached Shaftesbury Square I decided to phone Marie and have a chat with her. She seemed very happy about Luke coming over. I wish you were coming along with him.

Mommy, Daddy, Audrey and Olive are out again tonight so I am here by myself. You asked me where the plots are, well, all I know is that one of them is near Belvoir Park and the other is off some country road near Annadale Embankment.

Today Mommy hasn't mentioned your name. I'm hoping everything turns out OK as you say it will. Isn't it queer, Daddy never says a word to me. Auntie Vi once told me that she heard him telling Mommy to leave me alone. I have a good father and mother, Ray, but Mommy's love for me is such that she doesn't want me to ever leave her and go far away.

I think I'll end now and get something else done. I hope you're not missing Luke too much. —*Yours as always, Muriel*

Wednesday, April 14th

Dearest Muriel,

As you know I didn't write yesterday, I hope you'll forgive me. I had to work late but most of all I was sad because Luke had left and I was left behind.

Muriel, about the Red Cross pass, I really don't know what to say. I really don't want you to go but I guess it's OK if you don't go too often, leave early and get the last tram home.

Today was my day off. On the phone you sounded down-hearted, is there something wrong, Muriel, if so please let me know.

This afternoon I went into town and sent a telegram home for my mother's birthday then went to a show. I came out at seven and then went to the Red Cross, had supper and then came back. My cold is gone now so please don't worry about it.   —*Always yours, Raymond*

Wednesday, April 14th

Dearest Ray,

Before I write about anything else I want you to know that I am very sorry for the way I spoke on the phone today. Things went wrong in the office this morning and I got so worried and bad tempered that I couldn't be nice to anyone. This is what happened. Yesterday afternoon I was transferring new paper into a loose-leaf ledger and in doing so one of the old ones must have accidentally slipped off my desk onto the floor without me knowing. Anyway, this morning I missed it and though I hunted through every drawer in my desk I couldn't find it. I nearly went crazy, Ray, because all of the old pages out of that ledger must be kept safe for the auditors to check and I knew if the boss discovered it was lost he'd raise h---. When you phoned me I'd given up hope of ever finding it and was so worried and mad that I couldn't even be nice to you. It's not that I was caring what the boss would say to me because I'm not afraid of him. It's just that I don't like anything going wrong with the books I keep, and that page contained most important figures. To cut a long story short, I found it where I least expected to. After 5 o'clock at night two women come to clean our office and they empty the contents of all the wastebaskets into a big sack and when it's full it's taken to the wastepaper depot. Well, at 12:30 I suddenly had an idea that the women might have found the paper and thinking it was wastepaper put it in the sack. Peggy, one of the other girls and I went to the room where the sack is kept, emptied all of the paper out of it and after a bit of hunting we finally found it all crumpled up in a little ball. You've no idea how relieved I was, Ray, I was so glad I nearly hugged the life out of Peggy. The page was in such a state I had to make out a new one, but I didn't mind, all that mattered was I'd found it.

All afternoon I worried about the phone call but believe me, Ray, I'm sorry if I sounded awful to you or said anything to have you worried. You asked me if there was anything wrong but I had to say no just in case Miss Collins would be listening. When I finish writing this I think I'll go to the Regal and on my way home phone Marie. If Luke has two letters for me I certainly want to get them.   —*Yours always, Muriel*

Thursday, April 15th

Dearest Muriel,

Today I was very happy. I received two more letters from you of the 11th & 12th.

I'm sorry to hear about Aunt Vi's mother, when you see or write to her send my regards.

Muriel, I think it would be a good idea to go with your mother and father to the plot once in awhile. You could throw in a few good words for us—also I think they would like to have you with them.

About what your mother said, Muriel, I wish I knew what to do but with me over here there's not a thing I can do for you. The only thing you can do is keep away from arguments as much as possible—you know it's no use talking to her. I hope this letter finds you and your mother in a better mood. —*All my love, Raymond*

Friday, April 16th

Dearest Muriel,

Just finished work so I thought I would write you a few lines. It's now about 10 o'clock, you see I'm on emergency tonight and had to mop the floors and I just got done.

Today I received a telegram from my parents for my birthday on March 9th, but I received the telegram today because they had my name spelt wrong. They had a G instead of an F, isn't that crazy, they can't even copy straight, I mean the telegram people. I'm glad I got it even though it was over a month late. —*As always, Raymond*

Saturday, April 17th

Dearest Ray,

I am sorry for not writing on Thursday night. I phoned Marie on Wednesday night. Luke was there and they asked me to have lunch with them on Thursday. I said I would and told Luke I'd have his life if he forgot to bring your two letters along. We met at the Carlton and honestly, Ray, Luke teased me an awful lot. First he tried to make me believe he had forgotten the letters, then he started to tell me about the beautiful girl who works in the lab, he even told me her name but I can't remember it. He said the boys took turns at taking her out but I know he was only kidding so please don't say a word to him.

When I got back to the office I took on an awful headache, it got worse after tea time and I felt so sick I had to go to bed.

This morning I sent the office message boy to Louis Morrison for the proofs of my picture and when I saw them I couldn't believe it was me, they're so flattering. The girls in the office think they're very good and if you like them half as well I'll be satisfied. There's one good thing about them, my freckles don't show, that's one over on you.

I hope you aren't missing Luke too much. I missed Dot, Laura and Lily a little bit at first, but not any longer.   —*Yours always, Muriel*

PS Did you tell your mother I'm going to stay Protestant?

Sunday, April 18th

Dearest Muriel,

Tonight I went to town with the boys hoping to see "Springtime in the Rockies" but to our surprise it's not playing until Monday. I hear it's a wonderful picture, have you seen it yet? If not, don't miss it if it ever comes to town. Seeing there was nothing else to do we walked about town and then went to the Red Cross. It's about 9:30 now and we just got back.

How are you doing, still as lonesome as I am? I go around in a daze wishing you were here with me and when I see another couple walking along I think of the wonderful times we had.   —*I love you, Raymond*

Sunday, April 18th

Dearest Ray,

Auntie Vi, Betty and Raymond arrived back from England yesterday morning so I may go into her house when I finish writing and spend the evening there. In your letters you asked me quite a few questions so I will do my best to answer them.

About the kind of wedding I want—every girl dreams of a beautiful white wedding with the organ playing and choir singing as she walks up the aisle, a reception afterwards with all her friends invited and then a lovely honeymoon. Now with a war on people can't have that kind of wedding because they haven't coupons to spend on a wedding dress which they can't wear afterwards. Instead girls buy costumes or short dresses with accessories to match and then they can wear them after they are married. Ours will have to be a quiet wedding, Ray, with a best man and one bridesmaid because if my parents don't give their consent it will mean I have to save and buy all my trousseau myself. If they do consent, which is most unlikely, I won't have to worry about money. Another thing, Ray, I've often wondered where we'll go to get married. I mean if I don't get consent, it will be impossible for me to stay in the house until my wedding day, could you picture the scene that would be? As regards to getting married in a chapel here, that's impossible. There's a chance Mommy and Daddy would forgive me for getting married without their consent if I get married in church but if I get married in chapel they never would, I know that for certain. Even Auntie Vi says if you love me enough you'll marry me in church. There are two cathedrals here—one is St. George's and the other St. Anne's. They are high Church of Ireland and I know for certain either of them will marry a Protestant and Catholic. I know I'm giving up more than you so surely you could give up a little too and make what I'm giving up a little less. Besides, Mommy and Daddy will be more likely to give consent and come to the wedding if we get married in church and if that happens, I promise you I won't be a sad wife.

It's time for tea now so I must stop writing. Please be good and don't get mad at anything I've said.   —*Yours always, Muriel*

Monday, April 19th

Dearest Muriel,

I received two letters from home today. My mother said if I love you she wants me to marry you, if not now, after the war. I told her about religion and your parents not agreeing and she said not to worry about it, we could do whatever we wanted to do and be very happy. She's a swell mother, Muriel, she's always for me no matter what I do. So stop worrying about your mother and what she says. When the time comes for us to get married I know your mother will agree.

Tonight I'm working emergency, I wasn't listed to work but I'm taking over for another fellow who is going on leave.

Muriel, as you know this week is Easter and I have a two-day pass. The boys want me to go to Bournemouth, it's on the coast. I'm wondering if it would be OK with you if I did go. I'm going to try and call you up this week and ask you if it's OK, if not I want you to say so. I promise not to go out with any girl, etc. so please don't take me wrong, it's just that I have to get away from here once in awhile.

About Wednesday, I knew there was something wrong with you, Muriel, but I didn't want to ask you as I thought it was family trouble. I'm sorry about what happened at the office, knowing how important the papers were, but please don't get sick over something like that. Remember I'm going to marry you someday and I don't want you getting gray hairs like I have.   —*I love you, Raymond*

Monday, April 19th

Dearest Ray,

Today has been much like any other day except that I was more busy than usual at the office. I'm sitting next to Adeline now and honestly, Ray, I've got an awfully sore left arm. Every time she wants to tell me something she reaches out and gives me an awful thump on the arm. She does it unconsciously so now I've got that every time she hits me I hit her back, all in fun of course.

After lunch when I was going back to the office I met the postman at the end of Donegall Pass. He always kids me and tells me I'm very greedy for letters. I asked him why he didn't leave me one this morning and he said, "Trust me not to forget you, I've got one for you now." He gave me the one dated April 14th and I ran the rest of the way to the office to get reading it before work started.

At 1 p.m. I rushed into town to the photographers to leave the proofs in. I'm getting three of each position on Saturday and will send you two of each with the letter I write then. I asked the girl in the photographers if I could have six more of your photograph. She said certainly, but as they are very busy owing to the holidays it will probably be a few weeks before they are ready.

On Saturday night when I was going to the Majestic I met Greta at the tram stop at Bradbury Place. She had a date with someone who didn't show up and was going to the Majestic herself so we went together. She said she would call tonight but hasn't done so, so I guess I'll just go to the Regal myself. I'd rather go by myself than with Greta because she's a very depressing kind of girl. I like a girl whose good fun but Greta only makes me miserable the way she grumbles about being "fed up."   —*Yours as always, Muriel*

Tuesday, April 20th

Dearest Muriel,

There's really not much new here, I received a few more Easter cards from home but that's about all. Luke should be coming back in a few days—I hope so because I miss him. The boys just brought in some Coke and we have a few cookies so we will have our little snack, then lights out.

I guess that's about all for now. Just think, in another month or so maybe I'll be able to come over.   —*All my love, Raymond*

Wednesday, April 21st

Dearest Muriel,

I felt much better today after phoning you and seeing you were a little happier than the last time I phoned you.

Tonight I just got back from town and saw "Springtime in the Rockies" and it was swell. Harry James's band played in it. I danced to his band two or three time back home and when he started to play I could hardly stay still in my seat. To top it off he played "You Made Me Love You," that's the song that made him famous. I got more enjoyment from that picture than any other since I've been here.

The boys want the lights out so I better stop, but tomorrow will write again. *—I love you, Raymond*

Wednesday, April 21st

Dearest Ray,

Your phone call today made me very happy and I'm glad to know that your mother is quite agreeable to us getting married and me remaining Protestant. I hope you write and tell me in more detail what she said in reply to your letter.

About you going to Bournemouth, it's all right with me, Ray—I may be selfish but not that much. I mean I love and trust you and in a way I'm glad you're going to have that little bit of enjoyment. I only wish that I was there to go with you and hope this is the only Easter we'll ever be parted.

Yesterday morning when I was rushing down Cromac Street I met George Clarke and he stopped his bicycle to talk to me. He said he heard about the little quarrel I had with the girls and told me to forget about it and come up to the house any night I wanted to.

That was all that was said as I was late and had to hurry on to the office. As regards to visiting the Clarke house, I may be lonely but that would be the last place I would think of going. *—Loving you always, Muriel*

Thursday, April 22nd

Dearest Muriel,

Received your letter of Saturday the 17th today and was very glad to hear from you. I'm glad to see you contacted Luke and everything is OK. When he comes back I'll get even with him for him teasing you so much (kidding).

I'm glad to see you have the proofs of your picture, please hurry with them and send them over. I'm sorry your freckles don't show, darn the photographer, he probably took them out but I'll be satisfied without them. —*Always yours, Raymond*

Thursday, April 22nd

Dearest Ray,

Last night after I wrote to you I did some washing. It was about 9:30 when I finished and as it was quite clear I decided to take Scamp out for a walk as he hadn't been out all day. I took him up Botanic Avenue, cut through University Square into University Street and was walking down Bradbury Place when I met a girl I know. Her name is Hazel and although I seldom see her we used to be great friends at school. She said she went quite often to the pictures by herself and was coming from the Majestic when she spied me with Scamp. We walked down Shaftesbury Square together and before we parted we arranged to go to a show tomorrow night. While I was talking to Hazel I noticed she was wearing a little badge just like the one you gave me. I asked her how she came to have it and she told me her boyfriend who is in the 5th General gave it to her. She also told me the hospital had moved to England (as if I didn't know) and she was corresponding with the boy who gave her the badge. I can't remember his name, Ray, but if I find out perhaps you know him. He is one of the crowd who left here on January 16th, that should be a clue.

Mommy, Daddy and the children are out tonight and won't be back until around 10:30. I didn't go with them but I'll go some night next week perhaps. It will be better than sitting in the house alone. —*Yours always, Muriel*

Lockport, NY
Thursday, April 22nd

Hello Brother Brat,

We received your letter of the 5th today and as Mother is working at Gould's Flower Shop today and the rest of the week, I am answering your letter. So my brother went and did it, you are finally caught and by an Irish girl at that. How does it feel to be tied down? I have been that way since December 1st and by the time you receive this letter I shall be married. Yes, brother dear, I am going to get married. Wednesday of next week I am leaving Buffalo and will arrive in Fayetteville, NC on Tuesday and Wednesday night Stan and I will be one. Stan was stationed at Fort McClellan, Alabama, but about two weeks ago was transferred to Fort Bragg, your old hunting grounds. Ray, would you believe it, for the first week Stan was with the 66th General Hospital, your old unit. I thought that I would wait until the end of this war to get married but I find that I love Stan too much to wait, so we are going to get married next week. It is going to be hard for me to get married down there as I will be all alone as no one from home is going down with me. I shall tell you all about this when I see you. Stan is a grand person and I know that you will like him.

Ray, I shall probably get shot for this, so don't tell Mother. If you feel that you want to get married now, go ahead and take your happiness while you are still young and don't wait until this mess is over. If you love her and she loves you religion, hardships and everything else shouldn't stop you. Ray, now that you are engaged, don't you think that you better stay where you are and not try to join the Air Cadets? When you come home you can go to college and take up whatever you want, you won't be too old. Save some money now and later you can use it to a good advantage.

Ray, Grandpa is ill, and we do hope that he gets quite well soon. He has been sick for about a week now and last night had a temperature of 105. He is a little better today.

Mother will write to you sometime next week and we will keep your secret until you tell us it's OK to tell.

Well, brother dear, when you receive this letter I will be a Mrs. instead of a Miss. I will write to you from Fort Bragg so keep your nose clean. I promise to write you at least once a month and tell you all. Please stay where you are and don't join the Air Force—this is your big sister telling you! Be good and keep your chin up, we miss you and hope to see you soon. —*Love from all of us, Your Big Sister "Jo"*

Friday, April 23rd

Dearest Muriel,

Today is just two years since I was inducted into the army. It seems a lot longer but I imagine the next two will seem even longer.

In the letter you wrote Sunday about the wedding, Muriel, I'm going to leave everything up to you, you can plan it all. I'll marry you wherever you want to, in a church or a cathedral, if it's going to make you happy, well, then I'll do as you say. I love you and I want to see you happy.

Now I hope you feel better and stop worrying about it. You can tell your parents what I said and I know they also will feel better about it. Don't forget to tell them I'm only doing it because I love you so and couldn't be happy without you, also you are giving up a lot of things to marry me so in return I'm giving up some for you.

I thought you were teased a lot at the office but now if the postman teases you, that takes the cake. I don't know why but everyone likes to tease you, maybe it's because you're such a good sport.

I guess it's about time to turn in. They had a picture here at camp and now I'm getting my things ready for tomorrow, which I don't think I'll be using because all the boys are broke, me included so we may not go tomorrow. —*Always missing and loving you, Raymond*

Friday, April 23rd

Dearest Ray,

If you were here right now you would laugh at me, I have the hiccups. I'm in my bedroom writing this and Audrey is lying across the bed reading.

Isabel Ellis is getting married on Wednesday and everybody in the office contributed toward buying her a wedding present. The present was presented to her at 5 o'clock tonight and John, one of the boys, made a speech. She is going to Dublin for her honeymoon and after that she is going to live in Sydenham. That's the first place the train stops on its way to Bangor.

I'm going to the pictures tonight with Hazel so I'll have to stop writing now and get ready.   —*Yours forever, Muriel*

Saturday, April 24th

Dearest Ray,

In this letter I'm enclosing the photographs I promised you.

Hazel's boyfriend's name is Louis Cross, do you know him? He worked in ward G when stationed here. How do you like Bournemouth? —*I love you, Muriel*

Sunday, April 25th

Dearest Muriel,

It's about 8:30 and I just got back from Bournemouth. I didn't write yesterday but I'll explain in tomorrow's letter why and what we did, etc. I want to answer your two letters I received and then get to bed. Boy, am I tired, I played football and it almost killed me so if it's a short letter now please don't mind, I'll make it up tomorrow.

I'm glad to hear that everything is quiet at home and hope it continues so. About what my mother said, she didn't go into detail, she just told me to do as I wanted because she wanted me to be happy and she wouldn't stand in the way. As far as religion, she said we could still be happy and thought there wasn't any harm in it.

I'm glad you didn't mind me going to Bournemouth as I don't mind you going anyplace because I love and trust you.

My legs and back are so sore I can hardly move and can hardly climb into bed. I'll be lucky if I can get up tomorrow at 5:30. I'll never play football for three hours again, so help me.   —*I love you, Raymond*

Sunday, April 25th

Dearest Ray,

Yesterday's letter was rather short owing to the fact that Hazel called on her way from business and had so much to talk about that I couldn't write very well when she was in. She wanted me to go for a walk but it started raining so heavily that she left and went home. It was then almost 8:30 so with having nothing to do, I suddenly made up my mind to go to the Red Cross and spend the rest of the night there. Laura and Dot were there with Tex and Laura came over to talk to me for awhile. Since you've gone away the Red Cross dances aren't the same. I can't enjoy dancing with other boys so after a few dances I got my coat and came home.

At 2 o'clock today Hazel called round and as it was raining and rather stormy we stayed in until 4:30. It stopped raining then so we went to Isabel's house to see her wedding presents. We stayed with Isabel for about an hour then we left, took a tram into town and had tea in Whitehall Café. After that we walked home and Hazel is here now. She's a great bookworm so I gave her "Gone With the Wind" to keep her quiet while I write this to you and I must say, it has kept her quiet because she hasn't interrupted me once. As I've told you all the latest news I'll end now and get some supper for Hazel and me. With having her for company I'm a little less lonely the last few days but I'll never be happy until we are together again.   —*Yours, Muriel*

PS I'm glad your mother is on our side and I'm praying that Mommy gives her consent.

Monday, April 26th

Dearest Muriel,

I'm still sore all over, even more so than yesterday—I can hardly walk now and only hope I'm better tomorrow.

At about 2 o'clock on Saturday we got the bus and arrived in Bournemouth at about 4:30. We got our rooms at the Red Cross and went into town for tea, as you call it, at Bobby's restaurant. As there were five of us everyone kept looking at us, you see there are very few Yanks in Bournemouth. At about 5:30 we tried to get into a dance

hall, the Pavillion and others, but they were booked up weeks ahead. After walking around until nine o'clock we decided to go back to the Red Cross because there wasn't anything else to do.

Their dance was in a small room and the orchestra was a player piano, all in all it was pretty lousy. About eleven o'clock I was thinking of going to bed and an air raid started. The dance stopped and most of the people left especially when the guns started going off. To make matters worse it was windy and raining. The raid stopped about 12:30 so we went upstairs and just got into bed when another raid started. This time I said the h--- with this, I'm going to bed boys, so we stayed in and kidded around. We had a few RAF boys in with us talking, etc. At 1:30 the raid was over so we said goodnight. Sunday morning we got up at nine o'clock, believe it or not, and went to church, I even surprised myself. We walked around and took some pictures and then went back to the Red Cross where I almost killed myself playing football. I played until about 2 o'clock, went in for lunch and then went out for another hour. All this time I didn't feel too bad, a little tired but no pain. We then washed up and got packed, took another walk along the beach, took more pictures, came back and had a Coke, then got the bus back to camp. I can't say I had a good time but I enjoyed myself being away from camp. Bournemouth is really beautiful, it's the closest thing to home I've seen since I've been here. The place was packed with people on holiday—I bet it was swell in peacetime.

As I'm writing Luke and three other boys are here writing also (in the lab). Luke told me how he kidded you and thought you were looking very good. I was glad to hear that. *—I love you, Raymond*

Monday, April 26th

Dearest Ray,

You remember I told you I was going to Carrickfergus today with Aunt Vi, well, it has rained and been so stormy and cold that we both decided to wait until another day when the weather is better. I am at Hazel's house now and she is still reading "Gone With the Wind." When I finish writing this letter I'm going to tear the book away from her and make her come to the pictures with me. —*Loving you always, Muriel*

Tuesday, April 27th

Dearest Muriel,

No mail today so just a few lines to let you know that I'm well, I'm still stiff, but not so sore now.

How were your holidays? Did you have a good time? I hope so. Tomorrow I will try and call you up, I hope you're there. Tonight Luke remarked on how lovely you looked when he saw you. —*I love you, Raymond*

Tuesday, April 27th

Dearest Ray,

I've just got home after being to the Curzon to see a picture named "His Affair" and it really was a good picture. Yesterday Hazel and I went to the Regal and saw "Cross Roads," have you seen either of these two pictures?

Have you found out yet whether you're getting your next leave in June or July? Please let me know as soon as you do. I hope you are looking after yourself and being good. —*I love you, Muriel*

Wednesday, April 28th

Dearest Muriel,

I was glad to hear your voice again today—you were in a better mood today than other times. As I told you in my letters I would agree to the way you planned everything and would do as you wished. Everything you plan I know I will like so don't worry about me. I hate to have you do everything and me nothing, if I'm able to help when I do come over I will.

You asked me on the phone why I didn't write more about myself, well, Muriel, there's really nothing to tell. If I went out all the time maybe I would but I even doubt that because it's so dead here. Getting up at 5:30 every morning you have to get to bed early to get any sleep.

If there's a show here I go to that and then go up to the lab or to our day room where they have books, records and a radio, so that's how I usually spend my evenings. It's about 5:30 now—after I'm through with this letter I'm going into town with some of the boys to see a show. There are only three picture houses here so I'm not sure which one we will go to. After the show we'll go to the Red Cross and have a Coke (if there's any left) and then get a taxi and come back to camp. See what an exciting life we lead, so there's really nothing to write about except my work and I'm sure you wouldn't want to hear about that. Well, the boys just walked in and there they go ribbing me and making fun of me. Boy, what I have to put up with. It's a wonder they let me finish this, they all want to read the letter but I won't let them.
—*I love you, Raymond*

Wednesday, April 28th

Dearest Ray,

Your phone call today has made me happier than I have been for a long time. I'm so glad you've promised to marry me in church, it makes me love you more than ever and it also makes me realize how much you love me. Ray, please don't think you will be doing wrong by not marrying me in chapel, you won't, we will be married in the eyes of God no matter what anybody says and after all what else matters. You're a darling, Ray, for making that promise and I've thanked God for answering my prayers.

Hazel has just called—we are taking a tram to the end of the line and then going for a long walk in the country. It's such a lovely evening it would be a pity to waste it on the pictures.   —*Forever yours, Muriel*

PS Have you taken up football seriously? You'll maybe be able to run faster than me next time you come over.

Thursday, April 29th

Dearest Muriel,

I'm so happy, tonight at 6 o'clock they announced that the mail came in so I rushed over and sure enough, there were three letters and your pictures and honey you can't imagine how happy and thrilled I am. Honest, they're wonderful—you're looking sweeter than ever, I'm sure Mother will love them. I have them in front of me as I am writing this letter and all I can think of is that I'd give a million if I could be with you now. There's only one thing, I wish your freckles were showing but you look wonderful to me even if they aren't showing.

About the dance at the Red Cross, I feel the same way you do and never can enjoy myself. I also know why you left early, but I sometimes think it's because of what Laura says to you or other fellows say. I may be wrong, I hope so, but it's just a feeling I have.

I'm glad to hear that you and Hazel get along so well. I'm glad you found a girlfriend who thinks the same as you, yes, I know her boyfriend, when I see him I will tell him.

I didn't get through with work until eight tonight. This weekend we can't go out because we are having our anniversary of one year in operation, we are having visitors so that means cleaning up the place, etc. —*I love you, Raymond*

Thursday, April 29th

Dearest Ray,

Lately everything has been very quiet here, Mommy and Daddy have not mentioned your name for ages and I haven't said anything either because I'm afraid Mommy might start lecturing me again. Do you think I should keep quiet or tell them of our plans—I really don't know what to do. —*Forever Yours, Muriel*

Friday, April 30th

Dearest Muriel,

I have your pictures here in front of me, they're really lovely. I have been showing them to the boys and they want to know where I found such a pretty and lovely girl and most of all, how or why you go for me. I kid them back and tell them they can't find another girl like you, you're the only one. They all want to know if you have any sisters, I told them two. I have them believing they're about your age so now they want to meet them. What do you think—is it safe? They will really get a surprise when they find out how old they are. —*Loving and missing you, Raymond*

PS The boys want to know when the lucky day is.

Friday, April 30th

Dearest Ray,

Hazel is calling at 6:30 and last night she made me promise that I would have this letter written and be ready to go out as soon as she calls tonight. The show at the Majestic must be very good, Yvonne told me she tried to get in to see it last night but had to come away the place was so crowded. That's another reason I want to be ready when Hazel calls, I hate standing in line.

Tomorrow afternoon I think I have to work. We are stocktaking this week and boy, are we busy. Adeline and I worked until 5:20 tonight so we wouldn't have so much to do tomorrow. I have cured her of the habit of thumping me on the arm. She never does it now, I guess she suffered too much when I hit back. —*Yours as always, Muriel*

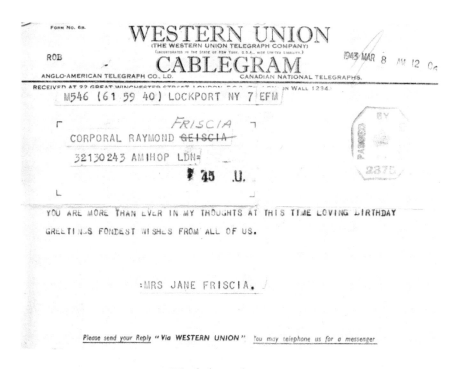

Birthday telegram.

Muriel

Ray

May 1943

Saturday, May 1st

Dearest Muriel,

It's just about nine o'clock now—I had to work all day. About six o'clock I lay down on my bunk and fell asleep. The boys wanted me to go with them tonight but I didn't want to, my heart is in Belfast so there's no point in going out. I'm all alone here now.

Last night at the Red Cross I listened to the band mostly, oh, yes, I had one dance. Every half-hour Luke and I would go and have a Coke, sit down and talk about you and Marie. Sometimes I think we're both crazy but I guess people in love are crazy.   —*I love you, Raymond*

Saturday, May 1st

Dearest Ray,

Most of the girls at the office had to work this afternoon but I managed to get my share of the work done this morning and the boss told me I could go home. The weather is beautiful today and if you were here now we could go to Bangor and bathe in Pickie swimming pool.

A new girl has started working in our office, her name is Maureen Graham, do you know her? The reason I'm asking you this is she used to work in the Telegram Office of the 5th General Hospital. She knew quite a few of the boys including Louis Cross but she didn't know you. The other day Maureen was talking about some of the boys and she mentioned Louis. I asked her if she knew him well and she said, "Certainly, he used to come in and talk to me, he also asked me to go out with him and wrote to me." She said she didn't go out with him because he is engaged to a girl back home and is one of the greatest wolves she has ever met. I got the shock of my life when I heard all this. Hazel doesn't know he is engaged, she thinks the world of him. He asked her to marry him but Hazel said no, it would be better to wait awhile—then they would know more about each other. Why should Louis make Hazel believe he wants to marry her when he is engaged to someone else? I know Hazel cares for him and is keeping true and would really hate to see her being let down. I haven't said anything to Hazel because it is none of my business and also because I don't want to hurt her feelings. Perhaps Louis really does care for her and does intend to marry her, but I think if he was on the level he would have told her about the girl back home. If you are ever talking to him please don't mention anything about this because if Hazel ever finds out that all the time I have known he was engaged and never told her she would never forgive me.

I was down at the photographers inquiring about your photograph. They are twenty-five shillings for six, but I am getting them for you and I don't want you to send the money, so please don't.

Everything is back to normal at home and Mommy is more like herself.   —*Yours as always, Muriel*

Sunday, May 2nd

Dearest Muriel,

This afternoon I had off and slept until about 4:30. I was going to tea, as you call it, when Luke came running in with two letters and also the pictures I had developed. After "tea" we didn't know if we should stay in or go to a show. I told him I had letters to write so in about ten minutes he's coming down and we're both going to spend the evening writing. Luke said Marie is going to write to his sisters soon, why don't you write to Dorothy, she is my youngest sister.

I can't say as yet when I'll have my leave. All I can say for now is that it will be in June or July.

About me thinking I'm doing wrong by getting married in your church, don't be foolish,

I'm doing right if I marry you in your church or mine. Don't worry about me, as long as we get married that's the main thing. I see we still have 8 month to wait, I hope it goes by fast.

I didn't have time today (or I slept) to look up Hazel's boyfriend, but will soon. Luke just walked in so now we'll start talking about Belfast and you and Marie.   —*I love you, Raymond*

PS What do you mean I may be able to run faster than you? I already can, I hope.

Sunday, May 2nd

Dearest Ray,

It's about 9:30 p.m. and I've just arrived home. Hazel called for me at 2:30 and about ten minutes later Greta came to the door. We stayed in the house until 5:30 then left and got a tram to Bellevue. We then climbed to the top of Cave Hill and boy, were we breathless when we reached the top. Do you remember how tired we were, or should I say you were when we climbed halfway? After that we came down again and when we got into town we went into the Lido and had supper. Ray, you should be here now, all the cafés are serving eggs, the Lido included, believe it or not.

THE STEPS, BELLEVUE, BELFAST.

Seeing Bellevue and the Cave Hill again brought back happy memories and when I was climbing the steps I couldn't help thinking of the time the apples and oranges fell out of your coat and rolled down the hill, do you remember?

How are you getting along, still playing football? I'm starting music again on Tuesday so that will mean I won't get out so often. I must end now and get to bed. *—Yours as always, Muriel*

Monday, May 3rd

Dearest Muriel,

Tonight I'm working emergency duty, Luke is here with me writing to Marie as we drink our Cokes. Last night after writing to you we made ourselves some coffee and I had a few cookies in my locker so we had them, Luke left and we went to bed. It's about ten o'clock now and it has been busy up until a half-hour ago.

I'm glad to see you and Hazel are together so much. I feel a lot better when I know you are not alone and have someone to go out with.

I'm glad to hear that everything is quiet at home. About saying anything about our latest plans, I wouldn't. Wait until I come over on leave, and then we can tell them. I think it would be much better, unless you think otherwise.

Say hello to Hazel for me.   —*I love you, Raymond*

Monday, May 3rd

Dearest Ray,

Hazel is calling tonight and we are going to the Regal to see a picture named "Are Husbands Necessary???" Ray Millard and Betty Field are acting in it.

We are having beautiful weather here now with plenty of sun and no rain.

As nothing interesting happened today and no letters came I haven't much to write about.   —*I love you, Muriel*

Tuesday, May 4th

Dearest Muriel,

Before I begin with anything else I want to tell you about Hazel's boyfriend. Monday night I was working and at eleven o'clock we have late supper. As I was having supper Hazel's boyfriend walked in and I called him over and asked him where he's been keeping himself. He has been working nights for two weeks—he said Hazel has been writing to him. I couldn't talk to him for long because I had to get back, but just as soon as he's off night duty we will get together. He said something about a furlough he's taking in July. If I'm able to come in July instead of June, which I don't think I can, we will come over together, is that OK with you?

Tonight we're going into town, I don't know what for. Luke, Howard (remember the fellow that you talked to at the Red Cross when I left) and a few other fellows want to walk in. Most likely we will go to the show.   —*Love, Raymond*

Tuesday, May 4th

Dearest Ray,

To begin with your letter of the 26th I see you had a very nice time in Bournemouth, please don't forget to send the pictures you took, I'd like to see them. If you enjoy getting out of camp and going to Bournemouth it's all right with me, I don't mind in the least, why should I object. If I took it in my head to go someplace here I'd hate to think that you didn't trust me enough to say go ahead.

As for visiting the Clarke house, I haven't the slightest intention of doing so, such an idea is far from my mind. I won't shock you by giving you my opinion of the girls because it hasn't been at all good lately.

I didn't go out tonight except for music. My examination is on the 1st June and between now and lunch hour tomorrow I've to decide whether I'm going in for it or not and if I am I have to sign the entry form then. As you know my music teacher was ill and unable to teach me for three weeks. That has kept me back a great deal and if I do decide to sit for the examination in June it will mean I'll have to practice in the mornings before I go to the office, at dinner hours and from 5:30 until 10:30 every night from now until June. Even with all that practice I might not be ready and as I'd hate to fail I think I'll wait and do the examination later.

As I have to wash my hair I'll stop writing now. —*I love you, Muriel*

Wednesday, May 5th

Dearest Muriel,

Today I was very glad to hear your voice again, you seemed to be so near and yet so far, if only I could reach out and touch you. After I phoned you I received two more letters which made me happier still.

Muriel, about the new girl at work, I don't know her, maybe I've seen her but as you know I never paid attention to any of them. Let me put you straight, you shouldn't believe all that girl said especially working where she did. She's probably trying to show off saying she had 20 boys after her, etc., you get the idea. Louis told me he loves Hazel and wants to marry her. As far as going out here, I haven't seen him and about the girl back home, I don't know if it's true or not. Don't forget he may have broken it off, anyway, I'll find out without letting him know what you said and let you know. Please don't say anything to Hazel, when he comes over he can straighten it out. If I do tell you everything please don't let her find out because it wouldn't be nice on my part. I don't think it's true but I will try to find out without letting him know what you said.

About the photographs, if I can't send the money I don't want them. You're spending enough now with your pictures and besides it wouldn't be fair to let you pay for them. It was swell of you to go through the trouble of getting them for me so I think you have done enough and I really appreciate it.

In six weeks time (I hope) you can be making some coffee for me so you better start to practice again—now don't get mad, I'm only kidding. —*I love you, Raymond*

Wednesday, May 5th

Dearest Ray,

The letter you wrote on Friday the 30th arrived today and it along with the phone call made me very happy.

Tonight I didn't go out. Hazel called for me at 7:30 and at the moment she is writing to her boyfriend. Tomorrow night we may go to the pictures. "Dangerous Moonlight" is showing at the Apollo and that is a picture I'd love to see, have you seen it?

As I have to do some washing and sewing I think I'll end now.
—*Forever yours, Muriel*

Thursday, May 6th

Dearest Muriel,

Today I received your letters of May 2nd and 3rd and as always was very happy to receive them.

I wish I was there when you went to Bellevue, it brings back happy memories, the steps and the apples and oranges, it all seems like it happened yesterday. What do you mean how tired I was, you were just as bad, almost. Didn't any Yanks help you to walk up or couldn't they make it? About them serving eggs, I see I'll have to come over soon and have some. I hope they still have some left when I come over.

Tonight Luke is working emergency so I'm staying here with him. I haven't seen Louis to find out anything as yet.   —*Yours always, Raymond*

Thursday, May 6th

Dearest Ray,

I'm very glad you like my pictures so well—they flatter me, maybe that's why.

A girl I used to go to school with got married to a Naval officer today. Mommy knows her people and as she was going to see the wedding she asked me to go with her. The bride was dressed in white and it really was a beautiful wedding. Mommy cried during the ceremony and believe it or not I began to cry too. Before the ceremony was finished I had to leave for two reasons. I didn't want Mommy to see me crying and I didn't want to be late getting back to the office. We were at the back of the church so no one noticed me slipping out.

Hazel is calling at 6:30 p.m. and we are going to the pictures.
—*Yours as always, Muriel*

Friday, May 7th

Dearest Muriel,

No letter today my sweet, and I really missed one. I know I shouldn't expect one every day but you know me, I'm very selfish when it comes to letters.

There's nothing much to tell, it's about 11:15 now. Tonight we went to the Red Cross dance, they had a good Yankee band but that's about all that was good. I danced a few dances and boy, I'll have to learn all over again when I come over, I'm really awful. At 10:45 we got a cab, it was raining and windy. The wind right now is blowing so it gives you a certain feeling that you want to be in bed, warm and comfortable.   —*Loving and missing you, Raymond*

Friday, May 7th

Dearest Ray,

Today I was delighted to receive the letter containing your pictures. They are all very good, especially the one of you sitting smiling on top of the haystack. It is the only one I have of you smiling and I love it, why don't you always smile when you have your picture taken? Was the one of you sitting in the snow taken at the hospital, I think it was.

Last night Hazel and I went to the Curzon to see a picture named the "Doctor and the Debutante."

When I arrived home Mommy told me that Dorothy Clarke had called about 7:45 p.m. She left a message that she had something to tell me and said she would see me again. She also wanted to know what picture house I had gone to but Mommy didn't know. I was greatly surprised to hear she had called, she must have had something to tell me or else she was at loose ends and had no place else to go. When I find out why she called I'll let you know.

Tonight I'm not going out and when I finish this letter I'm going to wash my hair, do some practice and get to bed early.

Ray, about writing to your sister Dot, maybe I'm silly but I think I should wait until I hear from your people before I write to them. They might think I'm forward if I write first. Why don't you ask your mother or Dot to write to me, I'd love if they would.   —*Forever yours, Muriel*

Saturday, May 8th

Dearest Muriel,

Tonight I'm working emergency. Luke is with me writing to Marie. I just got through mopping the floor and I really worked up a sweat. Boy, what a good husband I'll make, I can wash, dust mop, etc. now all I have to do is learn how to cook. Maybe you think this is funny (which it is) but it's the truth.

Muriel, about your examination, you promised me once that you would take it as soon as possible. I'm afraid you may give it up and I want you so much to have the degree. If it's not too hard for you I wish you would take the exam in June, but you know best so I'll leave it up to you.   —*I love you, Raymond*

Saturday, May 8th

Dearest Ray,

Audrey and Olive have gone to the pictures but Mommy and Daddy are still in the house, they couldn't go to the plot because it is raining very heavily. I knew the good weather couldn't last long. Tonight I don't know what I'll do. Hazel said she would call on her way from business but I don't think she will unless the weather clears up and that is most unlikely.

As soon as I finish writing I've got to brave the weather and go into town to buy myself shoes. I don't like buying shoes now because the shops haven't got the selection they used to have before the war and I hate parting with any of my coupons.   —*Yours as always, Muriel*

Sunday, May 9th

Dearest Muriel,

It's about 10:30 now, we just got back from town. They had a special show at the Red Cross for us tonight. They had a singer from the States named Yvette (I would listen to her quite often back home) and a show, the best one I've seen here so far. Luke was coming but he said he promised to call up Marie so he didn't make it. I'm really glad I did go because I laughed so much the tears were coming down my face. Honest, the Master of Ceremony was the best one I've seen in a long time. He went through an act of a lady getting undressed before taking a bath and I almost fell off the chair. I wish they could have shows like that more often—of course it was a GI show so it had to be good.

I guess we got back just in time as it's starting to rain, today it was very cold. I hope it's been better weather there.   —*Loving and missing you, Raymond*

Dearest Ray,

Yesterday afternoon I went into town to buy shoes. I only had time to try two shops and as neither of them had the kind of shoes I want I'll have to go into town next week and hunt around again. While I was there I went into the shop where Hazel works and bought some wool to knit myself a jumper, then I came home and had tea and about 6:30 Hazel called. She had her knitting with her and we both sat and knit until 11 p.m. instead of going out.

This morning the weather seemed bright but at lunchtime it started raining and has rained off and on since. It's 3:30 now and Hazel is coming round soon. I have lit the fire in the sitting room and we are both going to sit and knit for the rest of the day.   —*With all my love, Muriel*

Monday, May 10th

Dearest Muriel,

Today the weather has simply been terrible, rain and wind all day long, it's about 8:30 now and it's still raining. One thing that has made me happy and I don't care now how much it rains or blows is that we now have a radio. We all pooled together and bought one. Now I won't mind staying in nights because I'd rather listen to the music than go out. I have it on now and they just finished playing some American band music, some of which I danced to quite often back home.

I see Hazel is over again and I'm glad as I hate to think you're alone all the time. Her boyfriend has been very good and staying in nights. About the other girl, as yet I haven't had a chance to talk to him.

Well, I guess I'll close now and run myself down to the PX and have a Coke before it closes.   —*I love you, Raymond*

Monday, May 10th

Dearest Ray,

It's now three days since I received a letter, most likely three will arrive tomorrow and tomorrow night I'll be able to write a longer letter. At the moment I haven't very much to say as nothing of any interest has happened. Hazel will be calling at 6:30 and we are going to a show, we haven't decided where.

Everything is still quiet at home and I hope it stays that way. —*Forever yours, Muriel*

Tuesday, May 11th

Dearest Muriel,

Tonight I don't feel much like writing. Today I received a letter from home, I won't go into it tonight but my grandfather passed away April 28th. My mother didn't say much about it because it was at the time of his death she wrote the letter and was very busy. She has another letter following telling me all about it. I thought quite a lot of my grandfather and know I'm going to miss him. He was very good to me and we got along very well. I don't know how my grandmother will take it, but I'm afraid she won't live long now because the two of them were as much in love as the day they got married. —*I love you, Raymond*

Tuesday, May 11th

Dearest Ray,

When I arrived home at 5:15 I got a very pleasant surprise, five letters were awaiting me.

If you want to take your furlough when Louis is taking his it's OK with me. Louis maybe does love Hazel and want to marry her but Maureen wasn't telling lies when she said he was engaged to a girl back home. She has the girl's name and address and Louis used to send that girl telegrams every week up until the time he left Musgrave Park. He wrote to Maureen too but I haven't told Hazel anything and never will. It's none of my business so if you find out anything about Louis I'd rather not hear about it. All I hope is that Hazel isn't hurt and if she ever finds out about Louis I don't want her to know that I knew all the time and didn't tell her.

In one of your letters you asked me if any "Yanks" helped me to walk up the Cave Hill. Ray, you should know better than to ask a question like that. Most likely you meant it only in fun, but whether it was meant that way or not I want you to understand that I haven't been out with any boys since you went away. —*Loving you as always, Muriel*

Wednesday, May 12th

Dearest Muriel,

Today I'm very happy because of the phone call and I also received two letters from you. You sounded a little sad today, what is it, family troubles, I hope not. The darn telephone operator only gave us about three minutes and I put in eight shillings and we should have gotten seven minutes. Oh, well, maybe next time it will be longer.

About writing home, I wrote and told them to write to you so wait until you hear from them. I received a letter from my sister Jo and she also got married. She's my oldest sister. My mother didn't approve but she went ahead anyway, he's at camp down south where I was inducted into the army. Jo also wrote me about Grandfather. I was just thinking when I get back home how everything is going to be changed, I'm not going back to the same things I left. I thought an awful lot of my grandfather and know I'm going to miss him very much when I go back. He was sick about a week before he passed away.

Tonight we went to the Red Cross because we thought there was an American band but when we got there they had a six-piece band of some kind. To make a long story short, we got a taxi at about 9:45 and came back to camp. I don't mind when they have a good band but to sit and listen to what they had was not for me. —*Missing and loving you, Raymond*

Wednesday, May 12th

Dearest Ray,

Before I write anything else I want you to know that I'm very sorry for taking so long in reaching the phone today. Peggy told me there was a call for me and when I rushed to the Time Office the boss was using the phone there. Then I ran upstairs to Miss Collins only to find that some men were fixing the switchboard so I couldn't talk to you there. Miss Collins took me round to Mr. Ferguson's office (he's one of the directors of the firm) and as he wasn't in his office at the time I was able to speak to you through his phone. It must take quite a lot of money when you phone me, Ray, and it makes me feel bad when any time is wasted.

I'm very sorry to hear your grandfather is dead, was he your father's or mother's father? I hope you are not feeling too bad about it. As the connection of the call today wasn't very good I couldn't quite hear what you said about the letter you got from home

Hazel has just called, she has her knitting with her so we are both going to sit and knit the rest of the evening. —*Always yours, Muriel*

Thursday, May 13th

Dearest Muriel,

Today has been a real spring day, sunshine and warm. I would like to go walking or riding but I have to work tonight. Luke is here with me writing to Marie, he received a twelve-page letter from her today. I don't know what she has to say but she really can write. One thing I have over Luke is that she doesn't write everyday like you do, as long as I receive a letter everyday, long or short, I'm satisfied.

I see you and Hazel have taken up knitting. I hope when you are through with the knitting it comes out to be a jumper and not something else. Maybe if you're good at it I'll let you knit me some socks or something, is that OK? It will keep you in practice for later on if you know what I mean.

I received a letter from my sister Jo just before she got married. She told me to go ahead and get married and let nothing stop us, hardship, religion, etc.

As I told you on the phone my mother wrote and told me to think twice about taking you away to a strange country, she's afraid you might not like it. It's silly of my mother to say that but I guess it's my fault because I didn't tell her we had that all settled. She didn't say she didn't want me to marry you, but just to be sure we know what we are doing. I think the best thing to do is to go ahead with our plans and when you are twenty-one we will get married.   —*I love you, Raymond*

Thursday, May 13th

Dearest Ray,

Do you remember I told you I had to work on the Saturday afternoon before the Easter holidays, well, because of that I was allowed to take a half day off so I decided to stay off today. I am going to the pictures tonight with Hazel and I thought if I took the afternoon off I could do some washing, knitting and practice and also get this letter written. I already have the washing done and while I was doing it a letter arrived.

I can just picture you killing yourself laughing when the Master of Ceremonies went through the act of a lady getting undressed before taking a bath and I'm sure he made it look very funny. I haven't been to any of the Sunday Red Cross shows since before Christmas and I really miss going even though they weren't much good sometimes. Do they have the dances on Sunday afternoons the way they have here?

In your letter you have a sentence "I wish they could have shows like that more often, of course it was a GI show so it had to be good." What is that word between *a* and *show*?   —*Forever yours, Muriel*

Saturday, May 15th

Dearest Ray,

I really don't know how to begin this letter. Last night I didn't write to you because my mind was in such turmoil and I wasn't sure I should tell you what happened, but you have always told me to tell you everything no matter what it is.

On Thursday night after Mommy and the children had gone to bed Daddy and I started talking and gradually the conversation came round about music. I told Daddy what I told you about my Diploma Examination and he asked me when the next date was for entering for the examination. When I told him the next date was in December he immediately said, "Aren't you going to leave us to get married then?" That was how it all began. Daddy told me he was very disappointed in me, he also said that if you marry me you will have to do as your church tells you and bring any children up as Catholics. No matter what promises were made before marriage a Catholic always puts the rules of his church before anything else and when we would be married you would see to it that all the children would be your religion. He said even if we did get married in my church there would be some period in my life when I'd have to remarry in a chapel, and if I didn't do this you would be able to leave me. I told him it was only in Ireland things like this happened but he said no, it was the same the world over and what is more, when we do get married Mommy and he would not be at the ceremony.

That hurt me a great deal and it also hurt me more when he said, "It's too bad when a father and mother can't see to it that their daughter has a nice wedding and trousseau." He went to bed after saying that and on Friday night when I was about to go to my music lesson he told me if I didn't give you up I wasn't going back to music. When I heard that I didn't go for my lesson but went up to my bedroom so they wouldn't see me crying. After about an hour I came down and went round to Hazel's as we were expecting visitors and I didn't feel I could stay home and talk to them.

It's about 9:30 p.m. now and the family has been out since lunch hour. Ray, are those things that Daddy told me really true, and if so are you sure our marriage won't be that way, that we will live as we have already planned and you won't go back on any promises? Please don't think I don't trust you but I just want to make sure that you don't regret ever having made those promises.

I really and truly love you, Ray. I also love my parents and I don't want you to think badly of them. They believe they are saving me from unhappiness by talking the way they are and I've done all in my power to try and convince them that we will be happy but it's no good. Daddy is concerned about my happiness and Mommy is worried about losing me. I'm not going to think any more about this and when

you come over on leave perhaps we'll get everything straightened out.
—*Yours as always, Muriel*

Sunday, May 16th

Dearest Ray,

Although today has been one of the loveliest days we've had in a long time I haven't gone out. Mommy, Daddy and the children have gone for a walk and taken Scamp with them. Hazel was to call around 2:30 and we were to have gone out someplace but she sent her mother to tell me she couldn't come as she has gone away for the day. An American she knows called early this morning and coaxed her to go out with him. She often told me about this American calling for her and phoning her at business but she said she didn't like him very well and always refused to go out with him. I want you to promise never to tell Louis about this for he mightn't like it, she may write and tell him herself but please don't say anything, Hazel would be mad if she ever found out I told you. Besides, it's none of our business.

Mommy and Daddy haven't said anything more to me about us since Friday night but I've got so accustomed to being lectured now I hardly care. —*Yours forever, Muriel*

Monday, May 17th

Dearest Muriel,

I really don't know how or where to start this letter because I haven't written since last Thursday. I only hope you don't take me wrong and try to understand why I haven't written. I know I don't deserve it but I hope you forgive me for what I have done. Friday afternoon I was ordered to report to London to the 8th Air Force. Remember that fellow you talked with at the Red Cross when I left Belfast, well, he went with me. We arrived in London at 11:30 then went to the Red Cross and got our room. As we had to get up early we went right to bed and I didn't write thinking I would tomorrow. The next morning we reported to the headquarters of the 8th Air Force just outside London and we were there all day.

We came back to London at about five o'clock. I was going to write you a letter but there was a show in town that Howard wanted to see with Lana Turner and, oh, I forgot the fellow, well, anyway, we got out at eleven o'clock and went back to the Red Cross and got something to eat. As we sat there the girl in charge of the club came over and started to talk to us and before we knew it was one a.m. In the meantime, we got an invitation to go to church at St. James Palace,

Chapel Royal in London. (Sunday) Only three of us were invited and only a few other Yanks have ever been there. It's the King and Queen's private church but we were a little disappointed when the King and Queen didn't show up. I'm glad we went there even though they didn't come. The church was swell and in it I saw some great people of England, ambassadors, lawyers, etc. As it only holds about 60 people you have to be the King's guest just to get in.

We got back to the Red Cross at about 12:30 p.m. and had dinner. As I was very tired from Saturday with all the walking and running around I wanted to write you a letter and leave early to get back to camp but Howard, never having been in London, wanted to see a few places and take some pictures so we went sightseeing. Honest, I was never so tired in all my life—we walked all over London taking pictures. As we had planned to take the 9:30 train back to camp we came back to the Red Cross at 8 o'clock. Miss Davis, the director, had supper with us and made us stay. They had a little social party at the club and she wanted Howard and me to stay and help out because there were more girls than boys. They had dancing and games but it was very dead and most of the night I spent with Miss Davis—she treated us like kings. This happens to be a new club (the Liberty Club) and it's swell—away from the heart of London with only a few soldiers staying here.

It was very peaceful until about 11 o'clock when we had an air raid. During the raid from eleven till one we were trying to get a cab to get to the station. We finally made it just as the train was leaving. We arrived back at camp at about three this morning so you see I have been on the go since the day I left. Tonight I am so tired I can hardly write this letter. I know you're going to be mad at me, Muriel, and maybe I shouldn't be forgiven, but honest, I'm really sorry, everything happened so quickly.

There's a lot more to my visit to London which I can't say for now. This week we have to report back on Friday morning and may have to stay there Saturday also.

Muriel, I better tell you now so you won't be in the dark, you see Muriel, I have been called up in the Air Corps. I've been taking my examinations and if I passed the other two exams I'll be called up. Please try to understand, Muriel, it will be some time before I'm called up even if I do pass the exam. When I come over I will try to explain it all to you so please don't worry about me going away because if I'm accepted it will be quite a while before anything happens. I know you're going to get mad at me and think I don't love you, but I do,

Muriel, more than ever. I'll know more what's going to happen this weekend. I'm coming over this June or July, just as soon as I can and will explain it all to you.   —*Love, Raymond*

Monday, May 17th

Dearest Ray,

Today I was very happy to receive two more of your letters. On Saturday you seem to have been rather busy mopping the floor, etc. You should make a good husband if you can wash and dust, but I won't let you do that kind of thing if you help me by drying the dishes now and then and have a job of your own, I think you'll be able to leave the rest to me you crazy boy!

So your sister Jo went off and got married against your mother's wishes, why didn't she approve, if it's too personal don't tell me. I'm sorry you feel so bad about your grandfather dying. Your mother is certainly having a trying time with all this happening.

Ray, I am sure you were greatly disappointed to hear I have stopped going to music. When I received your letter saying you hoped I wouldn't give up trying for my degree it made me feel kind of bad so now I think I'll put past part of my pocket money every week and go independent of Daddy. Although I didn't go for my lesson on Friday night I didn't tell my music teacher I was leaving, so now I think I'll go to my lesson as usual.

Tonight I'm going to the Curzon to see "San Francisco." Hazel should be here any minute so I'll stop writing now and get ready.
—*Forever yours, Muriel*

Tuesday, May 18th

Dearest Muriel,

I'm writing this letter from the lab tonight as I'm on duty, after I'm through I have to do some studying. I have to go back to London this week Friday to take an exam and will be there for the weekend. I wrote and tried to explain what this was all about in yesterday's letter so I need not say much more about it.

I didn't receive a letter today but still have your other letters to answer so will do so now.

About the phone call, Muriel, I know it's not your fault but once I get on the phone I don't want to get off, if only they would give us a little more time.

Concerning the death of my grandfather, it was my mother's father and I will miss him a lot.

In one letter you asked me what GI stands for, it refers to soldiers, it really means Government Issue.

Muriel, about Hazel, let her be the way she is and don't interfere, as long as you both get along OK I wouldn't worry about anything else. How's the knitting coming along?

Have you heard anything more from Dot? If so, what was it all about?

As far as my furlough, I'm trying to come over in June so keep your fingers crossed.

As to London there is not much more I can say now but this weekend I can let you know more about it so please don't worry. I am leaving Thursday night so I will try and write to you from there. — *Yours forever, Raymond*

Wednesday, May 19th

Dearest Muriel,

I'm sorry I didn't call you up today but as I had to work I didn't have time. As you know tomorrow I'm going to London to take my test and will be gone until Sunday. I will try, if it is possible to call you up from London.

I received a letter from home—my dog died so my mother got another one for me. Here is a picture of the dog with my youngest sister. In her letter she said she received the pictures I sent her of you and likes them very much. This weekend I have to take two tests, one on Friday and one on Saturday so you see I'll be quite busy. —*I love you, Raymond*

Wednesday, May 19th

Dearest Ray,

It's just 8 o'clock now and I've just got back after leaving two cousins of Mommy's to the boat. Last night I didn't write to you because Mommy gave me a good talking to about us before she went out and when she did go out I felt so awful I went to bed and cried like a silly little fool. I guess you wonder at me calling myself a silly fool but that's what I've been and it's only tonight that I realized it.

Tonight when I arrived home from the office Mommy's two cousins were here and they asked me to go to the boat with them and I'm very glad I did. Edith and Evelyn are their names and now I'll tell you all about them. About four years ago Edith left her home in Ballymoney (that's a country town here) and went to England to train as a nurse. About 8 months ago she came back here because of her health and in the meantime got engaged to an American who is now in Africa. Evelyn was a Sister in a hospital in Salisbury and other parts of England and was home here on vacation. Tonight they were both going back to England and when I was leaving them to the boat they started talking about me being engaged and how Mommy was taking it. They told me that outside of Ireland people never talked about religion and they knew of many mixed marriages in England and they've all been quite happy. They say they can understand Mommy and Daddy's point of view. Mommy and Daddy have lived here all their lives and have seen so much unhappiness in mixed marriages that they think it's the same all over. To make a long story short they both told me I was silly to worry, Mommy might feel badly for awhile but she would soon get over it.

From now on I'm going to avoid all upsets in the house and stop worrying you by writing the kinds of letters I have been. You know exactly how Mommy and Daddy are without me writing and telling you all that they are saying. Anyhow, there won't be a word about all this 150 years from now.

I was disappointed when you didn't phone today but I understand you must have a pretty good reason for not doing so.

I guess it's about time I stopped writing. I want to wash my hair and do some knitting before going to bed. Hazel is out with the American I was telling you about and I haven't seen her since Monday night. She is calling tomorrow night and we are going to the Majestic. I hope and trust you haven't said anything to Louis, *please* don't ever tell him or I'll be landed in the soup for telling you.   —*Yours forever, Muriel*

PS I almost forgot, the boss says I've to take my holidays from the 3rd to the 13th of July. Could you come over then?

Thursday, May 20th

Dearest Muriel,

I'm writing this letter from the Liberty Club here in London. We arrived at about 3 o'clock and spent the afternoon getting things straight for tomorrow. We have to report to take our test at 8:30 tomorrow morning.

Saturday we are going to the 8th Air Force flying field to do some flying. We know one of the pilots and he is going to take us up in *censored*, we will be there all day.

Another good thing about this is that I'm getting paid one pound & five shillings a day for expenses, you see I'm under government orders and they give us that for our room and board, not bad is it. I keep wishing you were here with me so we could have a swell time in London together. Seeing I'm engaged and not going out with any other girls it's more like a business trip. —*Loving you always, Raymond*

Thursday, May 20th

Dearest Ray,

Another day and still no letters from you. I know it isn't your fault they are so long in coming lately, it's those old censors that hold them back and boy do they make me impatient. Today nothing worth talking about has happened, everybody in the office, including me, have been very busy so there wasn't any fun.

Tonight Hazel is calling and we are going to the Majestic. All is quiet at home. Don't forget to let me know if you can arrange to come over when I'm having my holiday. —*Yours forever, Muriel*

Lockport, NY
Friday, May 21st

Dear Son,

I really don't know how to start this letter. I hated to tell you about Grandfather but thought I should, I would have to tell you sometime. Grandmother is taking it very good because we all felt that if he had lived there would have been something wrong with his mind, so I think the Lord did the right thing. Rose wrote to your uncle but we have not had any answer yet.

Ray, about that Air Corps business, oh, I wish you would forget about it, I got a big kick reading your letters telling me you are old enough. Regardless of how old you are you are still my son, remember you will always be. I thought now that you had a girl you would forget about the air.

About your girl, I really don't know what to say. The pictures are very nice, I told you in my other letters she is a very sweet girl. I have her picture next to yours and they all give me the ah, ah about my son. Just remember, you are far away from home, are you going to like her as much when you bring her to this country. She will be far away from home and you will be at home. This is your home, your country, she will be a stranger, but you know best. Do not blame your mother, I am telling you to think twice before doing something that is for life.

We are not doing much at the other house just now, everything is pretty well done. Dad is fine and working hard. He comes home and has his dinner and can't even work in his garden, it's too wet. While I am writing this letter he has gone to bed at just 9:30. —*Goodbye and good luck to you, will write soon, Your mother*

Friday, May 21st

Dearest Muriel,

I was really glad to hear your voice today. As I told you all there is to tell over the phone as to why I'm here, I hope you understand.

Tomorrow we may go to the airport, if not, we are going to visit the wax museum, have you ever heard of it? It's supposed to be a wonderful place. —*Loving you more than ever, Raymond*

Friday, May 21st

Dearest Ray,

I can't say your phone call today made me happy, on the contrary it has me worried. When Miss Collins told me there was a call for me I was delighted because there haven't been any letters since Monday and I couldn't help wondering what was wrong. When you told me all that you did tell me I was very surprised and have pondered over it ever since. I honestly hope and pray you don't have to join the Air Corps, you seem to be quite sure you won't have to but how are you going to get out of it? There are lots of questions I would like to ask you but I know you wouldn't be able to answer them on paper. I can't understand why they are giving you extra money and also why any letters you write there don't have to be censored by the U.S. censorship, aren't you staying at the Red Cross? Perhaps I'm crazy to think of the worst but I can't help thinking of how awful it will be if you do have to join the Air Corps. I know you always had that ambition and I guess that's what has me even more worried. We must have been cut off at the end of the call because I didn't even hear you say cheerio. I guess I should be encouraging you to join the Air Corps if that's what you want, but I'm selfish and besides I'd always dread you might be killed. While you're in the Medical Corps I never think of that, but be transferred to the Air Corps I'll be picturing you dead every second especially if you qualify as a pilot, besides you're likely to be sent further away.

I know there's a war on and army orders are army orders. But I guess I'm not one of those brave girls who send their sweethearts off with a brave smile of encouragement to fight.

Well, Ray, I must stop writing now as supper is ready. I'm hoping and praying that next time I hear from you you'll still be in the Medical Corps. — *Yours forever, Muriel*

Saturday, May 22nd

Dearest Ray,

This morning I received the letter you wrote on the 17th and in the afternoon the one you wrote on the 13th arrived. It took a long time to reach me but better late than never.

About your mother writing asking you to think twice before marrying me and taking me to a strange country, I'm not worried, I think she is quite right in making sure we have talked over things like that. Ray, you never mention your father, doesn't he live home and doesn't he ever have anything to say about you getting married?

Ray, about this Air Corps business, I don't see how the army can transfer you into it unless you apply for a transfer. Perhaps I'm wrong but why did they pick you out of all of the boys in the 5th General. I know you got some papers at one time but you promised me that you wouldn't sign them or sit for any examinations. I guess I've no right to interfere in your army career so please go ahead and do as you please. If everything was all right for us getting married maybe I'd have more reason to try keeping you out of the Air Corps, but as everything is maybe it's just as well. When you join you'll probably be sent away, if not now later on, that means we don't get married until after the war.

Ray, I'm not really mad at you. I know I let my temper get the better of me at times and when that happens I always say things I regret immediately afterwards. Already I've regretted writing all this but I want you to know that I'm sorry and you are forgiven. I'll forgive you for almost anything and at least I'm glad you tell me the truth about everything. If you ever did anything and didn't tell me, that's when I wouldn't forgive you.

This afternoon Mommy and I went shopping and I got a pair of shoes. Hazel was to call tonight but it started raining so I guess that's why she didn't come. I'm glad, as I don't like anyone here when I'm writing to you and when the family's in I always go upstairs.

Tomorrow afternoon I may go to the Red Cross dance to break the monotony, it's ages since I've been there. — *I love you, Muriel*

Sunday, May 23rd

Dearest Ray,

Today I didn't go to the Red Cross dance although I said yesterday I might go. Hazel came round about 2:30 today and we started out to go for a walk. We had just reached Malone Road when it started raining so we got a tram and came straight home. Since then I've just sat around the house reading and knitting.

All day today I've been wondering how you are getting along in London and if you have to join the Air Corps. I really hope not. — *Yours as always, Muriel*

PS I have a lovely headache.

Monday, May 24th

Dearest Muriel,

I am writing this letter at camp, I came back Sunday night. I found your four letters waiting for me but before I begin with your letters I'll say a little about London. We didn't do too much. Saturday night we went to a show and Sunday we went to Richmond Park and played 18 holes of golf. We didn't do anything else to talk about.

As far as what your dad said, it's untrue, so forget about it and when I come over we will get things straightened out once and for all. I had been expecting this but was hoping it wouldn't happen. It makes me feel bad to see you there alone and me not being able to help you but I'm glad you told me. Muriel, about the music, it wasn't so much that I wanted you to take music lessons but I didn't want you to stop so they could blame me, but seeing they put it the way they did I wouldn't worry about it. If that's the way they want it, it's OK with me. We can do as my sister Jo did and I'm sure we'll be happy no matter how hard they try to make us unhappy. The best thing to do is what your cousins said and I'm sure your parents will forgive us so please don't worry about it, I know everything will be OK.

As for the furlough, I'm sure I can get it the same time you have your holidays so let's hope the time goes by fast until I come over.

Muriel, as far as me saying anything to Louis about Hazel please don't worry because I don't want to start trouble. I never say a word to him about anything you say.

I think I'll stop now and get to bed early. I wish I could explain in words how much I love you and what I think of you for putting up with what you have. I'll never forget it and it makes me love you all the more and more determined to marry you than ever before. —*Forever yours, Raymond*

Monday, May 24th

Dearest Ray,

Today I was glad to receive two letters from you dated the 18th & 19th.

I guess by now you'll know whether you have succeeded in passing your tests for the Air Corps. You know how I feel about it but I'll say nothing more, I'm ashamed of what I've said already.

No, Ray, I haven't heard anything more about Dorothy Clarke, most likely I'd have seen her if I'd gone to the Red Cross dances but I haven't been there for ages now and she hasn't called back at the house.

Thanks very much for the picture you sent me. I'm sorry to hear your dog has died but the new one you've got looks cute, do you like him? I think he's a lovely little dog.

Hazel is calling for me very soon, we are going to the Regal so I'll end now and be ready when she calls.   —*Yours always, Muriel*

Tuesday, May 25th

Dearest Muriel,

I just got back from the show here at camp. The name of the picture was "Random Harvest" with Ronald Coleman and Greer Garson—it really was a wonderful picture that I enjoyed very much. I wish you would see it when it comes to Belfast.

I read your letters over—the ones I received this weekend. It makes me very mad and upset, not because of what your parents say because I am going to marry you no matter what anyone says, but you being there alone with me not able to help. I may be crazy but I don't think it's religion so much that they're against us as you going away. They may think they will break us up but it's only bringing us closer. Next time they lecture you just think of how much I love you.   —*Yours forever, Raymond*

Tuesday, May 25th

Dearest Ray,

This morning I received the two letters you wrote in London. There's one good thing about you being in London and that is your letters don't take so long in coming.

You asked me the exact date of my holidays, well, I stop working on Saturday 3rd of July and don't start again until the 14th of July. If you can get your leave at the same time it will be wonderful.

At the moment I haven't very much to say as it's been very quiet here lately. By the way, the name of the picture Hazel and I saw last night was "True to the Army," it was very amusing and we really enjoyed it. *—I'll always love you, Muriel*

Wednesday, May 26th

Dearest Muriel,

Another lovely day for me as I received three more letters. I'm sorry to hear my phone call has you worried, as I told you before I can't tell you too much as I'm not sure myself what's going to happen. I stayed at the Red Cross, the Liberty Club, in London.

About the Air Corps, I had my application in before I came over here and when I was in Ireland, as you know, I told you I might be sent away. I put in before I met you so there's not much I can do now. I'm only trying to be someone and advance myself so after this is over I can support you. Maybe I can explain it when I come over, I hope so.

About my dad, he's quite good-natured and lets me do just about anything I want to. He doesn't worry about me as my mother does.

I don't mind you going to the Red Cross dance once in awhile because I know I can trust you and maybe it will help you forget a little. If you feel like going once in awhile, please do. *—Loving you always, Raymond*

PS I will try to call you up tomorrow. Tonight I had to move from my hut to another hut and boy it's hard to move. Mother wants to know if you need any lipstick, powder, etc., so let me know.

Wednesday, May 26th

Dearest Ray,

I've just got home from the office and want to get this written before I have tea. Yesterday I promised Daddy that Hazel and I would go up to the plot and help him to do some weeding. It rained most of the day but now it has stopped and the sun is shining so I guess I will have to keep my promise though I don't like the idea of weeding when the ground is all wet.

Today I haven't received any letters but as I've already had four from you this week I shouldn't grumble. I thought you would have phoned but I guess you had to work and couldn't get away.

How has Luke been keeping lately, it's a long time since you've said anything about him in your letters. If you go in the Air Corps won't you miss each other a great deal? *—Forever yours, Muriel*

Thursday, May 27th

Dearest Muriel,

I tried to phone you today but was too busy so I'll try tomorrow. I just got back from the show here—the name of the picture was "Stage Door Canteen." I don't know if you will see it because it's a special picture for the troops, it was a swell picture.

Muriel, after I think, June 9th I'll be able to tell you everything about what's happening but until then I can't say, one reason because I don't know, so please don't worry.

Hoping everything is quiet at home. *—I love you, Raymond*

Thursday, May 27th

Dearest Ray,

Last night Hazel and I went up to Daddy's plot and took Scamp along with us. We had some trouble locating the plot but it was good fun climbing over barbed wire fences. Every now and then some one of us would slip down a rabbit hole and sometimes we lost Scamp in the long grasses. When we finally arrived at the plot Olive took charge of Scamp and we helped Daddy for about an hour by doing some weeding. We got back about 10:30 p.m., tired out after the long walk there and back.

At the moment I'm in the house by myself, I'm not going out tonight as I want to wash my hair. Today at the office I had some good fun. Fred, Yvonne and I kidded each other the whole day and the things Fred said would have made anyone laugh. I'd love to tell you what it was all about but if I started to I would never have this letter written tonight. *—I love you, Muriel*

PS I still haven't heard from your mother or your sister. Have you told them about the Air Corps, if so I'm sure they'll be worried.

Friday, May 28th

Dearest Muriel,

I received your letter of the 24th today, it made good time. As far as you being ashamed of yourself for telling me off about the Air Corps, well, I can't blame you in a way but there is more behind it than you know or think. When I come over I'll explain it to you and maybe you'll understand.

Tonight I may go out to a show or the Red Cross—it will be the first time all week. Luke and some of the other boys just walked in so I better stop now and get ready. *—Always yours, Raymond*

Saturday, May 29th

Dearest Muriel,

Tonight I'm on duty so Luke is here with me writing to his Irish 'Spitfire.' Last night there weren't any good shows on and as it was a lovely night we walked around until about 8:30 then went into the Red Cross and had a few Cokes. Oh, yes, I had one dance, I hope you don't mind.

The pictures we took in Bournemouth will be ready this week sometime and the pictures of London in a week or two, when I have them I'll send them over to you.

I'd better stop now as I have to mop the floors and then get to bed. I wish you were here—maybe you would help me to mop the floors, or would you? —*I love you, Raymond*

Saturday, May 29th

Dearest Ray,

I received your letter of the 24th today. I hadn't time to write to you last night. Hazel and I went to the Ritz as planned and saw "Orchestra Wives." It's really a wonderful picture, Ray, Glenn Miller and his band played in it and I could hardly sit still in my seat his music was so good. I know it's the type of picture you would like so if you haven't seen it go see it if it shows over there.

Ray, by the sound of your letter you seem to be pretty mad at Daddy for saying the things he did. Please don't think little of him for it because he really is the best father a girl could have. Robert, Mommy's young brother, told me a long time ago that Daddy told him he would like to say yes to me but couldn't on account of Mommy. He said he was between two fires and didn't know what to do about it. Ray, do you remember you asked Daddy if we could become engaged, well, he said to wait until I'm 21 and I think he was mad because we got engaged right away.

As I haven't been to a dance in a long time I think I'll go to the Red Cross tonight. The band in the Ritz last night has put me in the mood for dancing. Along with your letter today I received a card from the Red Cross and it says on it; "The American Red Cross Service Club cordially invites you to attend a Birthday Ball in celebration of its First Anniversary, Sunday, June 6th, from 7:30 till 11 p.m." I would really like to go to that dance too, but if you don't want me to go, I won't. If you phone me next week I'll ask you then.

My Uncle Harold has come over from England on holiday and he along with Auntie Vi, Mommy, Daddy and Olive have gone to the plot. They've taken sandwiches and Thomas Flasks with them so they'll hardly be back again until 10 or 11 o'clock.   —*Forever yours, Muriel*

Sunday, May 30th

Dearest Muriel,

So you're finally going to be a farmer girl, maybe you don't like it but I don't think it will hurt you once in awhile. Maybe you can get your dad on your side—you know what I mean, try anyhow.

In another four or five weeks I'll be over and I can hardly wait until I see you again. I hope the weather is good.

There are other things I would like to say but they will only be censored so I hope you understand at times when my letters don't sound right.   —*I love you, Raymond*

Sunday, May 30th

Dearest Ray,

It's just after 7:30 p.m. and I'm only after having tea. Hazel came round today at 3 o'clock and as it was such a beautiful day we took a tram to the end of the Malone Road, walked way past Shaw's Bridge and when we got tired we sat down on a fallen tree to rest. We would have been there yet only we got hungry and that made us decide to come home. The country around Shaw's Bridge is really beautiful and I was wishing you were with me. When you come over try to bring a camera and we'll go there and take some snaps.

Last night I went to the Red Cross dance. Dot was there alone as Al, her boyfriend, had to take a patient over to a hospital in England and wasn't due to come back for a few days. Dot had quite a lot to talk to me about and she told me something which made me feel very sorry and sad. Do you remember Herbie, Lily's boyfriend who played with the Ambassadors of Swing, well, Marie Neill, Lily's cousin, had a letter from her boyfriend and another boy she knows to say that Herbie was killed in Africa. This was three weeks ago and a few days after hearing the news Lily received a little present from him but no letter. It seems he had been writing a lot to her and had sent home to his mother for an engagement ring. Dot said Lily is feeling awful and has cried ever since. She had been going out with a boy from the 10th station, but it seems only on a friendly basis as the other boy knows about Herbie. Lily must feel badly about Herbie and if she had been there last night I would have told her how sorry I am. I can just imagine how I'd feel if anything happened to you. I know I'd never be happy again.

Dot and I left the Red Cross at 9:45 and went round to the Lido for something to eat. While we were there Dot told me that George has joined the navy and was being trained at Plymouth. As I've told you all the latest news now, I'll end. —*Yours as always, Muriel*

Monday, May 31st

Dearest Ray,

I'm just after having lunch and want to get this letter finished before I leave for the office at 2 p.m. All this week "Me & My Gal" is showing at the Imperial, and as we've heard it's a good picture, Hazel is calling at 5:45 tonight and we are going into town to see it.

This morning we were very busy at the office and I don't think I had time to lift my head the whole morning. Please excuse this short letter, I'll write a longer one tomorrow. —*Forever yours, Muriel*

Ray in Green Park, London, May 1943.

Green Park, London.

June 1943

Tuesday, June 1st

Dearest Muriel,

Well, the great month of June is here and as far as the weather goes, it's not so good. I didn't write yesterday and I hope you'll forgive me. Some flying officers were in and I was talking to them last night from 7 till 11:30. They're a wonderful bunch of men and they told us a lot of stories, etc., and I completely forgot the time.

With me there is nothing new, everything is the same. I think our last trip to London is June 9th, so I'll know one way or another what's going to happen. *—Always yours, Raymond*

Tuesday, June 1st

Dearest Ray,

In Tuesday's letter you say that the letter I wrote you telling about the lecture Daddy gave me has made you very mad and upset. Please, Ray, you needn't worry about me being here alone and you not being able to help me. Lately those lectures have been few and far between. Since the last time Daddy lectured me everything has been quite normal and Mommy, Daddy and I just get along and talk to each other as if nothing was wrong. You say you don't think it's religion so much they're against, well, I think you're wrong because Mommy once told me she wouldn't care where you came from if you were the same religion. Ray, you may think you understand but you really don't. It would take you to have been born and lived here all your life to understand why Mommy and Daddy are so much against mixed marriages. You say that what Daddy told me is untrue, well, it may be as regards to Catholics living in America and England but it is quite true about the Catholics living here. In my opinion it's all wrong to fight about religion, after all if a person truly believes and trusts in God what else matters.

The reason I don't want you joining the Air Corps is because I love you and wouldn't like anything to happen to you. I know there's a war on and everyone should do his or her share in the fighting but isn't the work you are doing most essential. Think what it would be like if there weren't any hospitals for the wounded to come to. If you really think you can do better in the Air Corps then please go ahead. I won't be mad, Ray, I'll love you as much as ever. I don't want you ever to say I stood in your way and not only that, if being in the Air Corps appeals to you I want you to join it. If I was a boy the Air Corps is what I'd like to join and most likely I wouldn't let anything stand in my way, so I can't blame you.

It's getting late so I'll stop writing now.   —*Forever yours, Muriel*

Wednesday, June 2nd

Dearest Muriel,

It's been a happy day for me, after the phone call I received two letters. So you finally went to the plot, I'm glad you like climbing barbed wire fences, that's one sport I don't like, I always get caught in the most inconvenient places. Yes, I saw "Orchestra Wives" and liked it very much. We saw it here at camp a few weeks ago.

In your letter Saturday you didn't say much about why you didn't write Friday, did you go someplace else after the show?

Please, Muriel, don't take me wrong about your dad, I also think he's swell, you know that. It's just what he told you that night I didn't like. I can hardly wait until next month.   —*I love you, Raymond*

Wednesday, June 2nd

Dearest Ray,

I didn't receive any letters today but it made me very happy to hear your voice on the phone again. There's only one thing I didn't like hearing and that is you didn't feel well. Please, Ray, go and see the doctor, there must be something wrong when you get feeling sick as often as you do. Maybe you're taking too much out of yourself and getting to bed too late, if so go to bed earlier and see what happens.

Today a friend of mine got married to an American. They were married in St. Magdalene Church in Donegall Pass and Mommy and I went to see the wedding. Mommy was telling me about a girl who lives in Cromwell Road getting married. She isn't married yet as the American she's engaged to is waiting for his divorce papers to go through. He has a wife and two children in America and is divorcing his wife so he can marry the girl here. Ray, don't you think it's awful of him to do that? I blame the girl for letting a thing like that happen. All the girls at Inglis say they're going to be at the church the day I get married, they wouldn't miss it for worlds.

It's 6:45 and Hazel should be calling any minute. It won't be long now until you're over and then I'll be able to say all the things I can't write about. —*Yours as always, Muriel*

Thursday, June 3rd

Dearest Muriel,

I'm writing this letter from the lab as I am working tonight. I just got finished mopping the floors and I'm glad it's only once a week.

I received your letter of May 30th and was very sad to hear about Herbie. I feel kind of funny knowing him the way I did and now hearing that he's dead, but this is war and there's not much we can do about it. As for Lily, I feel very sorry for her, if she really did love him it's going to be very hard for her.

So George went and joined the navy, well, this is a surprise. I wonder why he went, I didn't think he would do that.

Last night I went to the Red Cross, they had a little dance going on and then a stage show, it wasn't too bad.

Today I received a postcard from my sister Jo, the one that just got married. She's down in North Carolina, about 1000 miles from home, with her husband. She didn't have much to say only that she was very happy and that a letter was being sent following the card.

I'm glad to hear that everything is OK at home. About myself, well, there is not much to say. Everything is the same—I still miss you more than ever. I sometimes think how wonderful it would be if we were here together. I keep thinking of a lot of different things, I wonder if you do the same. Someday we'll look back and laugh at all this and I hope it's soon. I better stop now as it's 11:00 and time for our late lunch, Luke is here waiting to go with me. He sends his regards. —*I love you, Raymond*

Thursday, June 3rd

Dearest Ray,

Two more letters arrived today and I was very glad to receive them. So Luke was writing to his Irish Spitfire, I wonder what Marie would say if she knew she was christened that by her American Thunderbolt. You say you hope I don't mind because you had one dance, not in the least, how could I object, occasionally I have more than one dance with the big bad wolves down at the Red Cross.

Last night Hazel and I went to the Royal Avenue Picture House to see "The Blues in the Night," have you seen it? It brought back memories of the time you used to sing that song. Ray, in one of the letters I received this week you say your mother asked if I need any powder or lipstick. I was able to obtain a box of Max Factor powder here and I know someone who may be able to get me a lipstick in Dublin, so tell your mother thanks for her kind offer, I don't need any.

As I've run out of talk, Ray, I'll end now.   —*Forever yours, Muriel*

Friday, June 4th

Dearest Muriel,

Today we were notified we wouldn't be going to London until July. I hope it doesn't interfere with our plans, but don't worry because I'll find some way to be over on your holiday.

Yesterday we had 200 new fellows in our hospital. They are in the outfit now so we are up to full strength. I guess most of them come from around New York City, the way they talk it sure sounds like it. I was asking one of the boys how New York was and after he got through I was homesick. It's not quite 10 o'clock so I think I'll run up to the PX and get a Coke before I turn in.   —*Forever yours, Raymond*

Friday, June 4th

Dearest Ray,

This is just a few lines to let you know that I am loving and missing you as much as ever. Tonight I was late leaving the office and as Hazel is calling around at 6:30 p.m. I haven't much time. We are going to the Regal to see "Cairo," some of the girls at the office have seen it and they say it is very good.   —*Yours Forever, Muriel*

Saturday, June 5th

Dearest Muriel,

Received your letter of the 1st today and was very glad to hear from you.

About what you said about the trouble being religion, well, maybe you're right. I can understand your mother and father's point of view and don't blame them but I wish they would just try to understand me and the way we think about it. Let's forget about it now, I'm sure we can settle it when I come over.

As for talking the way you did when I told you I was maybe joining the Air Corps, please, Muriel, don't think I'm holding it against you, in a way I don't blame you. I know you don't want me to go but you are being a good scout and letting me do as I wish. As much as you hate to see me go you're not standing in my way and that makes me love you all the more.

Now about myself, when I come to this part I never have anything to say. I worked all day, after chow (tea) I laid down for awhile and now I'm writing to you. —*Forever yours, Raymond*

Saturday, June 5th

Dearest Ray,

Last night Hazel and I went to the Regal to see "Cairo" but neither of us liked it very much. After the show we went to the Regal Café and had supper of ham and eggs. Tonight I'm not going out as I want to do some washing, wash my hair and then knit. At the moment I am here alone. Olive and Audrey are at the pictures and Mommy and Daddy have gone to the plot.

Just think, in another 30 or 31 days you'll be over here and boy will I be happy to see you again. —*Yours as ever, Muriel*

Sunday, June 6th

Dearest Muriel,

This afternoon about five of us went into town, they had a stage show at the Red Cross and it wasn't bad at all. There was some good acting and most of all it was very funny. After the show we had something to eat and came back to camp.

How come your mother went to an American wedding? I thought she didn't like them, weddings I mean. If all of Inglis comes to ours I see we are going to have a big crowd. —*Always yours, Raymond*

Sunday, June 6th

Dearest Ray,

It's after 1:30 p.m. and I'm just after having dinner. This morning Daddy and I went to the Church Anniversary and Flower Service. There was a parade of RAF boys there and Audrey, Olive, Betty and Raymond were in the choir.

This afternoon I'm not going out as Hazel isn't calling. I haven't made up my mind about the dance tonight but if I do go I'll let you know. When I was at the Red Cross yesterday week, Marie Neill and Dot said they were going to be there tonight so at least if I go I'll have someone to talk to and it will be better than sitting in the house alone. —*Yours forever, Muriel*

Monday, June 7th

Dearest Muriel,

Received your letter of June 3rd and was very glad to hear from you. I also received a letter from home. About the furlough, it will be on the 4th or 5th. I have it so it will be just right for us.

No, I haven't seen "The Blues in the Night," how was it, any good?

If you can't get any lipstick let me know and I'll send home for it. I'm in the lab writing this letter and have to write home now. I have some things I want my mother to send me. —*Yours forever, Raymond*

Tuesday, June 8th

Dearest Muriel,

I'm writing in the lab again tonight. Luke just left to see a show here at camp. There's no one here now and it's very quiet, just right to write letters.

So you had ham and eggs, I hope they hold out and have them when I come over. I bet the day I do come over they will stop serving them.

How is your jumper coming along, is it done yet? About the dance, no, I don't mind if you did go. Did you have a good time?

I have to go and cut the grass in front of the lab. We planted grass seed about three weeks ago and it's tall enough to cut now. Howard just brought the cutter over so I guess I better get started before it gets dark. —*I love you, Raymond*

Tuesday, June 8th

Dearest Ray,

Yesterday afternoon I was very happy to receive three letters from you. Last night I couldn't get writing to you as Hazel and I went to see "Footlight Serenade." It was showing at the Curzon and we had to leave at six o'clock to see it. When I got back from seeing "Footlight Serenade" and had supper I went upstairs to write but Audrey said she couldn't sleep with the light on so I had to turn it off and get to bed. As regards the Friday night I didn't write, no, I didn't go someplace else after the show. My Uncle Harold was over from England for a holiday and when I got home he was in. Do you remember I told you I had a row with him once and didn't speak to him since, well, when I found he was in I went into the sitting room with the intention of writing and avoiding him but he followed me. He sat down at the pi-ano and started to play and sing so I couldn't get writing. Ray, perhaps you don't know it, when I write to you I always like to be by myself. Mommy and Daddy know I always slip upstairs to my room to write you because if I write in their presence Mommy would be sure to start lecturing me.

Sunday night I went to the Red Cross, the hall was crowded and everybody seemed happy. If you had been there we could have had a marvelous time but as it was I couldn't enjoy myself so left with a girl I used to go to Sunday school with and got home about 10:30. Dot, Laura and Lily were there so I took the opportunity of telling Lily how sorry I was to hear about Herbie's death...

I had to stop writing Ray, to go for my music lesson. Yes, I'm back at music again. Mommy went round to my music teacher and gave her the money for another term. I told Mommy I was going back to music and paying for myself and when she heard that she went round to Mae Brown, gave her the money and told her to send for me.

I can hardly wait until I see you again because I've such a lot of things I want to discuss with you, things I just can't write about. —*Forever yours, Muriel*

Wednesday, June 9th

Dearest Muriel,

Today I had to work and it was a beautiful day. I wanted to call you up but didn't have time, so maybe tomorrow.

I just got back from the show here at camp, the name of the picture was "Always in My Heart," and it wasn't bad. Tonight Luke is working and I'm here with him. —*Always yours, Raymond*

Wednesday, June 9th

Dearest Ray,

Another two letters arrived today and they helped make up for the disappointment I had when you didn't phone. Maybe you went to London today after all and that was your reason.

I often wonder what it will be like when we are married and settled down after the war. I too hope it's soon when we can look back and laugh over all this, we'll be able to write a book together entitled "Love Finds a Way." Do you think that would be a suitable title or can you think of a better one?

Well, Ray, I'll stop writing now as Hazel is coming round but we're not going out as I want to knit and practice. —*Loving you as always, Muriel*

Thursday, June 10th

Dearest Muriel

I was glad to hear your voice again today, you sounded a little sad but so am I and always will be as long as I'm away from you.

It's about 10 o'clock now, I just got back from town. This afternoon I met a fellow I knew and we went around town together, shopping. They were selling strawberries on a street corner so we each bought a quart and went walking the streets eating them. I stopped at a few novelty shops and I got you a little pin, it's not much really. I got it for your black dress, remember, the one I told you to put a pin on? Now don't get mad, I'm only kidding, it's different and I thought maybe you would like it. I also found a shop where they sell lipstick so if you need any let me know, I can get all I want. I also bought some postcards. At about six o'clock we went to the show and saw "Dr. Gillespie's New Assistant."

Oh, about the strawberries, as we walked along everyone would stop and ask us where we got the berries and then we had to let them sample them so out of the quart I didn't have more than half. We finally ducked into the Red Cross, sat down and finished them, what we had left.

I received the pictures today. The place that made the prints did a terrible job, I'll have some new ones made soon if possible, if not I'll send you the ones I have.   *—Yours forever, Raymond*

Thursday, June 10th

Dearest Ray,

Today I was very glad that you phoned me, isn't it queer I was just thinking to myself, I wonder if Ray will call me this morning. I looked at the time and just at that moment I was told to go to the Time Office as the American Army was calling, yes, that's what the office girls call you now.

As I told you on the phone I had a letter today from Mommy's cousin Edith, and she is very eager that I go over to the hospital she's in and train as a nurse. Ray, I'd love to become a nurse but I wouldn't think of it unless you are sent away someplace else, in that case it would help to keep me occupied the duration of the war and maybe keep me from worrying.

As Hazel is due to call I'll stop writing now.   *—Forever yours, Muriel*

PS Do you know Arthur Rea, he is a doctor and one of the 200 newcomers you told me about.

Friday, June 11th

Dearest Muriel,

Today I was very disappointed, it's the third day and no letters, I hope there's one tomorrow.

It's about 11 o'clock now and I just got back from town. Luke, Howard and a few of the other fellows and I went to the Red Cross and had a few dances. The band was English, it wasn't bad but it was nothing like our bands. At 10:30 we called a cab and came back so here I am. I don't know why I go out, it doesn't do any good. I always have you on my mind. *—Always yours, Raymond*

Friday, June 11th

Dearest Ray,

Your letters of Saturday and Sunday arrived today and I was very happy to receive them.

You seem surprised to hear that Mommy went to an American wedding. The reason she went was she has known June Ferguson for years. She didn't say much about the wedding, only that it was very nice and they were both the same religion. *—Forever yours, Muriel*

Saturday, June 12th

Dearest Muriel,

Today after three days of no letters I received yours of June 8th and I'm very happy to hear from you.

I'm sorry you didn't have a good time at the dance, I guess you're the same as I am but we will have to make the best of it and try to enjoy ourselves as best we can. I'm glad you saw Lily, what did she have to say about Herbie?

So you're back at music, I'm glad to hear this. I know it's difficult for you, Muriel, but when I come over we are going to get things settled once and for all I promise you.

I received a letter from home today and my mother said she trusted me and if I was going to be happy with you she approved of us.

It's about eight o'clock now. Luke is here at the barracks with me, after I'm through we are going up to the PX and have a Coke. Luke sends his regards. *—Yours forever, Raymond*

Saturday, June 12th

Dearest Ray,

It's Saturday once again and I'm glad because I've had a busy week at the office. Yesterday the postman asked me if I wrote to myself because along with your two letters was a letter from the Red Cross asking me to attend some meeting on Wednesday night and also an invitation card for the dance tonight. They must have started to send out invitation cards again. Maybe I'll go to the dance tonight and ask Miss Anderson about the meeting. I don't want to attend it and perhaps she'll be able to tell me what it's all about. I hope you don't mind if I go tonight Ray, you know you can trust me and besides I've only been out twice this week.

I've been looking at the calendar and in three weeks time I'll be having my holiday and you'll be over on leave. It seems too good to be true and I'm still hoping nothing happens to prevent you coming. Everything has been very quiet and dull here lately. It won't be dull when you come over on leave but I sincerely hope it's peaceful, if you know what I mean. *—Yours as always, Muriel*

Sunday, June 13th

Dearest Muriel,

It's just about ten o'clock now and I just arrived back from town. I went with the boys to the Red Cross as they had a USO show. Adolphe Menjou was the star. The show lasted about three hours and it was very good with a lot of good acts. Luke is here with me writing to Marie telling her all about it. I just took my shoes off as Luke and I walked back to camp instead of taking the taxi. All the way back we talked about you and Marie, mostly about the future. Luke's parents said it's OK and are sending over the ring but don't ever mention it to Marie as Luke wants to surprise her.

You know from Mother's last letter everything is OK and she's very pleased with you. The only thing we have to settle is on your side and I'm sure when I come over we will do that. *—Forever yours, Raymond*

Sunday, June 13th

Dearest Ray,

Today I haven't been out at all. Hazel came round at four o'clock, it's 8:15 p.m. and she's here now reading a book as usual.

Last night I went to the Red Cross. Dot was there with Al and Lily was with a boy from the 10th station. She was talking to me for awhile and I think she is beginning to forget Herbie. She told me she didn't feel so bad about him now. I can't say I enjoyed the dance, all the time I kept thinking of you. Al kept kidding me and telling me to smile and not look so blue. After a few dances I left and as it was such a nice night I decided to walk home. I really wish you were back here with me. July isn't that far away but to me it seems like years. Mommy knows I'm taking my holiday in July but she doesn't know what week. The other night she told me I was going down to Omagh for my holiday but I told her I definitely wasn't so by now I guess she knows you must be coming. Daddy was taking his holiday from the 26th June until the 14th July. Now I think he's changed his mind and I can't really say when he'll be off, if I find out I'll let you know.   —*Forever yours, Muriel*

Monday, June 14th

Dearest Muriel,

It's about ten o'clock now, I just got up, after supper I laid down for what I thought was an hour, but when I awakened it was 9:30. I'm now up at the lab writing this letter, on my way up I stopped at the PX and had a few iced cold Cokes. I'm not so sleepy now.

I received your letter of June 9th and was very happy to hear from you. About the title of our book, I think it's very good but I'm afraid you will have to do most of the writing.

Today Adolphe Menjou was here visiting patients with the rest of his cast.

I see you're still knitting your jumper, you better have it done when I come over as you promised.   —*Forever yours, Raymond*

Monday, June 14th

Dearest Ray,

Owing to it being Whitsun I had the afternoon off. It's about 3:30 p.m. and I'm writing this letter now as Hazel and I may go to a show tonight. There was only one postal delivery and I was very disappointed when there wasn't a letter from you. I really hope you don't try phoning me this afternoon as I forgot to tell you I might have this afternoon off. At the moment I can't think of very much to say as nothing interesting has happened so I guess I'll end now.   —*Yours as always, Muriel*

P.T.O. Ray, where do you keep all these letters, I often wonder if you have them safely hidden.

Tuesday, June 15th

Dearest Muriel,

I'm writing this letter from the lab as Luke is working tonight. I received orders today that I have ------------------------*censored* ----------------------

----------------- meeting June 30th. I'm glad it came now so it won't interfere with your holiday. I was worried it would be in July but now that we know everything will be OK you can plan on me coming over the first part of July.

I know this is a short letter but I haven't anything more to say, not in writing anyway. I will close now and get to bed. It's about 10:30 p.m. now and it seems funny going to bed when it's still daylight out, I can't remember ever doing it in Belfast, can you?   *—I love you, Raymond*

Tuesday, June 15th

Dearest Ray,

Received four letters today—yes, four and boy, was I glad. Before I start answering your letters I must tell you where Hazel and I went last night. We went to the Regal to see a picture named "Sweethearts" and I think it was the best picture I've seen for a long, long time. We enjoyed it so much that we stayed to see it again.

About my jumper, no, I haven't it quite finished yet but I promise I'll have it ready when you come on leave.

Thursday's letter is really funny, did you and your friend actually walk along the streets eating strawberries, of course I don't blame you. I'd be glad to eat them any place myself. That reminds me, one afternoon a few weeks ago when I was coming home from the office some boys were selling scallions with heads as big as small onions. I knew Mommy would like them so I bought some. They hadn't any paper to wrap them in so I had to carry them without any. All the way home people were stopping me to ask me where I got them. Yvonne was with me and I think we laughed till we almost choked. We looked back once and everybody was rushing towards the corner where the boys were selling them. The war has really made big changes.

Thanks very much for buying me the pin, Ray. I'll always wear it no matter what dress I have on. About the lipstick, please don't bother buying any, I'll always have enough.

I'd better stop writing as I have to do some practice and go for my music lesson at eight o'clock.   *—Forever yours, Muriel*

Wednesday, June 16th

Dearest Muriel,

Today I was really surprised as I received four letters. I wish this was everyday.

So they call me the American Army, what else are they going to call me? If they kid about me that much I realize how much they must kid you.

About what Edith said, you know how I feel about you being a nurse. I won't go into detail now but will when I come over.

Muriel, in your letter you asked if I know Arthur Rea, no I don't, but how do you know he's here and why would he be here? If you explain yourself maybe I can help you, how do you know him?

So Lily was at the dance Saturday, I had an idea she would be. In a few weeks she'll forget all about Herbie but maybe it's the best thing because it won't do her any good to cry about it. I know I shouldn't talk like this but really, Muriel, she's young and has her life ahead of her. I don't think she ever was serious, maybe Herbie was but I'm sure she wasn't.

About the Red Cross, no, I don't mind because I know I can trust you and I want you to go once in awhile. About the meeting, that's up to you. —*Yours forever, Raymond*

Wednesday, June 16th

Dearest Ray,

I waited for a phone call today but no luck. I guess you had to work and most likely you'll phone tomorrow or Friday.

Tonight I'm expecting Hazel to call about 7 p.m. I haven't seen her since Monday night and before I left her she asked me if I would go on a message with her to the other side of town tonight and I said I would.

Last night after my music lesson I got my knitting and went in to sit with Auntie Vi. I'd only been there about half an hour when Olive came to the door to say that Greta was in our house. It was a surprise to me, Ray, because I haven't seen her in ages. Would you believe she doesn't like her new job and is going back to the Majestic. What a girl, I think she's crazy. At this very moment I hear Hazel at the door and Mommy is calling me down to her. —*Forever yours, Muriel*

Thursday, June 17th

Dearest Muriel,

It's about nine o'clock now and I just got back from the show here at camp named "George Washington Slept Here," it was very funny and I enjoyed it very much.

Today was my day off but I didn't go out as I had too much to do. This morning I had quite a time trying to reach you. At 10:00 I put the call through and they told me to come back at 10:30. When I got back there wasn't any telephone there, much to my surprise, so I had to run around and find another telephone box. In the meantime it was past 10:30 so I called the operator and told her the story. She told me to wait and she would try to put the call through again. I was lucky that the line was open and I finally got you. I wanted to talk longer to you but in the rush I forgot to get another shilling as I only had three. I will try to call you again on Tuesday, if possible.

Today I did a good housecleaning to my footlocker and barrack bags. I also packed a little package for you and will send it this week sometime. I received a letter from home today, my mother didn't have much to say only why didn't I write more. I write at least once a week, but she wants more. She told me Jo, my sister that just got married, came home with her husband to spend a few days, I guess he got a furlough, he's in the army also. —*Always yours, Raymond*

Thursday, June 17th

Dearest Ray,

It's 8:30 p.m. and I just got back from my music lesson. At the moment Greta is here, she actually kept her word for once and I can hardly believe it. Today I received your letter of the 11th, it was very short but the phone call made up for it. Honestly, Ray, I was very happy that you phoned me, the girls in the office tell me I've got it bad and God help poor Ray when he comes on leave.

Hazel is going to Portrush this Sunday to spend a week there and today Mommy told me to take my holiday then and go with Hazel. I told her when I was taking my holiday and also that I had to take it then or I wouldn't get off at all.

So you're going to London on the 30th, I hope it doesn't interfere with your leave. I'm not sure yet when the family is going to Omagh, but I'll let you know when I find out. Greta says hello. —*I love you, Muriel*

Friday, June 18th

Dearest Muriel,

Much to my surprise I received two letters and was very glad to hear from you. You asked me about your letters, don't worry, I have them under lock and key and I'm saving every one. I often wonder about my letters, with your two sisters. I don't trust them in the sense that they're young and full of the devil and they may get a notion to read some of them, so you better take care also.

Tonight I was going to the Red Cross Dance but after supper (tea) I fell asleep and didn't wake up until 8:30 and now I'm writing to you. I haven't sent the package but will soon, the pin will be in it.   *—Yours forever, Raymond*

Friday, June 18th

Dearest Ray,

Yesterday the weather was beautiful but today the rain has come down in torrents and it has hardly ceased for 10 minutes. If it's like this when you come over you'll probably grumble the whole time.

As of yet I haven't found out when the family is going to Omagh. If they don't go for the week before you come most likely it will be the week after you leave. Although I haven't mentioned that you are coming I'm sure they have a pretty good idea. Mommy seems reluctant to go without me. She seems to think I won't make myself proper meals and take them at the right time. The other day I told her I wasn't a child any longer—that I could take care of myself and she worries about nothing. If and when they do go Hazel has promised to come round and live with me while they're away. Honestly, Ray, Mommy's the limit, she has no desire to go anyplace and it takes her weeks to make up her mind to go on a holiday. Daddy has been coaxing her for the past month to go with him to Omagh and I don't think she has made up her mind yet. She seems to think that I'm helpless without her. What a mother, I can picture what she's going to be like when I get married. Daddy has to fire-watch all night tonight and if you had only heard the way Mommy talked she'd give you the impression she wasn't seeing him for years and the loss of a night's sleep was going to kill him.

Oh, I got a Max Factor lipstick yesterday. Yvonne and I went into the Chemist shop we always buy our makeup in and the boy who serves in it told me he had a Max Factor lipstick put past for me. I had kept asking for one for ages and when they did get a few in he kept one for me. It was he who sold me the Max Factor powder I told you about getting a few weeks ago.   *—Forever yours, Muriel*

Saturday, June 19th

Dearest Muriel,

I'm writing this letter from the lab tonight as I'm working. Luke and a few of the other boys are here also to keep me company.

I have a little package packed for you and will send it Sunday or Monday. I'm sending you another but I want you to save it so we will have it when I come over. The first one is yours but the second save for us.

I guess that's about all for now, I have lots to say but not in writing. I wish you had a phone so I could call you up and talk with you. —*All my love, Raymond*

Saturday, June 19th

Dearest Ray,

This morning I was happy to receive three more letters.

You want to know what Lily had to say about Herbie, well, she didn't have much to say only that she didn't feel as bad about him as she did when she first heard the news about him being killed. She told me that the boy from the 10th station was very good to her and I noticed she seemed more like her old self when in his company.

I'm very happy to hear that everything is OK for Luke and Marie to get married. What made his people change their minds? I promise not to say a word to Marie about the ring.

Audrey is just after coming upstairs to tell me that Mommy and Daddy are arranging to go to Omagh next week. They'll probably go next Saturday or Sunday.

Tonight I'm not going out as I want to practice and knit. —*Forever yours, Muriel*

Sunday, June 20th

Dearest Muriel,

Received your letter of the 16th and as always was glad to hear from you. Muriel, will you explain what a "message" means—I remember you would say that to me once in awhile and I never knew what you meant. I take it to mean to go see someone or go and buy something, am I close? So Greta quit her job again, what a girl. I pity the American she's going with.

At about six o'clock Luke and I are going into town and take in a show or walk around. I slept this afternoon as last night I didn't get to bed until three o'clock. I had some work to do and another fellow who works in the lab had some work so I stayed and helped him. Well, I guess that's about all for now, I will be seeing you soon. —*Yours forever, Raymond*

Sunday, June 20th

Dearest Ray,

Today has been a pretty dull day. The weather is a little better, but not much. At nine o'clock last night Greta came round to see me. I was in the sitting room knitting when she called and as I was feeling lonely I was glad to see her. She called at two o'clock today again, it's nine o'clock now and she's still here. We didn't go out at all, I've been knitting since four o'clock. I started knitting a sleeve of my jumper then and now I've almost finished the second sleeve. When it is done I've only to sew all the pieces together and the jumper is completed.

Right now Mommy is getting the supper ready and after that I'm taking a bath and going to bed. Greta is in great form, she has done nothing but laugh all day and I can hardly believe it. She says to tell you that I've sat night and day knitting. Then she starts laughing, what at I don't know, do you see anything funny about what she says? What a girl, I think she's gone nuts.

I have to end now, Ray, as supper is ready. —*Yours forever, Muriel*

Monday, June 21st

Dearest Muriel,

It's just eight o'clock and I'm in the lab here with Luke as he is on duty tonight. If you can't read this it's because I'm in an awkward position for writing. I'm sitting in a big soft chair with my feet stretched out on another chair and have a book as my writing table. A few of the other boys are here kidding around.

Last night we went to town and as there was nothing to do we went to the show and saw "Fire over England" and "Shut My Big Mouth." To make a long story short, I fell asleep they were so good. I didn't want to go but Luke insisted and he paid for it too. After the show we went to the Red Cross and had a few Cokes, met up with some more fellows, got a cab and we were back by 10:30. I hate Sundays because I remember the good times we had when we were together, and now I'm all alone with nothing to do and no place to go. I know you feel the same as I do but in another week or two I'll be there with bells on. —*I love you, Raymond*

Monday, June 21st

Dearest Ray,

Tonight I'm going to the Majestic by myself, I haven't been to a show since Monday night last. As you know I went on a message with Hazel on Wednesday night and those were the only times I was out last week. The picture showing in the Majestic tonight is named "Somewhere on Leave." Greta saw the trailer and says it seems pretty good. She is starting there today so I'll be able to come home with her after the show.

Ray, I can hardly believe I will be seeing you in two weeks time, it seems too good to be true...

I had to stop writing there for awhile, Greta came to the door. She worked all afternoon and at 3:30 p.m. the boss informed her that Monday night is her night off. With talking to her it is now too late to go to the pictures. I'll probably just go for a walk somewhere. *—Forever yours, Muriel*

Tuesday, June 22nd

Dearest Muriel,

Another happy day for me as I received your letters of the 17th & 18th. Tonight I'm working emergency, Luke is here with me writing to Marie.

I'll do more than grumble if it rains while I'm there. As for the family, I'm sure they have an idea I'm coming or they would go to Omagh. They want to make sure they're home when I arrive if you know what I mean. If your mother is the way she is with your dad I can see why she worries about you.

So you're making eyes at the boy in the Chemist shop. Muriel, I didn't think you'd do that just to get some lipstick and powder—I'm going to make you take it all back. I'll bring you some so you can make eyes at me. I better stop kidding now or you'll jump through the roof. All kidding aside, if you do need any let me know and I'll try to get some for you.

Well, I guess I better stop now and start mopping the floors. I wanted to call you up today but didn't have the chance, but will try tomorrow. *—I love you, Raymond*

Tuesday, June 22nd

Dearest Ray,

Today really has been a lucky day for me as I have received four letters from you and a postcard from Hazel. To begin with your letter of the 15th, there isn't much for me to say about it only that part of it was censored, but I think I know what you were trying to tell me. Probably you were telling me about going to London.

You'd never guess who christened you the American Army. Once when Miss Collins was phoning through to tell me to go to the Time

Office, the boss answered the phone and I almost had a fit when he said aloud, "Muriel, you've got to go to the Time Office, the American Army is phoning." All the girls began to laugh and ever since you're the American Army and I'm Yankee Doodle Dandy.

About Arthur Rea, I don't know him at all. I only asked if you knew him because he is a cousin of Phyllis Doyle, one of the girls who works in Inglis.

Tonight I went to music, got back at 8:45 and now I'm writing to you. After I finish this I'm going to practice for awhile and then get to bed early.   —*Always yours, Muriel*

Wednesday, June 23rd

Dearest Muriel,

I didn't receive a letter today but after that phone call I can't kick. I don't know who the operator was but I wish I could get her every time. Either that or they must have forgotten us. At the end I didn't quite hear what you said, but I think you said send a telegram when you are coming over. I'll phone you if I can, if not I'll send a telegram.

I expect to go to London this weekend to find out when and where I have to report next Wednesday, also if I can fly over and how much time I can have on furlough and when I have to leave. I may come over a little earlier than I expected.

Tonight Luke, a few of the fellows and I went to town to see "Casablanca." It was a wonderful picture so if you haven't seen it please do so when it comes to Belfast.

I got a GI haircut today. I have about one inch of hair left. Everybody here has been kidding me, they tell me I look like a young kid. I hope you like it when I come over. You know them as brush cuts and it really looks like a brush.   —*Forever yours, Raymond*

Wednesday, June 23rd

Dearest Ray,

Mommy had a letter from our friends in Omagh this afternoon, they want Mommy and Daddy to go to Omagh on Saturday 26th instead of Monday 28th. That means they'll probably be back again before you arrive. You seem to dislike the idea of meeting them again since we became engaged. In a way I don't blame you, but after all, I had to face them when you went back to England. I had the courage to do that and can't see why you haven't, a man is supposed to be more courageous than a woman. Please don't think I misunderstand, Ray, I know perfectly well how you must feel.

As I told you on the phone today, I'm going to the Majestic to-night to see "Somewhere on Leave." —*Forever yours, Muriel*

Thursday, June 24th

Dearest Muriel,

I received two more of your letters today. It's gotten so now that if I don't receive a letter I'm disappointed. Today has really been beautiful, after work I took a sunbath. I just finished taking a shower and now I'm all set to go out, that's if you were here with me. It's 9:30 now and it's still very warm, remember, just like that one day of summer we had last year in Ireland.

As to why Luke's parents changed their minds, I really don't know nor does he, they just did. If he ever does find out I'll let you know.

I see your jumper is coming along, I hope you have it done when I come over. Muriel, I'm surprised as to why you didn't realize why Greta was laughing at you. I won't say it now but don't forget to ask me when I come over and I'll explain. When you stop and think about it, it is funny. Don't worry, someday you'll be knitting for a baby, maybe, now do you catch on, that's what she was laughing at.

This afternoon we had to drill in the hot sun for about two hours and boy, my feet are sore but I'm not tired. Ha, Ha.

I'm going over now to have a Coke and then hit the hay, and I mean hay because our mattresses are filled with either hay or straw and they're not so good, but I guess you get used to anything in time.   —*Forever yours, Raymond*

Thursday, June 24th

Dearest Ray,

I really don't know how to begin this letter or should I say thank  you for the package which arrived today. I'm not very good at showing my appreciation in words, but boy, when you come over you'll really know how delighted I am. Honestly, Ray, the pin is beautiful, I just love it. Right now I'm wearing it and believe me I always will. I showed it to Elsie in the office this afternoon and before long all the other girls came over and asked me to show it to them. They all think it is very pretty and uncommon and I was very proud to tell them that you sent it. I just don't know what to say about the cigarettes and candies, you should keep them for yourself because I know you only get a certain amount for the week. I gave Mommy some chocolate and showed her the pin and she likes it very much too.

This last few day Mommy hasn't been feeling too well, but I must say she hasn't been lecturing me about you, on the contrary, she has been very good to me. I really am a lucky girl, I've got good parents and one of the best boys in the world for a boyfriend, what more could a girl want.

Last night I went to the Majestic, the picture was crazy but I enjoyed it, maybe because I've been in a crazy mood this last while back. After the show Greta and I came home together. As Hazel won't be back from Portrush until Sunday and Mommy and Daddy are going to Omagh on Saturday, Greta has promised to stay with me Saturday night. I told Mommy I didn't mind staying in the house one night myself but she said I would be lonely and insisted on me inviting Greta down. In a little over a week you'll be here so I needn't tell you how happy I am. *—Always yours, Muriel*

Friday, June 25th

Dearest Ray,

Today has been another lovely day for me, this morning I received two letters and in the afternoon another one.

So you pity the American Greta is going with. Once I thought she was a queer kind of girl and hard to understand, but not any longer. The other night Greta told me all about herself and her people. She also told me the real reason she started working in the Majestic and all I can say is I pity her and don't wonder she is the way she is. She's really quite a nice girl but she never had a chance, her home life is miserable and that's the reason she's so dull and lifeless at times. When you come over I'll tell you all about her and then maybe you too will understand.

Last night I finished my jumper, it fits me perfectly. Tonight I'm not going out—after I finish this I've to help Mommy with the packing. They are going to Omagh on the 12 o'clock train leaving Belfast tomorrow and don't want to leave everything to the last minute.

I'll explain what I mean by a message when you come over. *—Forever yours, Muriel*

Saturday, June 26th

Dearest Ray,

The phone call today was most unexpected and I can't tell you how glad I was to get speaking to you. Right now Greta is here or should I say she's upstairs having a bath. The time is 12:15 a.m., perhaps you'll think it's very late to be writing a letter but this is the first opportunity I've had today. This afternoon I had to go out and do some shopping. After tea I had lots of little things to do in the house and haven't had a minute to spare until now. After I write this Greta and I are going to wash our hair and when it's dry go straight to bed.

Even now I can hardly realize that you are coming over next week. This time I'm looking forward to seeing you even more than the last time. I guess it's because this is the longest we've been separated yet. —*Forever yours, Muriel*

Sunday, June 27th

Dearest Ray,

This afternoon Greta and I went for a walk, it was so warm I had to take my coat off and carry it and boy am I sorry now. My arms are red and absolutely covered with freckles. We got home again at 6 o'clock and at 6:30 Hazel called. If you could only see her now, her face is red like the rising sun. Her holiday in Portrush certainly did her good.

The thought of seeing you again has me feeling very happy for you'll never know how much I've missed you these past four months. —*Yours forever, Muriel*

Monday, June 28th

Dearest Muriel,

I really don't know where to start I have so much to tell you. I can't explain everything to you now but will when I come over. I'll give you a quick outline. As you know I left for London Friday night. Saturday, after I called you up, I left for the 8th Air Force Headquarters and spent the day there. That night we went to the Rainbow Club as they had a dance. Sunday morning we went to church, in the afternoon we went sightseeing, then went to the golf club and played golf. We got the 9:30 train and arrived back at camp at 12 o'clock. Today I was busy getting everything straightened out as I leave again tomorrow. It's 12 o'clock now. I just got through pressing my clothes and haven't had a minute all day. I hope you understand and don't get mad because I haven't written.

As you know I'm leaving tomorrow for London and staying until Thursday. This will be my last letter until I see you again. —*Yours forever, Raymond*

Back to England.

July 1943

Wednesday, July 14th

My Dearest Muriel,

I really don't know how to begin this letter, I have so much to say. When I got back to camp I went right to bed I was so tired. The boat trip was very rough and I didn't sleep all night. Today I tried to call all afternoon but couldn't make a connection until 7:30 this evening, I can't understand why but had to give up, I was really mad.

As I'm writing this letter I can't help but thinking of you coming around the corner to say cheerio again. Honest, Muriel, it was never so hard to leave anyone in all my life. I felt like coming back but knew I couldn't as I was late as it was. On the boat I couldn't sleep, I kept thinking of you and last night it was the same. When you came around the corner the last time I could hardly talk, honest, you did make it that much harder for me to leave but I was glad you came. Muriel, if it's one year or two don't let anyone tell you differently, I'll be back. I couldn't live without you. I love you too much & don't ever forget it.

I had two letters from home when I arrived back at camp. My sister Dot, has a new riding horse and my dad is building a stable for the horse. They're really going crazy back home, I wonder what else they're going to buy.

I have some of the pictures we took when I was over, some came out good but a few didn't. When I have the right paper I'll be able to have better prints made and when I do I'll send them to you.

Muriel, I know when everyone hears that I'm going back (to the States) they will start talking, you know what I mean, but don't let them get to you because I am coming back. Please don't pay any attention to them and don't let them get you mad.

I wish I could put into words how I feel, but that's impossible. I love you more than anything else in this world and always will.   —
Forever yours, Raymond

Thursday, July 15th

My Dearest Muriel,

As you know this will be the last letter from here. I won't be able to write to you until I'm settled. In the phone call today, Muriel, I felt very sad because I know you did. I feel the same way as you do, darling, but please try and be cheerful. I explained to you why I was going and you agreed. I'm going to miss you more than anything else in this world but we both made a promise. I'm coming back someday. It's going to be just as hard for me being away from you as it is for you being away from me. Someday we'll be together forever so let's look forward to those happy days. I'll write to you as long as I am in England and when I'm home I'll do the same. As soon as I have my new address I'll let you know. As for the camera, Luke will send the film over just as soon as it comes from home. As to Marie, you can call her up now and again and she will tell you what's new, so don't forget.

I'm all packed and will leave for a placement center tomorrow, the time I'll be there I can't say or know so if you don't hear from me for awhile please don't worry.   *—I love you, Raymond*

Thursday, July 15th

My Dearest Ray,

It's now 10:30 p.m. and I've just got home after being at the Curzon with Hazel. I have slept and eaten little since you went away and I do want to be a little fatter for you when you come back. Tonight in the Curzon I cried all through the show, I can't even tell you the name of the picture. Ray, I know I shouldn't tell you this because you have enough to worry about. *Please*, Ray, take care of yourself and write to me as often as you can. Maybe when your letters start to come I won't feel quite so bad.

Sometime next week I'm going to buy you an identity disc to wear on your wrist. Please don't refuse it, Ray, because I do so want to buy you something, you have been more than good to me. While you're away I'm going to save and buy some nice linens for our home when we get married. I'm also going to practice hard and get my diploma at Christmas. I haven't written to Edith yet, but when I do write I'll tell her I'm not going to become a nurse. You don't want me to be one and because of that I have no ambition to become one. Tomorrow night Hazel is coming round, she is going to write to Louis and I am going to write to your mother.

Honestly, Ray, every time I think of the coming lonely months I can't describe the awful feeling I get. I really and truly love you and if I were ever to lose you it would break my heart. Today Louis told me not to worry, maybe I would see you again. The word maybe has been in my head ever since and I can't explain how it hurts.

Please, Ray, don't fly, look after yourself and be careful. I'm praying that God keeps you safe. —*Always yours, Muriel*

Friday, July 16th

Dear Mrs. Friscia,

At last I have plucked up the courage to write you and I hope you don't think I am being forward in any way. Raymond arrived here on furlough on Saturday 3rd, and he went away again on Monday 12th. He should have left on Saturday 10th, but he phoned the hospital and got permission to stay a little longer.

Since he went away I have been utterly miserable and worried to death. I haven't been able to eat or sleep thinking about him. Yesterday morning he phoned me to tell me that he had to report to the 8th Air Corps Headquarters. He said he would be there for a week or maybe a few days longer and then he was being sent back to America for training. When Raymond first told me he was joining the Air Corps, I begged him not to do so. I love him with all my heart and if anything was ever to prevent me from seeing him again I don't think I could live.

Maybe you think I am crazy, Mrs. Friscia, but please try and understand, Ray is the only boy I ever loved or ever will love. When he left Belfast the day before Christmas I missed him more than words can describe, but somehow I didn't worry so much because I knew he would be pretty safe in England and I would be able to see him every time he had furlough. Now he is going in the Air Corps and after training likely to be transferred to any of the danger zones, it has me feeling terrible.

When he was here last he explained to me that he was most unhappy in the hospital for reasons which I cannot mention here. He told me he wanted to get a promotion in the army so that he could get a good job back home after the war and be able to provide me with all he wanted me to have. As far as I am concerned I love Ray so much I could live on a budget anyplace with him and be happy. I have told him that but he just would not change his mind. He told me that you didn't want him to join the Air Corps either and I can understand why.

Ray has asked me to wait for him and he will come back to me as soon as he can. He has also asked Daddy if he can marry me and as both he and Mommy like him a lot and know that we love each other, they have consented even though we are of different religion. The fact that Ray's religion is different than mine does not make any difference to me, we both believe in God and to me that is all that matters.

There is only one good thing about Ray going in the Air Corps and that is he will be able to see you and the rest of the family again. One thing I admire most in Ray is that he always talks a great deal about you, in fact, he has said so much that I feel I almost know you. As you never have met me I'm sure you often wonder if I will make a suitable wife for him and I don't blame you, but believe me no girl will ever love Ray more than I do, it couldn't be possible.

Please forgive me for writing this kind of letter but Ray told me to write and from all he's told me about you, I'm sure you will understand how much I care for him. Maybe when you see him you will be able to persuade him to give up the idea of becoming a pilot and train for the ground force instead. I really hope so.   —*Sincerely yours, Muriel*

Saturday, July 17th

My Dearest Ray,

Although I am writing this letter now I'm sure it will be a long time before you are reading it. I intend to post it as soon as I receive your new address. Last night Hazel and I set off for a long walk but I was so restless and unhappy that we took a tram home. When I got home I sat down and wrote a five-page letter to your mother.

Words can't describe how glad I was when you phoned me this morning, honestly, Ray, I'm going to miss those calls an awful lot.

At four o'clock today Hazel called and we went to the Regal, after the show we had tea in the café and then walked home. When I got in the house I played the piano for awhile and now I'm writing to you. At the moment Mommy and Daddy are at the plot but they should be home soon. My happiness depends on you, Ray, so please write often and make me feel better.   —*Forever yours, Muriel*

Sunday, July 18th

My Dearest Ray,

Once again I'm writing to you, it seems crazy doing so when I haven't an address to send it to, but anyhow it makes me feel a little better.

Today Hazel and I went to Bellevue, I didn't feel like going but there wasn't anything else for us to do. We lay down on the hill and looked out over the bough, and all the time I kept thinking of you.

Honestly, Ray, if it had been possible I'd have got on a boat and went across to England just to see you again before you went to America. There were crowds of people out and lots of Americans tried to get talking to us. That made me feel worse because there will never be anyone else but you. We stayed awhile at Bellevue and then we came into town and had something to eat in the Whitehall Café.

As I won't be getting anymore phone calls from you I'm going try hard to find another job. While I am working at Inglis the girls keep teasing me about you and all last week I couldn't do my work properly thinking about you. I tried very hard to be cheerful, but it isn't any good.

Tomorrow I hope to receive the letter you wrote containing the snaps and I also hope you have time to write to me while you are in ...., darn the censors, London. Please be good and take care of yourself.   —*Always loving and missing you, Muriel*

Monday, July 19th

My Dearest Muriel,

Tonight it's just a week ago since I left you and it seems like ages. I promise you, Muriel, after this war is over I'll be back for you. Please don't ever worry that I'll leave you, I couldn't live without you.

As you know I can't say where I am or when I'm leaving. I will write to you from here as long as possible. Letters to me you had better address home so I'll have them when I arrive.

We left camp Friday afternoon. We had a swell sendoff, all the boys and officers were there to say goodbye. In a way I was sorry to be leaving the boys I've known so long but I've finally got what I've wanted all my life. Now I hope I can carry it off and not flunk out because it means a lot to me, or should I say us. We stayed in London Friday night. Saturday we left and came to another camp and stayed overnight and Sunday morning we left again and came to the camp I'm at now. I wish I knew how long I'll be here, it may be a few days or a month. We haven't been able to go out of camp so far, but they may let us out later.

Don't forget to let me know what's going on at the office and at home, you know what I mean. I'm glad you wrote home to Mother. May I please read the letter you wrote to her?

Someday I will be back so don't worry about what other people say.   —*Forever yours, Raymond*

Tuesday, July 20th

My Dearest Muriel,

Another day here and nothing new only waiting and waiting, wish we knew when we were going. Muriel, yesterday you said something about buying me an ID bracelet, honest darling, you shouldn't have gone to all the trouble. When I do get it I will prize it very much. When I arrive home don't forget to let me know if there is anything you want. It's no trouble, I enjoy buying things for you.

You know, Muriel, I keep thinking of you coming around the corner when I was leaving. I'll never forget that, I almost didn't make the boat. I felt like coming back. It was never so hard for me to leave anyone in all my life.

Today we drilled in the morning, this afternoon they had me on a detail. What do you think, yes, mopping floors. Tonight we went to the canteen and had a few Cokes and that is how I spent my day, not very exciting is it? —*Forever yours, Raymond*

Wednesday, July 21st

My Dearest Muriel,

This morning at five o'clock I was told to report to the kitchen for KP. When I arrived Howard was there and we were told we had to wash pots and pans. That's what we did all day, I'm so tired now I can hardly write this letter. Honest, I never saw or washed so many pots and pans in all my life. I could hardly lift them let alone wash them. We were finally through at about eight o'clock, thank goodness.

There's nothing else new here. As yet I haven't received any of your letters that you sent to the hospital. The letters you write now—I think it best you send them home so they will be there when I arrive. I'm going to take a shower now and go to bed. Please don't worry about me. —*Yours forever, Raymond*

Thursday, July 22nd

My Dearest Ray,

This is the first time I've written since Sunday and I have such a lot to tell you. When you phoned me on Monday last it made me feel a little better but when I got home from the office and tried to write you, I couldn't. I also got your letter with the snaps in it. They didn't come out too well, except the ones of me on the bridge, everyone likes them here, but they make my hair look much darker than it really is. Please have some more of yourself taken and send them to me, after all, it's the next best thing to seeing you in person. Daddy is going to try and get some films and when he does, I'll have some more taken and send them to you.

Tuesday was another pretty miserable day for me so when I came from the office I went to the show by myself to try and help me forget. It didn't do much good. I might have stayed home but Daddy had a man in painting and decorating the kitchen and sitting room and I didn't like being around with that going on. My cousin, Pat Adair, was here when I got back from the show and I was really surprised to see her. She stayed overnight in our house and boy was I mad, I didn't get sleeping until around 4 a.m. You will wonder why so I'll tell you. She talks in her sleep and sleepwalks and the whole night she kept talking and getting out of bed, and I couldn't sleep with that going on. In a way it was very funny because I asked her questions and she answered them. Finally I had to waken her and we smoked a cigarette and after that I fell asleep, and if she talked after that I didn't hear her. The doctor has been giving Pat injections and sleeping draughts as he says she is using too much energy in her sleep.

Do you remember I told you I was going to try hard to get another job, well, on Wednesday afternoon I asked Mr. Johnston if I could stop working at 4:30 p.m. as I had to go into town on *an errand*. He said "yes" so I left and went to meet Hazel as she wants another job too. We went to the Employment Exchange and from there we were sent to the Law Courts. The Aeronautical Inspection Dept. has their office there and they offered us jobs as Inspectors of Aircraft parts. If we agree to take the jobs, we will be sent to England for training then we will be sent home again to work here, unless we agree to work in an Aircraft Factory elsewhere. As yet we haven't made up our minds. I'm absolutely fed up working at Inglis and I'd love to get a good job elsewhere. Other girls are earning 5 & 6 pounds a week doing war work and if I could get a job like that I'd be able to save quite a lot of money and buy lots of nice things for our home when we get married. Pat Adair has started working for the Lockheed Overseas Company, she knows the General Manager very well and she says if I like she will try to get me a job there. When you were over, Ray, you told me not to change my job but I've got to dislike working in Inglis and feel I'd like a change. I often wonder why you don't want me to work for the Lockheed Overseas Company. Maybe it's because you think I'd meet too many Americans, even if I did, Ray, I love you and only you and will never have anything to do with anyone else.

I started writing this letter in the house but Hazel called, she had a letter to write to Louis so as it was such a lovely night we took our writing pads to the Botanic Gardens. Right now we are sitting in the loveliest spot we could find. They have open air dancing in the Gardens now and where we are sitting we can hear the strains of the band. Honestly, Ray, I'd give anything I have if only you were here. The other night I dreamt that a taxi came to our door and you stepped out of it with three cases—what a dream, I really hope it comes true. Olive tells me I waken her every night talking about you in my sleep. She says I argue with you about which show we should go to, and shout, "Please, Ray, don't go away." Pat Adair talks a lot in her sleep but Olive says I talk even more.

Ray, when you finish your training I do hope you can be transferred back here again. A year is a long, long time, but two years is awful. I'm sending this letter along with two others to your home address. Please write to me often and above all take care of yourself and try to come back to me soon.   —*I love you, Muriel*

Friday, July 23rd

My Dearest Muriel,

Today, much to my surprise I received your letter of the 15th and I can't express in words how happy I was to receive it. Every day I would stop at the Post Office and ask if there were any letters for me. Each day I would be disappointed, but today I was lucky, and this was after the phone call. I was very glad to hear your voice but I could tell in your voice how very sad you are.

Muriel, sometimes I think I'm a rat for what I am doing, maybe I am in a way but I was only thinking of you. There are certain things in life I want to be able to give you and if it's possible I'm going to try. If I don't succeed, well, I can say I tried to do my best. Maybe you can't see my point now, but later on you will—I'm sure of it.

Yesterday I wrote you a letter but I tore it up because it was short and I was very depressed. Laying around here nights with nothing to do keeps me thinking of how wrong I am for what I am doing, but in another way I'm right, at least I hope so. I'm all mixed up. I could go on all night but I better stop and answer your letter. As for the identity disc, Muriel, my love, I don't know how to thank you. I'll never refuse anything you send me, never.

About you saving so as to buy things for our home, you really don't have to because I'm doing that now. I'm having 10 pounds a month put away for us but if you want to also OK, but maybe you need it to buy things for yourself. As regards to going out, please go anytime you want to because I know I'll never have to worry and I trust you. Maybe it would be best so as to keep your mind occupied, a little anyway.

Muriel, about you becoming a nurse, it's true I don't want you to be one but if you think it would help pass the time away, it's up to you. With me going away as I am I don't think it's fair of me to stop you. I think it's best if you stay home and get your diploma but if you think it's going to be too hard for you to stay home, I really won't mind too much.

Muriel, as far as Louis goes, maybe he has different ideas about Hazel so don't mind what he says. There's no maybe about it, I'm coming back for you and don't let anyone tell you differently. I'll be back no matter what anyone says or does, don't ever forget that. —*Always yours, Raymond*

PS When I get the identity disc I'll have my name and address put on one side and yours on the other. Here's three coupons I found, they're not much but maybe will help.

Saturday, July 24th

My Dearest Muriel,

Today has been quite an eventful one, Bob Hope was here at camp and I really enjoyed him. He was here for about an hour and a half (7-8:30) and I'm telling you I laughed the whole hour and a half. Honest, Muriel, he was swell. I was wishing you could see him but as he is only touring army camps I don't think you will unless he comes to Ireland. If you do get a chance don't miss it, they had quite a few civilians at camp to see him. After the show we went up to his car and talked to him for awhile before he left, then went to the canteen until eleven o'clock, drinking Cokes and playing records.

Tomorrow I'm to start pulling guard duty, how do you like that. I never did it before, I don't even know how to carry a gun let alone be a guard, but I guess they will show me. This waiting and waiting for something to happen is getting to me. I wish they would tell us when we are going and get it over with. —*I love you, Raymond*

Monday, July 26th

My Dearest Muriel,

I'm sorry the phone call was so short today, I couldn't get change as the canteen was closed, but the next time I'll be sure it is longer. Yesterday I didn't write as I was on guard duty. I didn't get much sleep but it wasn't bad. Oh, before I forget, have you called up Marie as yet? I think it would be a good idea once in awhile as Luke may have something to tell you. He is going to send you the film and the other part of the camera when my package arrives from home.

Boy, I wish I had a letter from you, I miss your letters very much but I know you are sending them home as I told you to.   —*Yours forever, Raymond*

Tuesday, July 27th

My Dearest Ray,

Once again I am writing to you and I have so much to say I hardly know how to begin. Perhaps you are mad at me for not writing every day, but I promise you I will just as soon as I receive your new address. Somehow, I don't like sending these letters to your home address because I don't know when you'll receive them.

Today I received two letters dated the 20th & 21st of July and was very happy to get them.

Ray, I'm sorry if I made it harder for you to leave by coming round the corner to say cheerio again, but I couldn't help it, I'd do the same thing all over again. When I started work again the girls in the office said they never in all their lives saw anyone so much changed as I was. They said I had got much thinner and didn't look at all well, no wonder when I couldn't eat or sleep thinking about you. All the time they kept asking when you'll be coming back so I told them you were training for a commission and it might be quite awhile before your training was finished and you would be able to return. I also told them you were being sent back to America and if there was anything else they would like to know about my private affairs not to be afraid to ask. Such a crowd, some of them are pretty nice and understanding but two in particular would just love if we broke off for good. Elsie and Adeline are two of my best friends and they always take my part. Elsie sits beside me and we cheer each other up. Her boyfriend is in the navy and reported missing. Although this is so Elsie feels sure he is alive and is always waiting for word from him. In the meantime she started going out on friendly terms with another boy. He was sent to England for about a month and the other day she got a telegram saying that he was back and wanted to take her out the following night. To make a long story short, we had a long discussion about boys and girls going out on friendly terms and it ended with Elise betting me 2/6 that although she was going out with the boy who sent her the telegram, he wouldn't kiss her. I bet her he would and the morning after he had been out with her I found 2/6 in the drawer of my desk. Boy, did I laugh, and I laughed all the more when Elise told me it was Bill who paid the bet. After he kissed her she told him about having made the bet with me. It amused him so much he insisted on paying the 2/6 and he told Elise to tell me to keep on betting, I wouldn't lose. Do you remember one night when you were on leave we went to Floral Hall and then to the Whitehall Café for supper, well, Elsie saw us when we were going around to the Whitehall and she said if she hadn't been in a bus she would have stopped to speak to us. She said she would have told you the way I kept her off her work the week before you came over. I have promised her that I will introduce you to her when you come back.

In a way I'm glad you're still in England, but in another way I'm not. It means the longer you are there the longer it will be before you are back here. Wherever you are, Ray, please be good and true to me and above all take good care of yourself. I read the war news all the time now and listen to the news on the wireless and the way things are shaping it looks like the war can't last much longer. If my prayers were answered it would be over tomorrow.

All day Saturday I stayed home and helped Mommy polish and dust the house. We had a man in painting and decorating and honestly, Ray, you wouldn't recognize the sitting room, it looks lovely now. The walls are cream and all the woodwork has been painted a colour slightly darker than cream. Daddy, Mommy and I put new covering on the floor. (I'll have to stop writing now and finish this letter tomorrow. Mommy went to the plot to get some vegetables and before she went I promised her I would prepare the supper. It's 10:15 p.m. now and about time I was keeping my promise.)

My Dearest Ray, I said I would finish writing this letter on Wednesday but with having so much to say and so little time yesterday, I thought it would be better to wait until tonight (Thursday). Now to begin where I left off. On Sunday afternoon Hazel called round and as it was such a beautiful day we decided to take a bus to Dundonald and then go for a long walk in the country. When we got off the bus we walked about four miles through lovely country lanes and gathered some beautiful flowers. We saw very few people and any that passed us said good-day or good-afternoon. On the way back to the bus stop we stopped at a farmhouse and had something to eat. Honestly, Ray, it was funny, the chickens were coming in the house while we were eating and Hazel and I almost tripped over them. When we got home again it was almost nine o'clock.

On Monday night we went to the Majestic to see "Desperate Journey," it was really a wonderful picture though a trifle far-fetched. Before I left Hazel I told her I couldn't see her on Tuesday night as I had to write a long letter to you. On Wednesday we decided to go to the Swimming Baths and then on to the pictures afterwards. Hazel wanted me to go out with her tonight again but I said no as I wanted to get this letter finished.

Now I think it's about time to answer the three letters I received from you this week. I only wish I was getting seven every week like I did before you joined the Air Corps. Perhaps it's hard for you to find time to write while you are being moved from one camp to another in England. When you go home please write every day and tell me how you are getting along. This coming winter is going to be very dismal for me and your letters will be all I'll have to look forward to. All the time I keep thinking of how wonderful it was having you here last year.

Do you remember we met practically every night in the week and went to shows and dances? I was very happy then, but I was always more happy when we were alone, even though we did fight a little, sometimes. You used to make me get mad, remember?

You asked me what made me change my mind about becoming a nurse, well, Ray, you want me to get my diploma at music and you would rather I didn't become a nurse, those are the reasons. Another thing, if I started training to become a nurse I mightn't be able to get away when you come back.

Ray, please don't ever say that sometimes you think you're a rat, you aren't any such thing. You went into the Air Corps because it was what you always wanted and because you want to get a better job back home after the war and be able to support me. In a way I admire you for what you are doing and I hope for your sake that you succeed in gaining what you want in the Air Corps. But please remember this, Ray, if you fail it won't make the slightest difference as to how I feel about you.

Daddy got a leather case made for the camera and quite by chance he managed to get film from his barber. Last night when Mommy and the children went to bed we got talking about the war. After a long discussion he said to me, "Muriel, you needn't worry, I don't think Ray will ever have to fly, I've an idea the war won't last that much longer." I could have kissed him when he said that, Ray, he really is very understanding. These last few days he hasn't been very well. Last night he called to see the doctor and the doctor told him he may have to go through an operation, but he isn't quite sure yet. Mommy and I are terribly worried.

Thanks very much for the three coupons you sent me. Now I'll be able to buy some wool and knit another jumper.   *—Forever yours, Muriel*

Thursday, July 29th

My Dearest Muriel,

I'm sorry that I haven't written in the last few days as there is really nothing to say. We still don't know when we are leaving. I'm on KP again tomorrow and how I hate that. I haven't gotten anymore letters from you, but hope there are some for me when I arrive home. As for calling you up tomorrow, I think that's impossible as we can't use the phones now until after 5:30 p.m. due to a new ruling. It may be awhile before we are together again, but when we do get together we will make up for the time we were apart, I promise you that. Whenever you are sad or blue think of me, my love, because I'm always thinking of you. When I'm sad I think of how much you love me and it makes me feel very much better, so much better I can carry on in life because I always know I have you.   *—Yours forever, Raymond*

Muriel Mitchell and Ray Friscia, July 1943.

9. PaC Ltr, Hq Eighth Air Force (Secret), Subject: "Orders", dtd 12 July 1943, the following named EM, Casual Pool, 12th Repl. Cont Depot, AAF Sta 591, APR and/or GMT fr AAF 591 to (destination as indicated in par 14 (secret) this order) for perm c of station, reporting upon arrival thereof to the CO. Cooked rations in kind will be furnished EM while travelling. TCMT. TDN. FSA 1-5600 P 431-02 A 0425-24.

Pvt. Edward B. Duncan, 35625264.

10. PaC Ltr, Hq Eighth Air Force (Secret), Subject: "Orders", dtd 9 July 1943, the following named EM, Casual Pool, 12th Repl Cont Depot AAF-591, WPR and/or GMT fr AAF-591 to (destination as indicated in par 14 (secret) this order) for perm c of station, reporting upon arrival thereof to the CO. Cooked rations in kind will be furnished EM while travelling. TCMT. TDN. FSA 1-5600 P 431-02 A 0425-24.

```
T/Sgt. William R. Wicks, 6830708
T/Sgt. Jean L. Vincent, 19032149
S/Sgt. Donald P. Anderson, 11068455
S/Sgt. Walter Skoniecany, 36176186
S/Sgt. Charles R. O'Flynn, 20452140
S/Sgt. Franon J. Musgrove, 14002070
S/Sgt. Clifford D. Mitchell, 19059093
S/Sgt. William J. Hammond, 32039394
Sgt. John G. Marsh, 17036561
Sgt. Rinaldo Yon, 16054424
Sgt. Francis O. Doggress, 12031102
Sgt. Berea O. Cromer, 34122901
Sgt. Charles W. Donohoo, 15300359
Sgt. Ledo J. Pastorelli, 33161262
T/4 Howard J. Merkel, 32039417
Cpl. William T. Schnieder, 33452807
Cpl. Norbert C. Van Tuil, 13040409
Cpl. Irving J. Fleischman, 14070007
Cpl. Thomas Williams, 19092823
Sgt. Ralph E. Draunstein, 35013816
T/5 Vernon O. Daniels, 37142646
T/5 Raymond G. Friscia, 32130243
Pfc. Robert K. Olson, 20739348
Pfc. Michael A . Hughes, 19013977
Pvt. Edward B. Scharoun, 12198712
Pvt. Joseph C. Donchin, 12070107
Pvt. David C. Crockett, 10600976
```

11. PaC Ltr, Hq Eighth Air Force (Secret), Subject: "Orders" dtd 26 July 1943, the following named EM, Casual Pool, 12th Repl Cont Depot, AAF 591, WPR and/or GMT fr AAF-591 to (destination as indicated in par 14 (secret) this order) for perm c of station, reporting upon arrival thereof to the C.O. Cooked rations in kind will be furnished EM while travelling. TCMT. TDN. FSA 1-5600 P 431-02 A 0425-24.

```
Cpl. Eldria A. Cummings, 18134854
Pfc. Joe Holmes, Jr, 39318122
```

(O V E R)

Orders Received

August 1943

Tuesday, August 3rd

My Dearest Muriel,

If you can't read this letter it's because the boat is rocking quite a bit. I'm not seasick but some of the boys are. I tried to call you up Saturday, the day we left. I had the call in but for some reason the phone went dead and I tried for an hour and a half to get through, but no luck. I was really mad and almost got caught but I didn't care, as long as I could have talked to you.

Muriel, as I lay in my bunk I keep thinking maybe you won't wait for me and it has me worried. I know I shouldn't have done what I did, I realize it now more than ever, but now that I've started I have to go through with it. I only hope I have done the right thing. Before I was sure of myself but now that I'm away from you I'm not so sure. Please, Muriel, write and tell me that I did so I'll have the strength to go through with it. You're the only thing in this world that keeps me going.

I have your pictures here next to me. I'm sitting near the ceiling on the fifth bunk next to a dim light writing this letter to you. The light just went out so I'll have to move to another place.

Saturday night they put us in trucks and took us to *censored,* from there we boarded the boat, that night we spent getting our bunks etc. set up. Sunday morning they had ----------------------- aboard the --------------
--------------------set and I --
---*censored*--

-- Sunday was spent mostly sleeping and talking to *censored.* Monday morning we left Liverpool and started on our way. I have lots of souvenirs from them and talked to quite a few, some speak English very well. They're very young fellows and to see the way they eat our food, it's pitiful. Sunday we had chicken and you should have seen them eat it. The food on the boat here has been wonderful but honest, my love, when I have these things I keep thinking of you and wishing I could give you some. Monday night we went to the show on board and then to bed, oh, on Sunday I

was taken down in the engine room and shown the boat from one end to the other.

It's starting to rain now, it's about 9 o'clock so we must still be around Ireland, now don't get mad. Every time it rains I think to myself and laugh at how I would carry on when it rained in Ireland. Every time it rains now I'll think of us. I'll probably go around with a smile on my face and everyone will wonder if I'm nuts or something. Honest, Muriel, the happiest moments in my life were spent with you and I'll never forget them. Someday I'm coming back so I can continue those happy moments with you for the rest of our lives. *—I love you, Raymond*

PS I'm mailing this letter as soon as we dock in NY.

Tuesday, August 3rd

My Dearest Ray,

Today your letter of the 29th of July arrived and I was very happy to receive it. I'm very sorry to know that you can't phone me because of the new rule. When you didn't phone me again last week I felt sure you were away, but I know if it had been possible you would have phoned me. If I thought you were going to be in England much longer I would send some letters there. All I have written I have sent to your home address, you should have plenty to read when you get there, one is a 15 page letter.

Gosh, Ray, I wish I knew when you were going to America and how long it will be before your training is finished and you come back. I know you love me and are coming back, but somehow I can't help but thinking that maybe getting home again and being in the Air Corps will dull your memories of me and help you forget. No matter where I am here I'm always thinking about you and wondering how you are getting along, in fact I'd give anything just to see you again before you go to America. At night when I'm coming from a show I think of how wonderful it would be if you were in the house waiting for me. Such a crazy thought, but I can't help it.

Tonight Hazel and I are going to the Curzon to see "Song of the Islands" with Betty Grable and Victor Mature, have you seen it? Tomorrow night we are going to the Ritz to see "Yankee Doodle Dandy." We've heard it's a good show.

I had a letter from Pat Adair today. She likes her new job and says it would be quite easy for me to get a job there too. I'm very undecided because I don't think you would like me working at Lockheed Overseas.

Well, Ray, I guess I'd better end and finish this letter tomorrow. It's getting late and Mommy has supper ready. Cheerio until tomorrow.

My Dearest Ray,

Today I received your letter dated Saturday the 31st of July. I was very glad to receive it, Ray, but very unhappy when I read the news it contained. Honestly, Ray darling, your inquiry about Scamp has made me feel awful. It's what I expected, but somehow I always kept hoping it wouldn't happen.

Hazel met me outside the office tonight and we went to the Ritz to see "Yankee Doodle Dandy." It was a little disappointing. After the show we came home to our house and I made us something to eat.

It's now Thursday night and here I am again writing, this time I intend to finish this letter and get it posted. I'm not seeing Hazel tonight as besides wanting to finish this letter I have to wash my hair, wash some clothes and practice a little. I haven't started music yet as Mae Brown is on holiday. Pretty soon she will be back and I'll have to start in earnest.

Lately the weather has been very good here, but yesterday and today it rained most of the time. Next week the clock is being put back an hour and that means it will get dark very early. Winter is coming in fast but I don't mind too much. The sooner it comes and goes, the sooner it will be spring and you'll be back again. Just think, in a little over four months I'll be 21 years and I'll have known you almost 2 years. To me it seems like 20 years since the night I walked home from Albert Whites with you. If anyone had told me then that all this was going to happen I wouldn't have believed them.

Ray, do you think you could succeed in becoming an instructor, it's much safer. I know you always wanted to be a pilot but please be on the ground staff, it will make me feel much better and your mother will feel much better, too.

Tomorrow night Hazel and I are going to visit her auntie and on Saturday afternoon two of the girls in the office (Elsie and Yvonne) and I are going to Rockport to have a bathe and take some snaps. If the weather doesn't get better than it is now we won't be able to go, but I'm hoping it's good because I want to have some snaps taken to send to you. By the way, Daddy managed to get another film for the camera.

As I want to get to bed early and I've such a lot to do before I go I must end now. —*Yours forever, Muriel*

Saturday, August 7th

My Dearest Ray,

It's about 2:30 and instead of being at Rockport I'm sitting here writing to you. You know what the weather is like here sometimes, well, just as I expected it rained today and spoilt our plans.

Last night Hazel and I went to visit some friends of hers in Balmoral. We had quite a nice evening and Mrs. Johnson went into the garden and gathered me a beautiful bunch of flowers. Most of them were carnations and I was delighted because carnations are my favorite flower.

Since I have come home from the office Mommy has been coaxing me to go into town and buy myself a new raincoat. I have developed an awful cold and she says it's because I run around in all kinds of weather just as I would if the sun was shining all the time. Elsie has a cold too and both of us sit in the office sneezing and coughing most of the time.

The first part of this letter was written yesterday, it's about 7 o'clock on Sunday now and I want to finish it tonight. When I began writing yesterday Mommy called me downstairs and sent me out to do some shopping. It was about 5:30 when I got home from town, after tea the family went out and as I was feeling pretty lonely I went into Aunt Vi's house to talk to her for awhile. About 8:30 she had to go out and as I had nothing else to do I thought if I went down to the Red Cross Dot would be there because last week Miss Anderson announced that a very good American band would be playing. Anyway, I got in the dance at about 9:10, Dot was there with Al and much to my surprise she was having a row with him. I never did like Al but I like him much less now. He takes Dot to the dances and then leaves her most of the night while he goes out drinking. I know it is none of my business but if I was Dot I wouldn't be there when he came back. Al is a hateful kind of person, since Dot told him you were going in the Air Corps he has kept telling me that you won't come back because you'll be killed.

I shouldn't tell you this, Ray, but that's what he's like and Dot gave off to him last night and told me not to heed him because he always got like that after he was drinking. After talking for awhile they got up to dance and in the meantime an Air Corps boy came over to me and sat beside me. I let him know that I didn't want to talk to him but he started talking about the war and the Air Corps, and as that interested me we got into conversation. After talking about 10 minutes he asked me to go out with him today and straight away I said no and when he got persistent I excused myself and left him.

After I left him another boy asked me to dance and while I was dancing with him I noticed someone smiling and waving at me from the other side of the floor. Although I recognized his face I couldn't think who he was, then it suddenly dawned on me he was Joe Goglia, the boy you introduced me to when you were here in March. After the dance I left my partner and went over to talk to him. He introduced me to another boy from the 5th General (I forgot his name) and then drew me to the side to tell me that Fay, his wife, had a baby boy and both mother and son were fine. The baby was born sometime this week, I forgot the exact date, and they are going to call him Peter Anthony. Joe has given me Fay's address and says he would like it if I would call sometime when she gets out of hospital. If I can manage to get some coupons I'll buy the baby something and pay Fay a visit. Joe wants me to send him your new address as soon as I receive it. After talking about Fay and the baby Joe asked me how I liked the idea of you being in the Air Corps. He told me that although the 5th General was breaking up none of them were being sent to any of the war zones. Some of them are being sent to other parts of England and a crowd of them are coming back here again. He is being sent back here and he said if you had remained in the hospital and tried hard enough, you too could have got transferred back here.

Ray, I needn't tell you how I felt when Joe said that, I was feeling miserable before but I almost cried after hearing that. Joe knows you weren't happy in the hospital but he thinks you were crazy to go in the Air Corps. Being a pilot may seem to you very exciting and interesting, but it is also very, very dangerous. I keep kidding myself that the war will be over when your training is completed but all the time I know it couldn't possibly be. When talking to Joe the time went very quickly and before I realized it was 10:55. Thinking I might not have missed the last tram I said goodbye and rushed out but I was too late and had to walk home.

On the way home a Marine passed me, and then he turned and came after me. He walked up beside me and started talking to me and the faster I walked, the faster he walked. Although this was happening, I was so busy thinking of you I didn't even realize someone was annoying me. The Marine kept trying to get me to talk but I never spoke one word. All the way up Bedford St. he kept hurrying along side of me but I was so worried about you and felt so much like crying, I completely ignored him. I'm sure the Marine thought I was crazy and wondered what was wrong, but I didn't care. When I got home I went straight to bed and cried myself to sleep. Ray, I know I shouldn't tell you things like that, but please don't worry, if I wasn't that way it would mean I didn't love you. There's a war on and there are thousands of other girls separated from the ones they love. I know if you come through safely you'll be back. All week long I have been wondering how you are getting along. You should be home by now and no doubt you'll be very happy to see all your friends again. —*Forever yours, Muriel*

Monday, August 9th

My Dearest Muriel,

Still at sea but as each day goes by we are getting closer to home. I haven't written since last Tuesday and I hope you don't mind, there's really nothing to say, these boat trips are all the same. The weather until Sunday has been awful, cold, wind, rain and boy did everyone get seasick. For three days I was in bed, the only time I got out of bed was at meal time. Not that I was seasick, but I had a funny feeling in my stomach and I knew if I stayed up, well, you know, it would be coming up also. The only safe thing was to stay in bed, which I did. This whole trip has been just sleeping, or trying to while the boat rocks around.

Muriel, my love, I keep thinking about what everyone is saying to you. I know they are saying that I won't be back and for you to start going out with other boys. I know it's going to be hard for you, Muriel, and now as I keep thinking about it maybe I was wrong to leave you. I promise you, Muriel, I will make up for it when I come back, and I am coming back, don't ever forget it. Don't let anyone change your mind because it will break my heart. If they start kidding you at the office tell them to mind their own business. It may be a year, maybe more, maybe less, until we see each other, but the next time I do see you, if it's only for a day, we are going to get married. So be prepared to get married on a moment's notice.

Muriel, this may sound funny to you but you can't ask questions. I want to know the size shoes, stockings and dress you wear. Please, if you love me you will tell me and if at any time, now don't forget this, if there is anything you need please let me know and if possible I will send it to you. Now don't forget or I will get mad.

They say we should be in NY on Wednesday, I hope so, I'm sick of the water. I'll leave the letter like this and add more to it before we get off the boat. The lights are going off now so goodnight and sleep tight. I love you. (Stop.)

Wednesday, August 11th

My Dearest Muriel,

I'm writing this letter in New York Harbor, it's about 8:30 now. We arrived at about 2:30 this afternoon and then tied up to the pier, and here we are, five feet from land and we can't get off. Today it's been beautiful, good American weather, warm and clear with lots of sun. All morning long we were on watch for land, saw it at about 12 o'clock and boy was it good. I'm very happy to be home but in another way very sad because I'm away from you.

Tomorrow morning we have to be up at two o'clock to start getting off the boat. When we are off we are getting the first train home. I'll send you a telegram before we take the train and when I'm home I'll write as often as I can and send you telegrams. We will spend ten days at home and from there we go to Greensboro, NC about 90 miles from where I was at camp before I came overseas. We may be there a day or maybe a month. I'll telegram you and let you know and also send you my address. There will be days when I won't be able to write but will explain in my next letters why and what I did. I promise to write as often as possible.

All the lights are on in the harbor and we can see the cars moving around and the houses all lit up, it's quite different alright. —*Forever yours, Raymond*

PS Let me know if these letters are censored.

Monday, August 9th

My Dearest Ray,

Tonight at six o'clock Hazel called and we went to the Curzon to see a picture named "Quiet Please, Murder." After the show we went into the Curzon Café and had supper. The family all went to the plot tonight and they only arrived home 15 minutes ago.

Maybe I'm crazy, Ray, but if only I could get one look at you I'd be more contented. I know how dangerous it is crossing the ocean at the present time. All through the day I keep trying to smile and to be cheerful, but there's always that awful feeling I can't describe.

Today I was thinking of how soon I'll be 21 years and how wonderful it would be if you could be here on my birthday. I'd love to have a party then, but not unless you were with me.

Believe it or not it's *Wednesday* and about time I was finishing this letter. On Monday night I had to stop writing as Audrey and Olive came upstairs and wouldn't give me peace to write anymore. Last night at 7:15 Hazel came around all upset about Louis and coaxed me to go with her to the pictures. She said she just had to get out someplace and try to forget what was on her mind. You remember the time when Louis asked Hazel's mother if she would consent to Hazel and he getting married, well, beforehand Hazel told Louis if her mother asked him what religion he was, he was to say Protestant as she didn't want to have all the trouble in her family that I had with mine. Anyway, when Mrs. T asked Louis what religion he was he did as Hazel told him to do and told her he was Protestant. To make a long story short, Louis phoned Hazel on Tuesday morning to say that he was sending the papers over to be signed and his religion would be stated on them. Now Hazel doesn't know what to do. They want to get married at Christmas and she says when her mother finds out that Louis is Catholic and also that he told her a lie, they'll probably be an awful row. She said she wouldn't mind so much only she won't be 21 until February 1945 and that's a long time to wait.

Ray, this all reminds me of the trouble we had, I have to laugh when I think of it now. Hazel asked me what she should do about it and I told her either tell her mother the truth now, or she could wait until Louis's next leave and they could face the music together. As it is Hazel doesn't seem to have the courage to confess so I guess she'll just wait until Louis is here.

What a predicament, I think it's even worse than the one we were in. I know what Hazel's mother is like and when she says no about anything she really means it. When Hazel wanted to take the job as Inspector of Aircraft her mother said *NO!* And I'll never forget the lecture that followed, it all ended up with her saying to Hazel, "Not another word," and marching out of the room. Boy, oh, boy, what a world, trouble around every corner. Anyway, as I told Hazel, I hope everything turns out all right because I do so want to be bridesmaid at Christmas.

Tonight after tea I went next door to talk to Aunt Vi, she isn't well and has to go into hospital soon for an operation. About 8 o'clock I left her and went out to phone Marie. I dialed the number several times but couldn't get through.

These last few days Daddy has been very ill. He is off work and last night he couldn't sleep because of the pains in his stomach. The doctor is sending him to the Royal Victoria Hospital on Friday to have an X-ray and most likely he'll have to have an operation. The pain must be awful Ray, because he's lying in bed and can hardly speak, and when he eats anything he's sick afterwards. All I hope is that there's nothing seriously wrong.

Please give my regards to all at home and take good care of yourself and try to keep away from danger, and I mean *all* kinds. —*Forever yours, Muriel*

PS They still tease me at the office but I'm learning to ignore them.

Friday, August 13th

My Dearest Ray,

As yet I haven't received a cable from you and you'll have no idea how anxious I am to know how you are and where you are. These past two weeks I've missed your letters and phone calls an awful lot. Yesterday I had to get a book out of the room where Miss Collins, the telephone operator works. As I expected, the first thing she said when I entered the room was, "How's your boyfriend and what has happened that he hasn't phoned you lately?" Honestly, Ray, I felt like telling her to mind her own business. She knew darn well that you were away and was just wanting to know how I was taking it. Anyhow, I told her you were away back to America to train for a commission and it would probably be six months before you could come back. She pretended to be all surprised and asked me if I was worried. I tried to laugh and then said, "Not at all, the only thing that worries me is his safety, as regards to anything else, I have nothing to worry about." The next thing she said was, "Why didn't you get married when he was on leave?" I told her we preferred to wait and was about to leave the room when Miss Witherow who works in the General Office came in. The first thing Miss Collins did was to tell her that you were away. Now everyone in the General Office knows and every time I go in there they say something to me about you. Someday I'm going to lose my temper and ask them why they're so anxious about us.

Lately, Peggy, one of the girls in the office has kept saying, "Ray has gone back to America and Muriel will never see him again." I ignored the remark but today she said it again and believe me, Ray, I wouldn't care to repeat the things I said to her in my temper. I told her I knew it would please her and a great many others in Inglis if you didn't return, but someday she and the others would be greatly disappointed. She has a boyfriend in the British Army and from what I hear they are getting married so I said, "Just hope your own boyfriend returns, there's always a chance they could both be killed." She stopped talking then and neither of us has spoken to each other since. On my way home tonight I told Yvonne about her and she said Peggy has often said that you'll meet someone else in America and desert me. The other day Victor tried putting his arms around me, I smacked his face and hit him several times and told him to go away and annoy some of the other girls. "Oh," he said. "If you mean Edna, she's engaged and I never touch engaged girls. You are engaged now but that will be all off sooner or later."Afterwards he said, "I'm sorry, Muriel, I didn't mean it." What a hateful crowd, the sooner I get away from them the better I'll feel.

I guess I shouldn't tell you all this, Ray, but you want to know what they are saying at the office and we both expected this. Please don't let it worry you, you know what people are like and their type is not worth worrying about.

I've told you all there is to tell about the office so now I'll tell you about Daddy. He isn't any better. Yesterday he went to the hospital and was examined by another doctor. Last night his own doctor examined him and this morning he had an X-ray. We won't know the results of the X-ray until next Monday. He's still got the awful pains and can't eat anything. There is a lump in his stomach and the doctors aren't sure whether it's gallstones or an ulcer.

As this is the last page of my writing tablet I'll have to stop writing. *—Forever yours, Muriel*

Saturday, August 14th

My Dearest Muriel,

Things are happening so fast I don't know where to start. When we got to New York we stayed on the boat overnight. The next morning we were taken to Fort Hamilton where we received our papers. I spent that night at my aunt's house and the next morning got the nine o'clock train from New York and arrived in Buffalo at eight o'clock. Boy, was there a mob there, it took me half an hour to say hello to everybody. When we got home the house was full of people, honestly, honey, it was really swell. I had to kiss quite a few girls, I hope you don't mind, most of them are married and I've known them most of my life. The first thing they wanted to know was where you were— they thought I was going to bring you over. It's really wonderful to be home but I still think of you every minute. I keep thinking of how wonderful it would be if you were here with me, but don't worry, someday it will be that way.

Mother told me she had received your letter and that I had one also. To make things even better I received a letter from you this morning. Mother says she knows she is going to like you very much. I told her all about you last night after everyone had left. So you see everything is OK here. I got h--- in a nice way for a lot of things,

Ray with his Mother.

mostly for leaving you and also for going into the Air Corps. This morning I got up at about 10:00 and went into town and sent you another telegram and mailed a few letters.

Tonight I am invited out for dinner. An old friend, Bill Zimmerman, is home on furlough but leaving tonight for camp. I get home and he is leaving, that's the way it goes.

Dad and Ray.

About the mail, Muriel, I want your letters as soon as possible but if you are going to write so often you can't spend all that money for stamps, it's too expensive. Send letters by regular mail, I don't think it will take that much longer.

I left this letter Saturday, it's now Monday. I'm at home with Mother and Father. Sunday I almost went crazy with company, people from all over.

When we get married, Muriel, I feel sorry for you because there's going to be so many people asking you a million questions. They all

Sister Jo.

asked me why I didn't bring you over, if they only knew how much I wanted to.

This morning I helped Dad build the horse stall (Dot has a riding horse now) and the rest of the afternoon people were riding the horse around the yard and asking me foolish questions.

My mother wants to know what size shoes, socks and dress you wear so don't forget to send me your sizes in your next letter, and don't ask questions. —*Forever yours, Raymond*

Saturday, August 14th

My Dearest Ray,

Another day is here and still no word from you. You have no idea how much I miss your letters and how much I am looking forward to the ones I hope to receive in the near future.

Today Daddy isn't any better, in fact he's much worse. He's just lying there and hasn't even the strength to talk. The doctor gave him sleeping tablets but even when he took them he couldn't sleep. Mommy is badly upset about him and today I discovered her crying. I wish we knew what was wrong with him.

This morning my Uncle Harold arrived from England and from what I hear he, Aunt Vi and the two children are going to live here for the duration. After the war they are all going back to England, or else going over to Canada or America to live.

As yet Hazel and Louis haven't settled the predicament they are in, but I'll let you know how everything goes with them later.

When you are writing please tell me all about yourself and how you are progressing, don't ever hide anything from me. If the news isn't good tell me just the same—I never hide anything from you. One thing I am very grateful for is that Mommy and Daddy have stopped lecturing me about you. I can mention your name anytime I like and it doesn't cause any trouble. They have both become used to the idea that we are getting married. Ray, please don't use the word someday anymore, it sounds so far away, just say—when I get back. —*Forever yours, Muriel*

PS Ray, if it is possible will you please send me an Air Corps badge?

Sunday, August 15th

My Dearest Ray,

Today after what seemed like an eternity your cable arrived and honestly, Ray, words can't describe how glad I am to know that you arrived safely in America. I'm very glad to know that already you have received three of my letters. I'm hoping it won't be long until I get one from you. You have no idea how eager I am to know what they are saying back home about us. In your cable you say "Arrived home everything wonderful." No doubt it is wonderful to you being back home but please, Ray, always remember Ireland and the times we spent together, to me they were the happiest days of my life.

At three o'clock today Hazel called and although it was quite a nice day we didn't go for a walk. She had tea in our house and afterwards we sat and talked about you and Louis. Louis has written and told Hazel that she needn't worry about the hospital being sent further away than England, in fact he says he is keeping his fingers crossed and hoping he will be one of the boys to be sent back here. Ray, I really hope you didn't know about this when you went into the Air Corps. You told me that the hospital was breaking up and most likely you would be sent further away, then Joe and Louis say differently. I believe you before anyone else and maybe things have changed since you were there.

Ray, if you only knew how much I worry about you, I try not to but when I face the facts I can't help worrying. I know quite a lot about the Air Corps now, and if I was rightly informed you will have four month training in America and then three months advanced training in Ireland or England—is that right? Anyhow, I'm hoping in four months time you will be sent back here.

Ray, if I had told you I would break up with you if you joined the Air Corps would you have joined, please answer that. I don't want to discourage you, Ray, but you know I don't care how good or bad the job you had back home was. Your life means more to me than the best paid job on earth.

It's almost suppertime now so I'll stop writing. Hazel and I are going to the Curzon tomorrow night and if we get back early I'll finish this letter. Goodnight, Ray.

My Dearest Ray,

It's Tuesday night now and I'm very sorry I couldn't get this letter finished last night. I got home from the Curzon about 9:15 intending to finish it but Uncle Harold and Aunt Vi were in and they insisted on me playing the piano. After that I had to help Mommy make supper and wash dishes.

Yesterday really was a happy day for me and it was you who made it so. At about 2 p.m. when I was just about to leave for the office, I got the loveliest surprise of my life. Another cable arrived and honestly, Ray, I felt better than if I had been handed a thousand pounds. Aunt Vi told me that Daddy told her about the cables and he also said that we were so dead nuts about each other he never again would try to prevent me from marrying you. Isn't that wonderful, Ray, all that trouble is over and we won't have anything to worry about when you come back.

Yesterday and today Daddy has been a little better and his pains have not been so severe. The X-ray he had didn't prove anything was wrong and when his own doctor heard about it he said, "Damned nonsense, there is something wrong." Pardon the expression, but that's what the doctor said and he is sending him to a Professor.

The news that you have gone to America is spreading through Inglis like fire and some girls I hardly know are saying to me, "I hear your boyfriend is away." It amazes me why so many people are taking an interest in us, but I don't care. I know you are coming back as soon as you can and it doesn't matter what the rest are thinking. —*Forever yours, Muriel*

Monday, August 16th

My Dearest Muriel,

I took a break since the last letter I wrote but before I start to answer your letters I can only say if there were words that could describe how wonderful you are, and how much I love you I would write and tell you, but there isn't. The feelings I have for you words can't describe. I keep thinking of how happy we will be when we are married.

Muriel, my love, I will write to you as much as possible, honest, the past few days I haven't had time for anything, I've had so much to do. I promise when I'm settled I'll write every day.

I'm glad you and Hazel went to Bellevue Park, I'll never forget the wonderful times we had there. I see the Yanks are still there as always, I hope they didn't bother you too much.

As to what the girls are doing in Inglis, I knew they would try that, they're just jealous. Tell them to mind their own business and that someday I'll be back to tell them what I think of them.

The letter you wrote to Mother was very sweet. She thinks an awful lot of you, Muriel, and will write soon. She said I never should have left you and hopes you will wait for me. I told her I didn't have to worry about that.

I see you found an easy way to make money betting with Elsie. Don't ever let it happen with you, I would go crazy, but I must say it was quite an amusing trick.

I'm sorry to hear that your daddy is sick and hope and pray he doesn't have to have an operation. Give your mother and father my regards, also the two brats (but I love them).

I had to stop writing and was going to continue last night but Rose invited us over for supper and we didn't get home until after 12:00. Today I drove Mother all over town, this afternoon I went to the plant where I used to work and spent the rest of the afternoon there. After supper I went with Dot to where she rides her horse and stayed there until now. I haven't gone anyplace, my family and relatives won't let me go. They still want to know why I didn't bring you (kidding me because they know I would have if I could).

Muriel, I think you should continue to send your letters here and my mother can send them to me. I won't have an address for a few weeks but just as soon as I think it will be for awhile in one place I'll telegram you my address.

Tomorrow I'm going with Mother to Buffalo to get a few things and darn it, see more people.

I haven't written to Luke yet, I tried to send him a telegram but didn't know his serial number.

Now it can be told.

Winston Churchill, Prime Minister of Great Britain, passed through Lockport last week, obviously en route to Hyde Park for his meeting with President Roosevelt.

Several Lockport residents reported seeing the Prime Minister's CPR train and some even said they saw Mr. Churchill on the observation platform on the rear car. In conformity with the Censorship Code, the Union-Sun and Journal omitted any mention of his passage through the city. Any intimation that the Premier had traveled eastward via Lockport following the story (cleared by the censors) that he had left Niagara Falls might have served to reveal his route.

Well, my love, I think I better stop now and get to bed as tomorrow will be a hard day. Give my regard to all your family and say hello to Hazel. —*I love you, Raymond*

PS This is a little clipping from the paper. I thought maybe you would get a big kick out of it. I love you.

Thursday, August 19th

My Dearest Ray,

Here I am again sitting upstairs writing to you and wishing I was talking to you instead.

Last night Hazel and I went to the Majestic but I can't remember the names of the two pictures we saw, they weren't much good anyhow. Hazel's mother still doesn't know that Louis is Catholic and on Tuesday night she wrote a letter to Louis giving him consent to marry Hazel at Christmas. Hazel isn't so worried now about the mix-up, she is beginning to think her mother won't mind too much and for her sake I hope she doesn't.

When I got home from the Majestic I suddenly thought of phoning Marie. Mrs. Roberts answered the phone and said that Marie was out, but if I phoned at six o'clock tonight I'd probably get speaking to her. After tea Daddy asked me to go to the library for some books and with doing that I didn't have time to phone until 6:30. Her mother answered the phone again and told me that Marie was out all day with Luke, but they had left word that I was to meet them for lunch at the Carlton on Monday. Hearing that Luke was here was a surprise to me. Mrs. Roberts said he arrived yesterday.

At the office this week there has been a lot of fun and I did my best to join in. The boss is on holiday and except for an occasional visit from Mr. Block, boss of the General Office and one of the most unpopular men in Inglis, we don't have anyone to look after us. Everyone hates Mr. Block because he's very sarcastic and if nothing goes wrong he invents something. Today I was sitting working at my desk and singing "You'd Be So Nice to Come Home To." There was other noise going on at the same time. Suddenly it all stopped but I didn't. I just went on working and singing at the top of my voice. Elsie, who was sitting beside me coughed and I turned around to find Mr. Block standing behind me. Boy, I nearly had a fit, it was so unexpected and I nearly had another fit when he turned and walked out of the room without giving me a lecture. Anytime he has lectured me I've always got mad and cheeked him back, so I guess he didn't want to have the others in the office laughing by lecturing me again. When he did go out of the office the noise all started again and they kidded me for long enough.

By the way, Ray, Mommy bought me a beautiful new coat and I'm delighted with it, it's the nicest coat I've ever had. The colour is light beige, almost cream and the material is curly fur. It's very warm and will certainly keep me warm in the winter time. I can't describe it properly, but maybe I'll get a picture taken and send it to you. Last week a friend of ours who lives in Dublin called and she brought me a lovely new handbag. It's a nice shape and inside there is a tab which says made in the U.S.A.

Gosh, Ray, I tell you everything and now I'm wondering what I can tell you about next. Oh, yes! Daddy is feeling a great deal better. He hasn't seen the Professor yet as he is still on holiday, but when he comes back Daddy is going to be examined by him.

As I've told you all there is to tell at the moment I'll end and practice a little before going to bed. —*I love you, Muriel*

PS Everyday I'm waiting for your letters.

Friday, August 20th

My Dearest Muriel,

It's about 2:30 now, Mother is here sewing, sitting next to me. Yesterday as you know we went to Buffalo and spent the day there, we went to dinner and a show and then to see more people! Boy, was I tired. Today I haven't been doing much—I can't get out of my mother's sight. After this letter I have to cut the grass, how do you like that?

I found some pictures to send you. I am going to take more and send them to you. You should see our horse, he's a beauty.

Mother says that just as soon as I leave she will write you and if there is anything you want to let her know. She already has powder, etc. for you and yesterday she made me go to the dress shop with her and wanted me to pick out some dresses for you, boy did I feel funny. She also wanted to know if she sends you the material can you have the dresses made. I told her yes, am I right, I hope so, and don't say no about the things I am going to send you, if you love me you'll take them.

I have been eating so much lately, honest, Muriel, every time I have something I think of you not having it and I get kind of sick. Maybe you think I'm crazy, but it's true.

I'm leaving for camp I think, on Tuesday. I'm going to spend a few days with my aunt in New York City. I have to be at camp in Greensboro, North Carolina on Friday, August 27th and from there I don't know so keep writing home and Mother can send me the letters. When I do get settled I'll telegram you my address.

I still can't realize I'm home, Muriel, it seems so funny. Only a month ago I was in England and now I'm home, what a change. It's really wonderful home, Muriel, I know you'll like it.

Well, my love, I guess I better get busy and cut the grass because there's a lot of it to cut.   —*Forever yours, Raymond*

Friday, August 20th

My Dearest Ray,

It's 10:15 and I want to write this short letter before Audrey and Olive come up to bed. As soon as I write it I'm going to bed too. Tonight I met Hazel in town and we went to the Classic to see "When Johnny Comes Marching Home" and "China Girl," both pictures were very good but as usual I was missing you and the pictures were just the type to make me feel even more blue.

As yet I haven't received any letters and you'll have no idea how eager I am to know how you have got along since reaching America. I hear Audrey and Olive coming upstairs so I must end. Please be careful and look after yourself. —*Forever yours, Muriel*

Saturday, August 21st

My Dearest Ray,

Tonight Hazel isn't coming round and I'm wondering if I should go to the Red Cross. Adeline is going out with a technician now and I'm the only person in the office who knows. She doesn't want the others to know and start talking about her the way they are me. She has applied to join the Red Cross and wants me to go with her on the nights she isn't seeing her boyfriend.

Next week I think I am starting music again and when that happens I'll hardly ever have time to go out. It's not quite four months until my examination and I'll have to practice very hard. I've never failed in any examination so far and I'd hate to fail in the last one, so pray for me, will you?

Last night I had the funniest dream. I dreamt a letter came and thinking it was for me I opened it, and then I looked at the name and found it wasn't for me at all. Another night I had a queer dream and don't laugh when I tell you about it because it isn't funny. I dreamt that you came back and with you were a girl and a little boy about two years old. You told me the girl was your sister. We all sat and talked for awhile and the little boy sat on my knee and wanted to play. Then you called me into the sitting room and told me the little boy was your son, I got very mad and told you I never wanted to see you again. I can even remember what the boy looked like—he was the image of you except that his eyes were blue. What a crazy dream, sometimes they are even crazier and I hope they never come true.

As there isn't anything else to tell you now, I'll stop writing and finish this letter later.

My Dearest Ray,

It's about 11 o'clock and I've just got home after being at the Red Cross. When I got to the Red Cross I met Dot and Lily in the cloak room and we went upstairs together. We were just going down the room to find some seats when what do you think happened, Luke and Marie came rushing over to me. Ray, I was so surprised I almost had a fit and Luke almost shook my hand off. They took me over to the side of the room to have a chat. Luke said he hadn't heard from you since you left the 5th General and was wondering how you were getting along, he says he misses you a lot. Luke was in a very good mood. He asked me to dance and told me not to tell you, as if you would mind—

he's crazy. All the time we were dancing he talked about you and every now and then he'd say "Isn't Marie wonderful?" In a way I'm sorry I went to the Red Cross. You are on my mind all the time and all I do is worry about you and wonder how long it will be before you come back. Another thing, if we aren't married before the end of the war it may be years before we can get married, for reasons which I'm sure you know.

After I left Luke and Marie, Lily and I got talking, her brother is very ill now and she's afraid he won't live much longer. As Lily and I were feeling pretty miserable we left the dance about nine o'clock. We had supper in the Lido and afterwards we walked to Botanic Gardens and then came home. From Lily's talk I gathered that she hasn't got over the news of Herbie's death. She isn't going out with anyone else now and she says she has no desire to do so. I felt very sorry for her. Before I left Lily she asked me to go to the Red Cross on Sunday with her, but I said no, not because of the row we had so long ago, but because it only makes me feel worse about you.

My Dearest Ray,

It's Sunday now and as I didn't get yesterday's letter posted because the Post Office is closed, today I thought I might as well just continue from where I left off. Last night I didn't sleep too well with the result that I didn't rise until 12:00 today. After dinner Hazel came round and started reading a book and I sat and played the piano. About 3 o'clock Marie Neill, Lily's cousin, called. I was very surprised because she hardly ever calls for me. She asked me to go down to the Red Cross with her and Hazel said, "Go ahead, Muriel, I want to read this book and it isn't a good day to go for a walk." I said, "No, I wasn't going," but Marie coaxed me and said if I didn't like the dance she would leave early and come home with me. Anyhow, for the first Sunday since Christmas I went to the dance. Luke and Marie were there and I was talking to them for awhile. They looked very happy and seeing Luke again more than ever reminded me of the days when you were stationed here. He gave me the flash bulb for the camera and also a bottle of petro for my cigarette lighter. After leaving Luke and Marie I found Marie Neill and told her I was going home, she left with me. After tea Hazel and I went to church and then walked through Botanic Gardens and now I'm home writing to you. Thanks very much for the flash bulb and fluid. I gave the bulb to Daddy and he is very pleased with it. Luke said something about not being able to get the films for me as the packages were returned to your home address. He says he will explain it to you when he writes.

As it is getting late I must end... Please be good and always love me. —*Forever yours, Muriel*

Monday, August 23rd

My Dearest Muriel,

It's about two o'clock and a warm and beautiful afternoon in Lockport. I haven't written since Friday and I'm sorry but honest, I just haven't had the time. Today I was very happy as I received your letter of August 7th. It's been quite awhile since I received a letter from you. I don't expect a letter from you every day, but when you don't write, let me know.

Friday night I was out with my mother visiting different people, they all ask the same silly questions over and over again. Saturday morning I was driving my mother and dad all around and Saturday afternoon had to take my sister Dot, and her two girlfriends to their horses. Dot and her two girlfriends had supper here and after that I took them to town (Park Hotel) and we had a drink, just one, and then came back here and they stayed another hour with Dot, then I took them home. Sunday was the horse show (about 300 horses) and Dot won a prize for one of the races. We stayed all afternoon and I came back with them at about six o'clock. In the meantime, Sunday morning, a fellow I hadn't seen in about 2 ½ years called me up. Bob Secrist and I had paled around for about ten years, honest, I was so glad to see him, he was with us all day. After supper I had the car and we went into town to a pub, now don't get mad, it's only once in awhile. All the boys started buying drinks and I got to feeling pretty good. I stayed at Bob's house for the night and this morning I don't feel so good. Mother gave me h---, but I didn't mind too much because it's the most fun I've had since I've been home.

Tonight I'll have to get packed because I'm leaving for New York to spend a day with my aunt and from there have to be in Greensboro, NC by Friday. If I don't write for a few days you'll know why.

Now to answer your letter. So you like carnations—I'll have to remember that. I have the radio (wireless) on and Harry James is playing. I wish you were here next to me listening to him. Muriel, please take care of yourself, it worries me when you get colds all the time.

Al may just be trying to get you mad. Just because I'm joining the Air Corps doesn't mean I'm going to get killed. Don't pay any attention to him, as for Dot, tell her to wake up.

I'm glad you met Joe again and glad to hear about the baby, give them my regards.

Ray, Jane Friscia and Bob Secrist, Lockport, New York.

I'm sorry you had trouble going home, Muriel, did that Marine hurt you in any way?

As I told you before, maybe I did make a mistake but now we can't cry over it. If I knew then what I know now maybe I wouldn't have transferred, but I'm happy in the Air Corps, Muriel, it makes me feel like a new man. It's always been what I wanted and if I didn't join I never would have been satisfied with life. I know it sounds crazy but it's true. I love you more than anyone else in this world so please have faith in me. I'll be back I promise you that, so please don't worry. Don't ever worry about me not being true, I haven't been out on any dates. I've talked to a lot of girls I've known all my life and some have even come over to see me but that is all there is to it. They all know about you and have been kidding me. A lot of them have been saying, "I'm Irish, what's wrong with me?" We've had a lot of fun with that. They want to know what your secret is, what made me fall for you. So you see there is nothing to worry about. Well, Muriel, I have to start packing now so will close. —*I love you, Raymond*

Tuesday, August 24th

My Dearest Ray,

Tonight I'm staying home because I want to write to you, also do some practice and theory.

Yesterday I met Luke and Marie at the Carlton for lunch. We talked over old times, especially the day we went to Bangor and I scratched my knee, remember? Luke has a picture of you bandaging it and he's promised to let me have it sometime. Luke was very jolly and he and Marie were kidding me about the time when we'd all be married and they would be visiting us back home. Luke is coming over again in November.

Last night Yvonne called and we went to the Majestic. After the show we walked home and Yvonne gave me a lecture for worrying so much. Tomorrow night I'm meeting Hazel and we're going to the Ritz to see "Casablanca."

Yesterday and today I felt sure there would be a letter from you and was very disappointed when there wasn't. Please let me know how you like the Air Corps and Ray, will you try and give me a better idea of how long it will be before your training over there is finished and when you can come back. I'm hoping it isn't long until then, and when you do come back the war ends shortly afterwards and you never have to fly over enemy territory. The idea of dropping bombs on innocent people is all wrong to me. I know the Germans deserve it but I'm sure there are decent people among them who don't.

My Dearest Ray,

It's 9:30 p.m. and I've just arrived home after having been at the Ritz with Hazel to see "Casablanca." What a picture, Ray, it was wonderful but very sad and I didn't like the way it ended. Ingrid Bergman is really a wonderful actress. It's the best picture I've ever seen. The song "As Time Goes By" is so lovely and I want to buy it and play it for you when you come back.   —*Forever yours, Muriel*

Saturday, August 28th

My Dearest Ray,

Today is one of those rainy dismal days I detest and here I am writing again only this time I haven't very much to say. On Thursday night I didn't go out and to pass the time I got busy and did some housework for Mommy. Last night I met Hazel when coming from the office and we went to the Regal to see a picture named "Pittsburgh." It was an awful picture and I was glad to see it end. When I got home there was a gentleman in seeing Daddy. People are calling all the time to see how he is and some of them have never met him before. Daddy looks and feels a lot better now, the doctor is still attending him but as yet he hasn't seen the Professor as he is still on holiday.

The crowd in the office still kid me and ask about you. Every time George sees me he asks how you are, only instead of saying, "How's Ray?" he says, "How's Hack?" Today I went to the office to get my pay but George wouldn't give it to me. I told him I was busy and had to hurry but he wouldn't listen. Finally I got mad and went right to the Works Office to tell Miss Ferguson. That made matters worse because as soon as I did that Graham and George caught hold of me and began to tickle me. I gave Graham a push which sent him staggering backwards, and then I lifted a book and hit George with it. After that I darted out of the room and told them in future they could bring my pay to me as I wasn't going down for it anymore. About 15 minutes later George brought it to me—he knew I wouldn't go to the office a second time.

When I received my pay I got a very unexpected surprise. Inglis has given me another increase, can you believe it—and about time. It doesn't make any difference, I still intend to get another job even if they were to pay me twice as much again.

As yet I haven't received any letters from you and words can't describe how much I'm longing to know how you are and what's been happening since you went away.

Everything is fine at home, Mommy and Daddy don't seem to mind us getting married now, in fact Daddy often talks to me about you and tells me to be cheerful, nothing will happen to you. What a change from the way things used to be. It would be wonderful if you were back, then we could get married on Christmas Day the way we planned one time, remember?

Please don't worry about me, Ray, just study and make good in the Air Corps. Let people back here say and think what they like. Just as you said, someday we will look back together and laugh at them and then when we grow old we can tell our grandchildren of how we met and all the obstacles we crossed before we were able to get married. — *Forever yours, Muriel*

Sunday, August 29th

My Dearest Ray,

It's Sunday once again and I'm just after having lunch. Today is another wet dismal day with not much to do and no place to go.

Last night I played the piano for awhile and then began reading a book. About 9:30 p.m. I went around to Lily's house to find out how John, her brother, was keeping. Lily was in and seemed very glad to see me. She hasn't been out all week and I never saw her looking so pale and tired in all my life. The doctor doesn't think John will live much longer and Lily has taken the news badly. With attending John she hasn't been able to get any sleep at night. Some of the neighbors volunteered to take turns at looking after him and giving Lily a rest, but he just keeps calling for her all the time. Sometimes when he becomes more sick than usual he catches her hand and won't let her leave him for even a minute. Poor Lily, I feel sorry for her with one thing or another happening. She has had a pretty bad break in life. There was a time when I grew to dislike her for reasons which you know, but that's all finished now. I know you don't like me going into Lily's house because of John's ill health so because of that I only stayed about fifteen minutes.

Hazel is due to call for me and most likely when she does we will go for a walk and after tea, to church. Greta called about an hour ago and I had to stop writing. She has just gone and says she will be back at 6:30 to go to church with Hazel and me.

Tomorrow begins another week and I'm looking forward to it because there should be a letter from you, maybe I'll receive three or four all at once.   *—Forever yours, Muriel*

Monday, August 30th

My Dearest Muriel,

It's been a long time since I last wrote to you so I hope you'll forgive me. I left for New York Tuesday evening and arrived the next morning at about nine o'clock. I went to my aunt's house and spent the day there. That night I went out with my two cousins, Nick and Patricia. Nick had his girl and we went to Hotel Pennsylvania and danced to Glen Gray music. We had a good time—as good as you can have with your cousin. The next morning I stayed in and Howard and Bill arrived (I had left the day before them). We got the 6:30 train from New York to Greensboro, arrived Friday morning and spent the day getting settled in. As you know, my sister Jo got married not long ago and her husband is in the army. As it happens he's at Fort Bragg where I was before, and as it's only 100 miles or so from Greensboro he and Jo drove up Saturday and spent the day with me. They left at about 11 p.m. as he is being moved. Isn't that awful, I come down here and my sister and her husband are moving out. I've only seen her for a few hours in over a year and a half, but that's army life. Sunday I was given a special pass and spent the day with my uncle. My cousin Bob is in the hospital here and my uncle was down here visiting him. I left him at the train station on Sunday night.

Today we started training and have been busy all day. They have been very nice to us here, we put in for a leave and if we are lucky will get 15 days from September 3rd.

Well, my love, how are you doing? I am always thinking of you and haven't changed my mind about you and never will so don't you worry about me. Have you gotten a new job? If you feel you don't like it where you are go ahead and get your new job but promise me, not in England.

I want you to stay home, you may wonder why but I have my reasons.   *—Forever yours, Raymond*

PS Regards to the family. Don't forget your clothing sizes, Mother wants them.

Tuesday, August 31st

My Dearest Ray,

It's very difficult for me to be patient when I love you so much but nevertheless I'm trying. The postman knows I'm waiting for letters and every time he see me he just shakes his head before I have time to ask him if there are any. I'm really glad you sent the cables because if you hadn't I would have been thinking something had happened to you.

Last night Hazel and I went to the Apollo to see "Road to Morocco" with Dorothy Lamour, Bing Crosby and Bob Hope. It was a silly kind of picture and not much good. Tonight I'm not going out but tomorrow night Hazel and I may go to the Majestic to see "Tales of Manhattan." Mommy and the children are at the plot and Daddy is next door talking to Uncle Harold. At the moment I'm feeling very lonesome and wishing more than ever you were here. Please be good and look after yourself. I hope you are writing every day. —*Forever yours, Muriel*

September 1943

Wednesday, September 1st

My Dearest Ray,

It's about 10:00 and I'm upstairs trying to get some of this written before I go to bed. Hazel and I went to the Majestic to see "Tales of Manhattan." We heard it wasn't a good picture but we liked it. As yet none of your letters have come—this waiting is driving me nuts. Audrey and Olive have come to bed now so I'm sorry I can't write more. —*Yours forever, Muriel*

Thursday, September 2nd

My Dearest Ray,

Today has been another disappointing day as no letters have arrived. Why on earth are they taking so long in coming, a plane only takes a short while to reach here and yet letters take weeks. Of course there is a war in progress but even so I'm in no mood for excuses. Here I go talking nonsense. It has only been weeks but it seems like years since I've heard from you. Gosh, but I miss the letters I used to receive so often from England and the phone calls every week.

In the office when I'm trying to think of something else other than you for a change, an aeroplane has to fly over Inglis and when that happens someone in the office remarks, "Here's Ray coming back." Today again Victor began annoying me by putting his arms around me and trying to kiss me. I got really mad and my face went a deep red. George was in the office at the time and when he went back to his own office he told the staff there about the lovely temper I have. Victor is the comedian in our office, every time the boss goes out he begins to tell funny stories and has everyone laughing, then he begins annoying me and they laugh even more. What an office, you've no idea how they carry on.

The other day Margaret had three lovely pears. She began eating one and put the other two in the drawer of her desk. I watched her do this and as soon as her back was turned I took the other two out of the drawer and gave one to Elsie and ate one myself. This may not sound nice but everyone does it. There's always fun finding out the culprit.

Yesterday I brought a bar of milk chocolate, after eating some and giving some to Elsie I hid the rest in my drawer. When I looked for it again it had disappeared and I discovered later that Edna had taken it. All this is done in fun and afterwards we always pay each other back—for instance, I gave Margaret an apple and a pear yesterday and today Edna gave me some chocolate and an apple. In case you're wondering where we're getting all the apples and pears, this is the season for them and the shops are full of them.

Today Uncle Jack, Aunt Jean & Anne came up from Omagh. Aunt Anne has gone into hospital for treatment and Jean and Jack are living with us for awhile, but I'm not sure how long.

Tomorrow is the National Day of Prayer here and most of the girls in the office including myself are going to church instead of going home for lunch. I'll end now and practice a little before I go to bed. —*Yours forever, Muriel*

Saturday, September 4th

My Dearest Ray,

Yesterday at lunchtime I went to St. George's Church with the girls in the office. The service was lovely but very sad. At 5 o'clock I came home from the office expecting there would be a letter from you but none had arrived. When Hazel arrived at 6:30 I was in terribly bad form, she asked me what on earth was wrong and when I told her I didn't get any letters she said, "Just as I thought, but you needn't be so mad about it, after all he'll have such a lot to do when he gets home he won't have time to write to you." When Hazel said that it was just like throwing petrol on a fire and I got madder still. I was mad and I made her mad. After arguing for awhile I began to laugh and before long we were both laughing at how silly we were. Later Hazel had supper in our house. Aunt Jean and Uncle Jack were in and we all sat talking about the war until bedtime.

Now for the most important news—at 1 o'clock today I came home from the office almost sure to find your letters awaiting me, but once again I was disappointed. After dinner Audrey washed the dishes and I dried them, and while we were doing this we argued. As Audrey was hurrying to get out to the pictures she didn't wash some of the dishes right and I kept putting them back into the basin to be washed over again and boy, did she get mad. Just at that the postman came to the door and Olive came in with four letters from you. Now when I think of it I have to laugh. Poor Audrey, as soon as I got the letters I flung the dish towel at her and raced upstairs to read them leaving her to wash and dry the rest of the dishes by herself. As Audrey hates doing the dishes she raced after me and told me she wasn't going to finish them. To get her to do them I gave her a shilling and then she left me in peace to read the letters I had so long and impatiently waited for.

In your letter you keep thinking maybe I won't wait for you, well, never say or think that again because if you do I'll get mad.

You say it's raining so you must still be around Ireland, I like that. Because of the nice refreshing rain we do have here at times the grass is the greenest grass in the world and I'm proud to live in such a beautiful country! Do you remember the night you put my umbrella on the air raid shelter and the wind blew it onto the top and you could hardly get it down? I have to laugh every time that I think of it now.

Please don't worry about what the crowd in the office are saying, and above all don't ever think that they will make me change my mind. They all know I'm very much in love and maybe they think that you're not so much in love with me and just went into the Air Corps to get away from me. What a crowd. About getting married, don't worry, I'll be ready at a moment's notice. ----------------------------------
--*the bottom of this page and top of the next were cut off by the censor*--

Mind you, Ray, if I wasn't engaged to you I wouldn't tell you such intimate things. I'd still like to know why you're asking me to do this—even if it was possible to send things like that over here I wouldn't want you to do it. Please don't be mad, Ray, it's not that I wouldn't appreciate them, it's just that I'm funny about accepting things. Sometimes I even save to buy things for myself rather than let Mommy or Daddy buy them for me. Please don't feel hurt, Ray, you're a darling and I love you.

So Dot has a horse, that's wonderful, I love horses, ask her if I may ride it when I come over, that is if the horse hasn't died of old age (I'm pessimistic, the war can't last that long).

As it's tea time now I'll stop writing.   —*I love you, Muriel*

Sunday, September 5th

My Dearest Ray,

As Uncle Jack has his business to attend to he left yesterday for Omagh. This morning Mommy and Daddy and the two children went to Bangor to spend the day. Some friends of ours that live here have a bungalow in Bangor and they invited us all down but Aunt Jean and I decided not to go. After dinner we went to visit Aunt Anne in hospital and after tea went to church and we've just returned.

Last night I went down to the Red Cross because with receiving your letters I thought I might enjoy myself a little better than usual. Dot, Laura and Lily weren't there but Marie Neill and her boyfriend Joe, were. You met Joe last time you were here. He's in the 8th Air Corps and he told me that very soon he was returning to America to become a pilot. Marie danced a lot with other boys and Joe danced most of the night with me. He told me I looked a lot happier than usual and teased me a lot about you. The dance was crowded as usual and all the time I kept wishing you were with me. One of the boys from the 5th General was there but I can't remember his name.

As Aunt Jane is sitting downstairs by herself I think I better end now and go down and talk to her. Please write to me every day when you're settled, Ray.   —*Forever yours, Muriel*

Tuesday, September 7th

My Dearest Ray,

All day I kept hoping there would be another letter from you and there was one when I arrived home from the office at 5:15. It seemed too good to be true after receiving four on Saturday.

So your mother won't let you out of her sight, I don't blame her, I'll be just the same when you come back, in fact, maybe I'll be worse.

So everybody back home is talking about me and expecting to see me, gosh, but I'm going to feel funny meeting all your friends, what kind of questions did they ask and why didn't you answer them? Do you think they will like me when they meet me?

Ray, I hardly know what to say as regards the things you're going to send. You say if I love you I'll take them. It's very thoughtful of you and your mother to think of sending them but the Post Office won't allow it. As I can't decide whether to say no or yes I'll just leave it to you and if you do manage to get anything across I'll think of some way to repay you and your mother. Please don't get mad at me, Ray, it's just my nature and I can't help it.

No, I don't think you're crazy when you get kind of sick when you eat things that we can't get here. I'd be just the same if I was getting things you couldn't get, but please don't worry, Ray, I enjoy what I do get to eat and never think of what I did eat before the war. I've lived four years without dainties and now I've got used to it.

It's about 9:00 now and as I want to wash my hair before going to bed I'll stop writing. Please forgive me for not writing yesterday but I promise you I'll write everyday when I get your new address. Always be good, as I am.   —*Forever yours, Muriel*

PS Daddy is much better but as yet he hasn't gone back to work, his doctor won't allow him to.

Wednesday, September 8th

My Dearest Muriel,

I'm writing this letter from home—yes, I got another fifteen day leave. I'm sorry I haven't written since last week but I have been busy getting settled at camp. We didn't expect a leave so soon but we took it. As you know my sister had been over to Greensboro to see me and then left for New York. Well, I arrived in New York Monday and we both stayed with our aunt and yesterday morning we left for home. My sister had her husband's car so I drove it home. It was a wonderful drive through the mountains—I only wish that you were with me.

I see that Italy is out of the war now. Maybe by Christmas it will be over and if we're lucky I will be with you again. I'm wishing now more than ever that I was still there. I would have to be sent back now that all the action has started.

They have been very good to us at camp, in fact, too good. It's been so good to be home but it's still you I'm thinking of every minute of the day.

Muriel, my love, keep sending your letters home as when I do go back to camp I'll only be there a week. I will be at school for five or six months and not until then will I have a permanent address. —*Forever yours, Raymond*

Wednesday, September 8th

My Dearest Ray,

At five o'clock Hazel met me outside Inglis and we went to the Hippodrome to see a picture named "The Lady is Willing." The picture was very amusing and during it the news that Italy had capitulated was put on the screen. When that happened I was so delighted I could hardly watch the remainder of the show. Isn't it marvelous, the war shouldn't last so long now. I don't understand why Italy fought against us anyhow and I'm sure old Hitler isn't a bit pleased with what has happened. Wouldn't it be marvelous if Germany and Japan would capitulate, as sure as the skies above I'd go crazy the day this war ends and so will everybody. I hope we are together that day, if so we will have a great celebration.

As supper is ready I'll have to stop writing now and continue this letter tomorrow. —*Forever yours, Muriel*

My Dearest Ray,

Today I received an airgraph and could you guess who sent it? It was from Alan, the Air Force boy I went out with before I met you. Fancy him writing to me after all these months. He is in North Africa and has been there since last December. The letter is quite friendly and he thinks the scenery in Africa is beautiful and also that the war will be over soon. He didn't mention you and wants me to write to him. I guess boys who are stationed so far from home and especially in places like Africa do like receiving letters. No doubt I'll have to answer his letter but when I do so I'll tell him I'm engaged and kept very busy writing to you. It would be rude not to answer his letter and I'm sure you won't mind.

Do you remember I told you I would be starting music soon, well, as yet I haven't as my teacher can't begin teaching again until she finds a new nursemaid to take care of her baby. She had better hurry and start teaching again because if she doesn't I'll never be ready for the diploma at Christmas. —*Forever yours, Muriel*

Thursday, September 9th

My Dearest Muriel,

I was very happy today as I have six letters from you but when I read them and found out you hadn't heard from me I almost went crazy. I sent you three telegrams but from the sound of your letters you haven't received any of them. When I read your letters today I rushed down and sent you another one. I don't blame you for being worried and upset—I can't understand why you haven't received my mail, those darn censors are a pain in the neck sometimes. I haven't written anything about the army or anything about military doings so that shouldn't stop them. I can really understand how you feel.

Yesterday was quite a day for Mother and Father. It was their 32nd wedding anniversary and it was the first time in two years that we were all together. It was a wonderful day for all of us and last night the house was full of people as it usually is and it was quite late before we got to bed.

I'll begin to answer your letters now and what beautiful letters they are. I only wish mine were half as good. I'm hoping your dad will be OK—I'm really worried about him and hope everything turns out for the best. If there is anything I can do please let me know.

Muriel, I won't mind if you change your job as long as you stay in Belfast and at home. Don't ever accept a job away from home. I sent you a telegram to that effect but I guess you never received it. I hope you don't mind, my love, but I have my reasons.

Yes, it has been about two years that we've known each other and yes, it seems like I have known you all my life also and I'm very happy about that.

Muriel, please stop worrying about me becoming a pilot. For your sake and my mother's I will try to become an instructor, but let's not worry about it. The war may be over by that time and if not you still shouldn't worry.

I'm sorry to hear about Louis and Hazel, I know how they feel, I hope it turns out OK.

I'm glad you're ignoring them teasing you at the office.

Muriel, it's starting to rain and the only thing I can think of is Ireland and you. Someday we will be in this chair together looking out at the rain. —*I love you, Raymond*

Friday, September 10th

My Dearest Muriel,

I'm all mixed up as far as the mail goes. I received two more of your letters today and don't need to tell you how happy I am. Yesterday I sent you a telegram because I didn't think you had received the ones I sent before but today in your letter it's a great relief to know you have.

Yes, I was excited and happy to be home but it wasn't my friends I was happy about. It was my mother and father and sisters, that's what was wonderful, but don't ever worry about me forgetting you or Ireland Muriel, that's something in my heart that I'll never be able to forget. You know it's funny, you worry about me maybe not coming back and I worry about you, thinking you may find someone else. I guess we're both crazy.

Muriel, about the hospital, at the time I was there they were talking about breaking up the hospital and sending it away but that wasn't the main reason I joined the Air Corps. I admit it now, I made a mistake leaving you but it's over with now so let's make the best of it. Please don't ever ask me about it again, I'm trying to forget it.

About my training—the time and place, etc., I don't know—it all depends on what I qualify for. I honestly don't know if I'll be there for Christmas, it may be a long time after but let's not worry about that now. When I start training I'll be able to tell you more about it, I hope. No, Muriel, I never would have joined if you had told me you would break off with me, but do you think that's fair? It wouldn't have been the right thing to say, or would it? Try and understand why I'm doing what I am. I know how lonely you are and it hurts me to hear you say it, but don't forget I'm feeling the same way you are.

I'm glad to hear that you have a beautiful new coat but don't forget to send me or Mother your sizes and don't ask questions.

I'm glad you told Miss Collins what you did, that's the way, Muriel. If they give you a dig, give them a dig right back but don't lose your temper, that's what they want you to do. Just be calm and cool and always have an answer for them. As to what you told Peggy, I'm sure she won't say anything now. Keep it up, Muriel—don't let them step on you. When I do get back that's the first place we'll go together. *(Stop, more people have arrived.)*

I'm finally back to finish this letter, today is Sunday. I'll try to explain why I didn't write yesterday. Friday after everyone left I went to the plant where I used to work and stayed until five o'clock. After supper I drove Mother about five miles out into the country and we got some chickens, corn and pears for the weekend. When we came back I went to a show with my Uncle Ray. His name is the same as mine and he's about a year younger than I am and he's my uncle, believe it or not.

Yesterday I was a working man. In the morning I had to cut all of the grass and after that I had to clean the darn horse stall and brush and feed him. After lunch I was informed I was going to help fix our furnace and at about five o'clock my Aunt Rose called and invited me over for supper. After supper Ray and I went to the Park Hotel to have a drink. My sister Dot was there as where she works one of the girls is getting married next week so they were having a party. Dot introduced me to the girls, about twelve of them, and then you know what she said, she only meant it in a kidding way but I'm proud of it. She said, "Lay off my brother girls, he's engaged to an Irish girl." Boy, from then on they asked me a million questions and kidded me all night. We had a lot of fun and at about eleven o'clock Ray, Dot and I left as I had to get up at six. I went fishing with my two uncles. Ray's older brother Sam has an eighteen foot boat hitched to a trailer. We attached it to the car and took off with it to Lewiston, about eighteen miles from here. We fished all morning and darn, not one fish so we took the boat out and before we started for home Sam went and bought four pounds of fish. How's that, we didn't catch any fish but we sure came home with some. They have been kidding us about it.

I wanted to continue this letter but I think I'll mail it today and start another tomorrow as tonight I have to visit a sick aunt.

Honestly, Muriel, I'm thinking of you every minute, no matter where I am or what I'm doing. I dream nights that I am with you and then in the morning I'm so sad when I awaken and find it's only a dream. I made a mistake and I'm paying for it and I'm sorry that it has to hurt you also. I am being true to you, don't ever doubt me. I love you too much to be anything else. Today Sam said for me to hurry up and get married to you so he and his wife and you and I can go fishing together.

Mother, Father and my sisters send their regards.   —*Forever yours, Raymond*

Saturday, September 11th

My Dearest Ray,

As the last letter I received from you is dated 20th of August I was almost sure I'd get one today, but the postman passed by without leaving me any and once again I am very disappointed.

Last night Hazel came round and asked me to go to the Curzon with her to see a picture named "My Gal Sal." Rita Hayworth and Victor Mature were the actors. When we came out of the Curzon it was very dark and raining heavily and we had to race over to get a tram. Do you remember we used to do that and when a tram did come it was crowded with people? Do you remember we used to look to see what number was on our ticket? I still do that, often I get three but I never get the kiss that it's supposed to represent. Before you left here you got lots of ones, remember, one is for sorrow, are you superstitious?

A girl I know got married to a staff sergeant in our church on Monday. Her husband is an American stationed here and they have rented a furnished flat in Eglantine Avenue. Do you know what I saw the other day, a young girl and an American. The American was wheeling a baby in a baby carriage. That is becoming a common sight over here.

This morning I had to go down to the General Office and do some work. Harry, George and Ken work there and honestly, Ray, they teased me something awful but I just worked away and completely ignored them. Miss Fritz, one of the girls I like said, "Let them talk away, Muriel, they're just jealous, that's what's wrong with them." Yesterday when I was putting some books away in the Strong Room Harry came in. He slipped up behind me and before I knew he had his arms around me. I struggled with him and then I drew out and banged his head against the edge of an iron safe. He let go of me and I left him rubbing his head, his face all screwed up with pain. Harry is engaged and really deserved that bang on the head. I've no sympathy for him or anyone else who acts the way he does.

I haven't mailed the identity disc, I am waiting for your new address, but if it doesn't come soon I'll just mail it to your home address. I heard of a girl who gave her boyfriend an Identity disc, on one side she had his name and address printed and on the other side "hands off he's mine." What do you think of that? —*Forever yours, Muriel*

Sunday, September 12ᵗʰ

My Dearest Ray,

This morning I received a very pleasant surprise, a cable arrived from you and I don't need to tell you how happy I was to receive it. The cable is worded "Received letters have written and telegram home again, Regards to all love." I'm glad you have received some more of my letters but don't quite understand why you put—have written and telegram and home again. Maybe the next letters I receive will explain what you meant. I wish I knew how you are getting along in the Air Corps... Hazel just called—I'll stop writing now and finish this letter later.

Tuesday, September 14ᵗʰ

My Dearest Ray,

I'm sorry I didn't continue writing this letter earlier, but I'll explain later the reason why.

Hazel called on Sunday and we stayed home, had tea together and after tea we went to church. A RAF padre was preaching and a RAF choir was there. As always the prayers were for the boys fighting for freedom. After church it was too dark to walk so we came home.

On Monday night as no letters arrived from you for me to answer, Hazel and I went to the Curzon to see Loretta Young in "The Men in Her Life." Have you seen that picture, it was quite good though a little sad. After the show I hurried home intending to write to you but when I got in the house Mommy told me that Mae Brown, my music teacher, had left word that I was to call and see her as soon as I got back. I went round to Mae Brown and she kept me talking so long that I couldn't write to you when I got home again. I have to start music again on Friday night and believe me, Ray, I'll have to practice so hard I won't have time to go out at all. Mae Brown is a very good teacher and she has over 100 pupils. Out of all of them six are going in for the diploma at Christmas and as Mae is going to have another baby she isn't going to teach more than six of us from now until then. Olive and the rest of them haven't to go back until January. She says I'll have to spend hours upon hours practicing and also attend theory classes several nights in the week.

Tonight I'm not seeing Hazel. When I got home from the office I had to go up the Lisburn Road and do a message for Daddy. After that I came home and now I'm writing to you. By the way, Daddy is feeling fine now and he started work yesterday.

If it wasn't for you and the letters I look forward so much to receiving I don't think I could bear to stay home so much. I love going out and having fun—but since you've gone away I can't have fun and I just can't enjoy myself going out. The thought of how happy we'll be when we're together again helps to make me content, so please, Ray, try and get in the least dangerous branch of the Air Corps and I'll not worry so much.   —*Forever yours, Muriel*

Monday, September 13th

My Dearest Muriel,

I received your letter that you wrote on Tuesday, August 31st and was very unhappy to hear that you haven't received any of my mail. I really understand how you feel and just hope you start receiving my mail soon.

Not much excitement here because I'm not going out and besides most of the boys I know are in the army. Mother keeps me occupied by making me work. I had to make a few repairs on the washing machine this morning. I fixed the heater on my car this afternoon and changed the spark plugs. Then I had to fix my sister Jo's car. Mother came out and took a few pictures of me working so when I have them developed I'll send them to you. Tonight I have to help Dad with the furnace so I'll be busy all night.

I'm sorry to hear that Lily's brother is so sick, please, Muriel, don't go near the house, I'm afraid you may get his sickness. I know that I shouldn't say this but I'm worried about you.

My Dearest Muriel,

Today is Tuesday. Yesterday I had to stop writing to you and go and get Dad at work. After supper I helped Dad put in the new furnace, we worked until eleven o'clock and tonight we have to finish it.

I'm going to start back to camp Thursday night or Friday. This morning I went and got a haircut. Mother asked me to tell you if there is anything you want to let her know. I know you won't tell Mother or me so if you don't I'm going to send you things I think you may need, so be good and tell me what you want.

I'm glad you had dinner with Luke and Marie. I told him to take care of you and take you out and he kept his promise. I see he gave you the flash bulb and lighter fluid—I'm glad he remembered. When I get the package back I'll send you the film.

It's about time Inglis gave you an increase in pay. I see the boys there are still giving you trouble. Yes, don't go to the Works Office—let them bring your pay to you. —*I love you, Raymond*

Wednesday, September 15th

My Dearest Ray,

Last night for almost half an hour I sat at the window and watched an aeroplane circling around in the sky. It was a beautiful clear night with a full moon and I couldn't help remembering and thinking about the nights we walked home together. I kept wondering how you are getting along and wishing I knew just what you were doing as I sat at the window. If I could only get a glimpse of you now and then it would satisfy my heart.

Today I received a letter from the Red Cross but none from you. If it hadn't been for the cable you sent I would be thinking you were killed in one of the two railway disasters you had over there—I had to stop writing for about 20 minutes as Hazel called to tell me her mother isn't too well and she couldn't go out with me tonight. Hazel said she received a letter from Louis today and he says he won't be able to have his furlough until November.

Today was pretty quiet at the office, nothing worth telling you about. I want to wash my hair before practicing so I'll stop writing now. —*Forever yours, Muriel*

Thursday, September 16th

My Dearest Ray,

Tonight I'm going down to the Red Cross and I want to write to you now because it will be too late when I get home. I don't really care about going but there isn't anything else to do and besides, I won't be out all winter.

Please Ray, get in the safest branch of the Air Corps that you can because if anything ever happened to you I'd die of a broken heart.

As it's about 8 o'clock and time for the Red Cross, I'll finish this letter later.

It's Friday now and I want to finish this letter. Last night I went down to the Red Cross, Dot was there alone and I was talking to her for a short time. The dance was very crowded, a great many navy boys have landed here and quite a few of them were at the dance. For most of the night I danced with a boy whom I met about five weeks ago. When I first met him he asked me to go to one of the picnics the Red Cross have on Sundays. I told him I was engaged and didn't go out with any boys. He said he understood and admired me for being like that. Ever since he has danced with me anytime I go. He was there last night and talked to me for quite awhile. Later his pal came over and I was introduced to him. He danced with me several times and then they both sat talking to me about their hometowns and the war, etc. They left about 10 o'clock to go back to camp and shortly after a sailor asked me to dance. After the dance I tried to get away from him by rushing over to Dot, but he followed me and insisted on giving me some chocolate. He sat down and began talking and before long his pal came over and asked him was I his girl. He turned around and asked me if I was and then Dot lifted my hand and pointed to my engagement ring. He danced the next dance with me and while we were dancing he said he might have known a girl like me wasn't disengaged and he was sorry he couldn't call me his girl. Maybe you don't believe me but I don't like fellows flattering me and what is more I never believe they mean a word they say. About 10:40 I left the dance and was in good time to catch a tram home. When I got home the key was in the door and I couldn't help thinking of the nights you left me home. Remember I used to have to powder my nose and comb my hair and you used to hold the mirror for me. Gosh, but I miss you an awful lot Ray, my hair is never tossed now and I very seldom have to comb it. Please try your best and get back soon. I keep thinking that maybe you won't be sent back here, and maybe you'll be sent over to the Pacific or some other dangerous place.

By the way, I haven't to go to music tonight. I received a note from Mae Brown to say I've to begin taking lessons next Tuesday— after arranging definitely to go tonight, she sends a note. At this rate I'll never pass the examination. Tonight I'm not going out, I guess I'd better stay home and give my scales a good run over.   —*I adore you, Muriel*

Saturday, September 18th

My Dearest Ray,

All morning at the office I kept wishing it was time to go home as I felt I'd receive some letters from you. The postman doesn't deliver letters until 2 in the afternoon but I met him at 1:15 when I was walking home with Yvonne. Words can't describe how disappointed I was when he said there weren't any letters. The last letter I received was dated the 20th of August.

When I was at the Red Cross on Thursday night I was speaking to Marie Neill in the cloakroom. She said that Lily's brother was so ill the doctor didn't think he would live over the weekend. This afternoon I told Mommy about him and said I wanted to call and see Lily. She said she didn't want me going into Lily's house but I coaxed her and promised I wouldn't go upstairs to see him. Anyhow, I did call and took some vegetables, onions and my egg ration with me. Onions are hard to get and I knew John would need eggs. Honest, Ray, I felt like crying when in Lily's house. John's little pal called to see him and it was so sad. Lily said he thinks he'll get better and be out soon, and the doctor was surprised to find him living when he came this morning. It seems there is a hole in one of his lungs and the other one is collapsing too. Mommy can't understand why he isn't in hospital because it really is dangerous to the others in the family having him in the house.

When I left Lily's house and was walking up the street past Marie Neill's house, Marie came to the window and called me in. She asked me to go to the Red Cross with her tonight but I said no, I didn't feel like going. Then she said as she was going alone she would call for me at 7:45 and maybe I would change my mind and go with her. Right now it's about 6:30 and I am here alone as Mommy and Daddy are at the plot and Olive and Audrey are at the pictures. Maybe when Marie does call I will go with her as there isn't anyplace else to go and I feel very lonesome. —*Forever yours, Muriel*

Sunday, September 19th

My Dearest Ray,

Last night when Marie called I wasn't ready to go to the Red Cross and I really didn't care to go but Mommy came in from the plot and told me to go as I was sitting about the house too much and I might as well go out now because I'll be in all winter practicing. Anyhow, we arrived at the dance about 8:30 and honest, Ray, it never was so crowded before.

A band named "The Sad Sacks" was there and the floor was so crowded that everyone was bumping against each other. While I was dancing with some fellow he asked me if I would join his party as they were going around to the "400 Club" and needed another girl to make the party complete. I immediately refused, he wanted to know why not, but I gave him no reason. I left him to look for Marie but when I found her she was sitting talking to some American so I walked away and sat on another seat. Later on when I was dancing I noticed a boy nodding and smiling at me and who was it but Joe Goglia, he was there with Fay. Joe sends you his regards, he is stationed here now. He gave me his address and wants me to send him your new address when I receive it. After talking to them for about 10 minutes I went down to the cloakroom. I stopped to look at a map of America which was hanging on the wall. You remember that map, Ray, it's the one with all the little flags pinned on it and it's right beside the cloakroom door. I went over to it to see if I could find Greensboro, North Carolina. While I was looking some boy came up behind me, asked me which town I was looking for and offered to help me find it. By that time I had located North Carolina so I told him I was just curious and walked into the cloakroom. By the way I had my hand placed on the map he must have known it was North Carolina I was looking for because he said, "Is it North Carolina you want, that's where I come from and I wouldn't mind being over there with you right now." When he said that, I just looked him up and down with disdain and went in to get my coat.

When I got out of the Red Cross and was walking up Chichester Street I passed a crowd of Americans. In the glare of the passing trams and cars, the boy who had spoken to me while looking at the map must have recognized me because he shouted, "Hello, North Carolina." I pretended I didn't hear him and the next thing I knew he was coming after me. He walked up beside me and asked me where he could get a taxi. I told him I didn't know and to ask someone else. Then I saw my tram, left him standing there and ran to get it.

By the way, Ray, Greensboro must be a great distance from Lockport. I'm sure it's at least 1,000 miles, is that right? Are you still there? As yet I haven't received your new address. I'm hoping I receive some letters from you tomorrow. I have read the letters that I have received so often that now I know almost every word by heart. Every night before I get into bed I read them and Audrey keeps telling me I'm nuts. She's an awful wee girl, when she's saying her prayers at night she spends so little time over them that I sometimes think she only says "Amen." Olive is entirely different—she takes ages to say her prayers. The other night I asked her what she prays for and why it takes her so long and this was her reply. "Well, I say the Lord's Prayer, and then I ask God to keep Ray, Alan and Uncle Bobby safe in this war." I could have hugged her, fancy a child like her remembering to pray for the only boys she knows in the army.

As this is all the news I'll stop writing and get this letter and yesterday's mailed. —*Forever yours, Muriel*

Monday, September 20ᵗʰ

My Dearest Muriel,

Here I am back at camp after a 15 day furlough. All day Friday I went around saying goodbye to everyone and the payoff was when I got home at about four in the afternoon. In the driveway there were two big trucks full of hay. As you know the people next door have three horses. The hay was in bails and we had to pile about a third of it on the upper floor of our barn for Dot's horse. When we were through I was so tired I couldn't move.

That night the usual mob was there to see me off. The next morning I got on the train and on the way picked up Howard in Rochester and Bill in Syracuse. We got into New York City at about three o'clock and then got the train to Washington, DC at 4:30 and arrived there at 8 o'clock. Our next train to Greensboro wasn't until 11:30 so we went and had supper and walked around Washington until it was time for our train. We arrived in Greensboro at 8:30 Sunday morning and boy was I tired because it's hard trying to sleep on a train. I slept all day Sunday.

Today we didn't do much as it's been raining. I went to the dentist this afternoon and had four of my teeth fixed so that's about all I've done. I saw Bob tonight, remember my cousin that was in the hospital. He's out now and OK. Bob and I are going out Wednesday night if it doesn't rain. He's only 18 years old so I have to look after him, orders from home. He's a swell cousin, about as tall as me and he hasn't stopped growing—good looking too.

Muriel, before I forget, I've been trying to find out if it's possible to have you come over now but so far I haven't succeeded. When you have time go to the American Consulate—see what they have to say and I will do the same thing here the first chance I get.

Mother is sending you a package soon and later on I will send you another. Please, Muriel, if there is anything you need let me know and I will be more than glad to send it to you.

I hope by now you have received some of my letters because I know how you must feel. Have you gotten a new job yet or are you going to stay at Inglis? How is your dad coming along? Give my regards to all and take care of yourself, Muriel. —*I love you, Raymond*

My Dearest Ray,

It's 5:15 and I want to write a few lines to you while Mommy is preparing my tea and before Hazel comes around at 6 o'clock to go to a show. Today I received the letter you wrote on the 20th August with the snaps in it. I was very happy to receive it, Ray, but as yet I haven't received any letters written later than the 20th August and I'm worried. By the way, it wasn't opened by censors.

The snaps you sent are very good, especially the one of you standing by your car. I'm thinking of having it enlarged so I can put it in a frame and set it on my dressing table.

Last night I had to stop writing as Hazel called and was eager that we should get to the pictures early, just in case we wouldn't get in. We went to the Apollo to see Ann Harding in "Eyes in the Night" and it was different but quite good. About 9 o'clock we came out of the show and went into a café on the Ormeau Road for supper, after that we got a tram home. Hazel was telling me that Louis is in hospital ill with his stomach and she seems pretty worried. Not only that, he wrote and told her that rumors were going around that the hospital may be moved to Africa or Italy and it may even be before his next leave in November. I phoned Marie on Sunday night and had a talk with her.

She told me that Luke had heard from you and I was very glad to hear that.

Nothing very interesting has happened here lately except that I have been transferred into another department at the office. Now I am working beside Yvonne and Fred. Victor has left (thank goodness), Peggy has left and so has Miss Todd. I am doing Miss Todd's work now.

Now for some sad news, last night when I got home Mommy told me that she had read of the death of John, Lily's brother, in the "Telegraph." I was very sorry to hear about it. John was buried at 2:15 today and at 1:30 I called to see Lily. She was upset but she was taking it better than I expected she would. I guess it was better that he did go because he never could have been better in this world, and now all his suffering has ended.

It's time I was going to music so now I must end. —*Always forever yours, Muriel*

Wednesday, September 22nd

My Dearest Ray,

Lately the weather hasn't been too bad here, it hasn't rained for quite awhile but it is very cold. I don't mind the cold but it reminds me of the nights you used to share your overcoat with me and I miss that so much. As it is time I was leaving for the office I'll stop writing now and continue tonight... Now it's 5:20 and I've just arrived back from the office. No letters again today. I know you're writing all right but it's the mail that's holding them back.

In my other letter I told you I was transferred, I'm in the same room I always worked in only at the other end. Elsie says she misses my chatter and wishes I was back beside her. I go to speak to her sometimes and sometimes she comes down to see me. At other times when the girls are having a silly talk about something they call me up so I can give my opinion. They all still ask how you are and I tell them very well. By my attitude I think they're quite convinced that you are coming back (most of them anyhow) and they often ask me if I am preparing my trousseau. I guess the reason they are all so interested in my affairs is because you're an American and I'm the only girl in Inglis engaged to one. —*I adore you, Muriel*

Thursday, September 23rd

My Dearest Muriel,

I'm sorry I'm not writing everyday as I should, but we are so busy.

We have started our training and boy it's tough—up at five o'clock, breakfast from 5:30-7:00 (we have to make our beds and mop the floors, etc.). We fall out at seven and go to the drill field where we stay until 11:15, we have lectures and commando style drilling, you know running, jumping, climbing fences, etc. From 11:15 until 12:45 dinner and mail call (that's the only good part—mail call). From 12:45 until 4:30 it's about the same as in the morning with more drilling—boy, my feet are sore. Supper is from 4:30 until 6:00, a parade usually from 6:00 until 8:00 and lights out at 9:30. Tuesday night from 6:30 until 10:30 we had to do written examinations and last night we had to move to different barracks.

Right now I'm writing this at the dentist's office while I'm waiting and have some time. It's about 1:30. I thought maybe we could go into town tonight but they said no passes. How long we will be here training I don't know. We have a few more tests to take before we start college, I hope it's soon.

Mother is sending you a package soon and later on I'm sending you one for your birthday and Christmas. Please, Muriel, don't send us anything as you will have to pay too much duty. If there is anything you want please let me know. How is your dad, your mother and the kids? I guess I'd better stop as I'm next in line for the dentist. *—I love you, Raymond*

Friday, September 24th

My Dearest Ray,

When I got home from the office yesterday your letter of the 10th September was awaiting me and I needn't tell you how happy I was to receive it.

About your training—you say that how long you'll be away all depends on what you qualify for. Have you chosen what you want to be, if so what? You want to know if telling you I would break off with you if you joined the Air Corps would have been the right thing to say. In one way yes and in another no. You see, Ray, you didn't tell me about it until it was too late to drawback. I'll admit you did mention it to me shortly after you went to England, and when I said not to think of joining you promised you wouldn't. However, you have done what you wanted to do and I guess there's nothing either of us can do about it now. Ray, please understand—I'm not mad at you and what's more I don't blame you for what you did. If you weren't happy in the hospital and are happy now in the Air Corps then I'm glad, I want you to be happy no matter about me.

Ray, I'm so mixed up I can't put what I want to say in words. You have asked me not to mention the Air Corps to you again and said you admit you made a mistake leaving me. I promise I won't say anymore about it, what good could it do anyhow.

Ray, there are lots of things I don't understand about your letter. In the first place it was written at home and yet your camp address is on the envelope. As yet I haven't received any letters explaining why you're home and not at camp. Weren't you supposed to start training the 27th August? Also, I'm not sure which address to mail my letters to. Today I received a letter dated 23rd August but it hasn't enlightened me. Ray, I guess I'd better stop writing now, I'm all confused and can't think straight. I haven't answered your letters properly but I'll do so tomorrow and also tell you what I've been doing last night and to-night. —*Forever yours, Muriel*

Saturday, September 25th

My Dearest Ray,

You seem to be having a wonderful time going places and visiting the Park Hotel, etc. but please, Ray, when you're settled write to me more often. Right now I'm trying to understand why you can't while you're home.

So you went fishing with your Uncle Sam, didn't catch any fish and bought some on your way home. That was really funny, Ray, did you make those at home think you caught them?

So you had just one drink with Dot and her girlfriends. I feel like saying something but I won't, I'm crazy, besides I give up. Anyhow, maybe I'm too old-fashioned. I see you went out with the boys and got tight, well, I can't or won't say much because sometimes I feel like doing that myself.

Since Monday night I haven't been out, I've had to sit home and practice. I don't mind the examination pieces but the scales are driving me nuts and I absolutely loathe practicing them.

This morning in the office Elsie and I arranged to go into town this afternoon as she had some shopping to do. I went into a music shop and bought "As Time Goes By." When I got home I tried playing it, it's quite easy.

Right now everyone is out and as it's about 6:30 p.m. and I haven't yet had tea I'll stop writing and make some.

It's about 11:15 p.m. and about 15 minutes ago I got back from the Red Cross. After tea I practiced for about two hours and then got feeling so bored I had to go out or go crazy. Marie Neill and Lily were there and for a short while I sat talking to them. Just as they were getting up to dance a technician asked me to dance and after the dance he followed me and sat down beside me. For half an hour he sat there and talked and all the while I was itching to be on the dance floor. Once again he asked me to dance and then for the remainder of the night we sat and talked. He was quite interesting to talk to, we talked about voting rights for women, clothes rationing, and he gave his opinion of Ireland and its people and told me a great deal about America. What a conversation, I think we talked about almost everything. Early in the night he asked me to go to church with him tomorrow... he told me he was Protestant. I told him I couldn't go with him as I was engaged and didn't go anyplace with any other boys. He seemed to think me very extraordinary. When it came 10:30 I told him I would have to go and because I refused to let him leave me even to the tram he was a little mad. "Surely there's no harm in that," he said. "I'm sure your boyfriend would be glad to know I got you safely to a tram instead of you going there yourself in the blackout." At that I laughed and said I was quite capable of getting there safely by myself. Maybe I'm nuts, Ray, but I just don't want any other boys walking with me, I'd feel guilty and in the wrong. —*Forever yours, Muriel*

Sunday, September 26th

My Dearest Muriel,

It's just about 2:30 Sunday afternoon here at camp. I haven't written since Thursday or Friday, the time goes by so fast here. Thursday night we had another test and Friday morning I woke and was sick and went on sick call at seven o'clock. I had a head cold and was sore all over. They gave me a lot of pills and I spent the rest of the day in bed. Friday night the boys wanted me to go into town to a dance but as I could hardly move I stayed in. Saturday morning I took another test and in the afternoon there was an inspection and a parade. Saturday night I went to a football game in Greensboro, the teams were Duke and North Carolina. I don't think you know how football is played so I won't go into detail. It was a night game as we call it here. It started at 8 and ended at 11 o'clock. They have big floodlights that light up the field just as if it were daylight. That is one of the first things I am going to take you to when you come back with me. Duke won 7 to 0, they are one of the best teams in the States. After the game we three

(Howard & Bill were with me) went to the USO, it's a club like the Red Cross in Ireland. They had a dance but it was over so we had something to eat and as we had to be back at camp by 12 o'clock we didn't stay long.

Today Bob, my cousin here at camp, Bill, Howard, Bud and Chuck—you don't know Bud and Chuck but they came over with us— we're all going out. I don't know what we're going to do but they're talking about going to the show, there's an airplane picture on. I don't know the name of it but as long as there are airplanes in it we're satis- fied. Bob just walked in—we are waiting for the other boys to get ready.

I hope by now, Muriel, that you have started to receive my letters. I have been so worried over the fact that you haven't. It's been over a week now since I've heard from you. Mother may have some home but I told her to send them to me right away. I just wish I had you here with me now, Muriel. As things look now maybe this war will be over by Christmas and then, oh boy, don't forget to start packing the minute it is. —*Loving you always, Raymond*

Sunday, September 26th

My Dearest Ray,

This morning I called and asked Hazel to come to church with me. She was in bed but I made her get up and come. She seemed very hap- py and pleased and could you guess what made her like that, well, I'll tell you. She received a letter from Louis telling her he was out of hos- pital and he thinks he is getting his furlough at the end of next week. I only wish you were coming then too. If you were still with the 5th General it would almost be time for your next leave and I'd have been so very happy and excited about it. —*I love you, Muriel*

Monday, September 27th

My Dearest Muriel,

Today I received two more of your letters, the first since I left from home—it sure felt good to see your handwriting again. Mother wrote and told me she had the pictures we took developed and is send- ing them to me. After I see them I'll send them to you. Mother also sent you a package, it will take five or six weeks so don't worry if you don't receive it for awhile.

Last night nothing much happened. We walked around so much my feet ached all morning. We went to the USO show (like they had in Belfast after the dance at the Red Cross, remember the good old days). It wasn't bad—after the show we went and had a bite to eat and then came back.

I take it you have received some of my letters and that makes me very happy. I'm also glad to hear that your daddy is much better. I wish you wouldn't worry about me, Muriel. Just because I'm in the Air Corps doesn't mean something is going to happen to me.

My Dearest Muriel,

It's Tuesday now, yesterday I had to stop as we were told we were going to have an inspection. After dinner we had to start cleaning the barracks. The inspection was at 9 o'clock and lights out at 9:30 so I didn't have time to finish this letter.

So the boys at the office are still kidding you about me. I'm glad you gave Harry a bang on the head—maybe it will teach him to keep his hands off you, so keep it up.

As to the identity disc—my, you really want me to stay far away from girls, well, my love, that's one thing you won't have to worry about, I promise you that. No other girl could ever take your place and as far as going out with them, it doesn't interest me in the least so don't ever worry.

I was wondering if any of my mail has been cut up by the censors, I would like to know if I'm writing anything I shouldn't be. Your letters are censored, not all of them, but so far no cutouts.   *—Forever yours, Raymond*

Monday, September 27th

My Dearest Ray,

After I finished writing to you yesterday afternoon I called to see Hazel. I had tea in her house and at 6:30 I came home to practice. It was very cold so I lit a big fire in the sitting room. The past few weeks the weather has been icy cold and some people say we're going to have a very severe winter.

Tonight when I came home from the office I got a very big surprise. Mommy told me that Gloria and Pearl Adair (my cousins) had called this afternoon. I can hardly believe it. Gloria went to America 4 years ago this month and couldn't get back here because of the outbreak of the war. Anyhow, she's back now and I'm dying to see her. Before she went to America we were great pals and used to spend our holidays together.   *—Forever yours, Muriel*

Tuesday, September 28th

My Dearest Ray,

This letter is going to be written in an awful hurry as I have to practice for a few hours before I go to bed. I'm just back from a music lesson and honestly, Ray, the amount of scales I have to learn is driving me nuts. Mae Brown has told me if I don't think I can manage to get them all learnt before the examination I'll just have to wait and try for it in June instead.

This morning I received a postcard from you and it made me very happy, although I was a little disappointed because it wasn't a letter. —*Yours forever, Muriel*

Wednesday, September 29th

My Dearest Ray,

It's 1:35 p.m. I'm just after having lunch and want to write to you now as I won't have time tonight—practice again. So far no more letters have arrived but I'm really hoping for one or two this afternoon.

Last night I practiced until 11:45. Hazel called at 6:15 on her way to a show—she borrowed some sweet coupons from me. I would have loved to have gone with her but I couldn't.

Nothing worth talking about has happened here lately. All I do is go to the office, come home and sit practicing from 6 o'clock until bedtime. Gosh, but I wish I had this examination off my mind. How are you getting along? —*Forever yours, Muriel*

Thursday, September 30th

My Dearest Ray,

Last night when I arrived home from the office your letter of 13th September was waiting for me and honestly I was very happy and delighted to receive it. So your mother is keeping you busy. I'm very happy to hear that. What with fixing the washing machine, furnace and cars you certainly have been busy. I'm glad I'm marrying a man who can do all those things.

So you had to return to camp on Thursday night or Friday. I'd still like to know why you were sent home again, as yet the letters you wrote explaining about that haven't got here.

So you and your mother are still wanting to know if I need anything or if there's anything I want. You're both very good but you should know me better than to ask such questions. If I did want anything, Ray, I just couldn't bring myself to ask you, at least not until we are married. —*I love you, Muriel*

Muriel Mitchell, Belfast, Northern Ireland, 1943.

October 1943

Friday, October 1ˢᵗ

My Dearest Ray,

I'm just after having tea and want to get this letter written before I go for my music lesson at 7:15. Last night I practiced until 11:30 and I'll have to do the same tonight.

This morning Hazel called in the shop for your identity disc and she brought it around to me at lunchtime. Tonight I'll get it ready for mailing and will mail it to you tomorrow afternoon.

Ray, did you write to me between the 23ʳᵈ of August and the 10ᵗʰ of September? So far I've only received a card written between those dates. By now I expect you have really started your training and are being kept very busy.

Yesterday Adeline received her invitation card for the Red Cross dances. Do you remember I told you she was joining? She wants me to go with her tomorrow night and I think I might as Mommy has invited Mr. & Mrs. Templeton over to the house and she says I can't practice while they're here. Gosh, but it's funny, Ray, every night when I'm practicing while Audrey and Olive are in bed, Audrey keeps shouting down, "Mommy will you make Muriel stop that racket, I can't sleep." She says she wouldn't mind listening to decent music but she hates my examination pieces and scales and I don't blame her, they're awful to listen to. I wish it were next year then you'll be back and my examination over, maybe the war too—what a hope!   —*Forever yours, Muriel*

Saturday, October 2ⁿᵈ

My Dearest Ray,

After lunch I took the identity disc around to the Post Office in Bradbury Place. I asked the girl in the Post Office which would be the best way to mail it and she advised me to have it registered and send it ordinary mail. I only hope it reaches you safely as lots of mail is lost through enemy action.

At 5:30 Mr. & Mrs. Templeton are due to come. They are bringing along a boy who is a friend of theirs. He is a musician in some dance band but I'm not sure whether it's a piano or piano-accordion he plays. At 7:45 I have to meet Adeline in town, I really wish you were here— I'd give anything to have you with me tonight. Today again I didn't receive any letters so now I'm hoping to receive some on Monday.

By the way, Mae Brown says my playing is so much better than many she's put through the diploma, but she says my scales aren't so good and if I fail that will be the reason. Monday night I've to attend a theory class, I'm going to be really busy next week.

The visitors have arrived now, Ray, so I must end and help Mommy prepare tea. —*Forever yours, Muriel*

Sunday, October 3ʳᵈ

My Dearest Ray,

At 3 p.m. Hazel called and wanted me to go for a walk with her but I told her I had to write to you, also practice scales. She stayed for about half an hour and before she left borrowed two books to take home and read. Hazel told me she had a letter from Louis, he can't have his leave until November.

Last night I met Adeline in town and we went to the Red Cross. It was Adeline's first time there and she enjoyed it very much. Two technicians wanted to take us out but we both refused. The dance was very good and there was a big crowd there but as usual I couldn't enjoy myself.

When I arrived home from the dance a party was going on. Mr. & Mrs. Templeton and friend were still here and Aunt Vi & Uncle Harold were in. Mr. Templeton is a comedian and he sang some funny songs and made us all laugh. We had some liquor in the house and Uncle Harold & Mr. Templeton got feeling good, but Daddy didn't touch it and I was glad. I didn't get to bed until 2:30 a.m. and the visitors didn't leave until about 3 a.m. You would have enjoyed listening to them. Tea is ready so I'll end now. —*Forever yours, Muriel*

Monday, October 4ᵗʰ

My Dearest Muriel,

I don't know how to start this letter because I'm ashamed of myself, please don't get mad at me because I'll never let it happen again, I promise. I haven't written since Tuesday. Wednesday and Thursday I stayed in as I was so sore and I mean sore. Every bone and muscle in my body ached so I couldn't even walk. Having 8 hours a day of drilling and exercise is more than I can stand. I hadn't done any of that for two years so I was pretty soft but I'm getting hard now, the hard way.

Friday, Saturday and Sunday I was given a three day pass with Bill and Howard so we went to Raleigh, North Carolina. It's about 100 miles from camp. We left Friday morning on the bus and arrived there about two o'clock. Friday night we went to a show then went to bed as there was nothing else to do. We took the trip to get a lot of sleep and boy, we did. Saturday we called up some girls we knew back in 1941, to pay our respect, and we were invited over to dinner. At eight o'clock we left them and went to a dance they had in town. It was so good that I was in bed by eleven o'clock. Sunday morning we came back to camp and got things settled up.

You may think I was out with a girl but honest, Muriel, I wasn't. Two of the girls I knew are now married—in fact one has a baby about 5 months old. Her husband has been in England for five months so naturally she wanted to know all about England. I showed them your picture and told them I was engaged to you. They liked it very much and asked when we were getting married. Everything has changed for me, I knew these girls and went out with them but now things are different, other girls don't mean a thing.

Today I received a letter from Luke and he told me he may be getting married in November. When he told me that it really hurt but it's all my fault. Luke told me he took you out and saw you at the Red Cross, also that he misses me very much, well, I miss Luke an awful lot also. Mother sent me the pictures we took at home. The ones that came out I will send to you in a package soon. Muriel, if there is anything you want please let me know & I'll be more than glad to send it.

As to the time we will be here, we expect to be moved this week, to where we don't know but I hope it's close to home

I guess this letter on the whole is pretty sad, well, that's the way I feel tonight and I can't help it. I'm all through my tests for now and have come out on top, way above average so I'm starting out OK. I'm so restless I can't sit still one minute. Mother has been mad because I haven't been writing but honest, Muriel, I'm nervous and can't sit down and write. The nights after I came back from the field all tired and sore I just took a shower and went right to bed.

Please, Muriel, don't let this letter worry you, it's just one of my off days. Take care of yourself and be cheerful, not like me. Say hello to everyone there for me and write more often than I do. —*I love you, Raymond*

Monday, October 4th

My Dearest Ray,

Tonight I came home from the office hoping to find some letters but there weren't any and I was very disappointed. I wish they'd come more often and then maybe I'd feel better.

Tonight Hazel is going to a show by herself and I'm wishing I could go with her, instead I have to attend a theory class and after that I have to practice. Mommy is trying to make me wait and go for the diploma next June instead of this December, she says it isn't good for me to sit in every night but I want to get it over with now.

Please tell me this, Ray, when your training is finished will you be stationed here or in England? If I thought you would have to stay in America I'd go crazy. Please try and find out these details and let me know, right now I can't help wondering and worrying.   —*Forever yours, Muriel*

Tuesday, October 5th

My Dearest Ray,

Today again I was very disappointed, no letters arrived. I just got home from the office and while Mommy is preparing tea I want to get this letter written. After tea I have to go for a music lesson and practice the rest of the night. That's how I'm passing the time, not very exciting, is it? Ray, I'm feeling pretty miserable these days.

If I was receiving more letters from you it wouldn't be so bad. Now that you're settled in camp they'll come more often, I hope so. —*Forever yours, Muriel*

Thursday, October 7th

My Dearest Ray,

Yesterday I didn't write because I didn't feel well, today I don't feel any better but I'm writing to you anyhow to tell you what it's all about. I hardly know where to begin, but I'll try. Before I went to bed the night before last Mommy and I were downstairs alone and somehow the conversation came round about you. Until that night she didn't say anything about us getting married and I thought she had changed and didn't mind anymore. Anyhow, I told her we were getting married as soon as your training was completed and you came back. That started trouble and do you know what Mommy said, she said I was only infatuated and I wasn't marrying you. I told her I wasn't infatuated and to try and realize I was marrying you, also I would probably be married this time next year. She said she would never realize it and she was praying that God would guide me. Mommy also said something else which hurt me very much. She just said it to annoy me and I can't forgive her for it. Since that night I haven't spoken to her. She has spoken to me at the table asking me if I wanted anything more to eat, etc., and all I've said is yes or no, beyond that I've just went about the house without speaking and intend to do that from now on. If Daddy asks me what is wrong I'm going to tell him how things are, maybe he'll understand.

Since Friday last I haven't felt too good, I've lost my appetite and everything I have eaten has made me sick. Mae Brown noticed I wasn't well and the girls in the office have too. Yesterday morning I felt very depressed and Yvonne wanted to know why I wasn't talking and making fun. She knows Mommy doesn't want me to get married so I told her that I thought Mommy had changed her mind and I discovered she hadn't. That started more trouble. Yvonne said she put her mother before any man and if she loved someone and would hurt her mother by marrying him she wouldn't. Honest, Ray, I felt so awful I cried. When Yvonne saw me crying all she said was, "Is that how love gets you?" I didn't answer or speak to her for the rest of the morning and at lunchtime she rushed out and didn't want to walk home with me. After lunch I called around to see Hazel and ask her to go to a show with me. Yes, I was so mad and miserable I decided to take the afternoon off. As Wednesday afternoon is Hazel's afternoon off she was delighted that I had decided to stay off too. Anyhow, about 3 o'clock we went to the Classic to see a picture named "The More the Merrier." Hazel was amused at me. I sat in the show and now and then I'd say, "I don't care two hoots, I'm sitting here when I should be back at the office working, why don't I do this more often." After the show we went and had something to eat and then I went to Hazel's house with her. It was about 8:30 when we got there and her mother informed me that Mommy had sent Olive down at 6 o'clock to inquire if Hazel was home and if she knew where I was. Mrs. T said she wasn't sure but that she thought that Hazel and I had gone to the pictures. At 8:45 I left Hazel's house and came home, no one was in and as I had a headache I went straight to bed.

This morning when I arrived at the office everyone wanted to know why I didn't come back yesterday afternoon (everyone except Yvonne and Maureen). They thought I went home and went to bed but I told them I went to the show. All day Yvonne and Maureen didn't speak to me, they were very mad because I stayed off and left them to do my work along with their own.

As I have just lately been transferred into their department I'm not quite sure of the routine yet, and today I had to ask Maureen what had to be done next. Every time I asked her anything she hardly answered me and once I got so mad I asked her if she lost her voice and did it hurt her to speak. Fred, who is in charge of our department wasn't too happy about me staying off either but before I came home tonight he playfully hit me with a book, told me he liked me and hoped I wasn't mad at him too.

Gosh, but I've felt awful these past few days, the least little thing annoys me. Maybe when I receive some more letters I'll feel better. Please, Ray, don't let what I've written annoy you. I shouldn't tell you all these things but you're the only person I have to confide in.

All that's wrong with me is that I'm missing and thinking about you, worrying about this music examination and Mommy. Right now it's about 8 o'clock so I must stop writing and practice. I feel much better since telling you everything. —*Forever yours, Muriel*

Friday, October 8th

My Dearest Muriel,

I have so much to tell you I really don't know where to start. Tuesday was another routine day here and that night we went and saw Howard as he is in the hospital with a cold. Afterwards we went to see "Best Foot Forward." The Harry James Band was in it so if it ever comes over don't forget to see it. Wednesday I was on a detail all day and that night Bill and I went to a fair they had in town. It wasn't very good so we came back by ten o'clock. All this time I'm going to write to you but kept putting it off. Honest, Muriel, I'm always doing something.

Thursday I went into town to get my clothing I had cleaned and was short a shirt, tomorrow I'm going back to try and get it. An old favorite was playing at one of the shows, remember "Orchestra Wives?" Bill and I went to see it again as Glenn Miller played in it. After the show we got a bite to eat and came back. Tonight we just got back from seeing Howard in the hospital, he's getting out tomorrow.

We are restricted again as we had an inspection today and it wasn't too good. We're also restricted tomorrow and Sunday. Tomorrow we'll have another inspection and Sunday we move to another barracks. They said we may be shipped out of here on Monday.

Today I received two letters from you. The two letters I received from you last week were written after these were but as long as I receive them I'm happy.

I have two packages I'm sending you, no, I won't tell you what they're for, it's a surprise so let me know when you receive them and how you like them.

I hope the letter I wrote on Monday didn't get you down, I have been kicking myself ever since for sending it. Boy, I was down in the dumps.

It makes me very happy as I read your letters, Muriel. I know how you feel because when I receive one from you I feel 100% better, too.

How can I ever forget about the umbrella on the air raid shelter, how can I ever forget about the shelter, period.

Muriel, pages 7 and 8 were cut in two, did you do it or was it the censor? Page 7 starts with—"About getting married, don't worry I'll be ready at a moment's notice"—then the page is cut in half. Page 8 starts with— "Mind you, Ray, if I wasn't engaged to you I wouldn't tell you such intimate things." I think it's your sizes I asked you to send but I don't see why they censored that, unless they don't want us to send things to you over there. Write it out again.   —*I love you, Raymond*

Saturday, October 9th

My Dearest Ray,

Last night I didn't write because I felt too unhappy even to write to you. All day in the office I was miserable, Yvonne and Maureen are still the same and I'm too proud to start talking to them. They just sit talking to each other and now and then say something catty which is meant for me.

Yesterday Yvonne had some sweets and she began sharing them with Maureen. She flung one at me, it landed on my desk, but I just let it be there. If she had offered it to me the right way I would have accepted it and thanked her. Anyhow, I didn't eat the sweet and later it disappeared.

Although I'm in misery sitting beside them I try not to show it. I really wish I was back in my other department sitting beside Elsie. It hurts me to be unfriendly with people and I hate rows. If Maureen and Yvonne keep on acting like they're doing I'm going to leave Inglis. You remember the job in Uncle Harold's firm I told you about, well, he said I could have it only I might be sent to England after a few months. As regards to the Lockheed job, the hours are long and I wouldn't have much time to practice. However, if I can still get a job there, I may take it.

Last night I went round for my music lesson, but Mae Brown's father has died and she isn't teaching again until next week.

You remember I told you about Mommy giving off to me about us getting married, well, on Thursday night after I finished practicing and I went into the kitchen, I noticed she had been crying. Since then she has been quite herself, she talks to me as usual, but I'm not feeling so good and don't say much.

Ray, I feel like saying plenty about receiving no letters, but what's the use, maybe you are writing everyday and maybe I'll receive a lot of letters on Monday and then feel very sorry for what I feel like saying now. —*Forever yours, Muriel*

Saturday, October 9th

My Dearest Ray,

It's about 11:20 p.m. I'm just after having supper and I feel I can't go to bed unless I write to you. Today after I wrote to you I had tea and then practiced a few hours. All the time I felt restless and unhappy so I decided to go to the Red Cross and try and be cheerful. Dot and Marie Neill were there and so were Joe and a few of his pals. Dot has stopped going out with Al and he was there coaxing her to go out with him again. By the way, Dot told me she had two letters from Zane in South Africa and he wanted to know if you and I were married yet. Poor Zane, I think he was the nicest boy Dot ever went out with and I don't think much of the ones she's going around with now.

As usual Joe inquired about you, and then he began betting me you wouldn't come back. Later one of his pals came over and began getting fresh. He put his arms around me and I felt like smacking his face. Joe told him to lay off as I was engaged and my boyfriend was in America. "Would you believe it," he said, "Her boyfriend joined the Air Corps and left her to go back to America." The other fellow (I forgot his name) said, "That's fine, now the coast is clear, will you come out with me." He asked me to dance and while we were dancing he asked me to go out again, I said no and he said, "Why not, the coast is clear, your boyfriend is thousands of miles away and he'll never know." I simply said no again and he said, "Boy, you're one in a million."

Anyhow, after the dance he sat talking to me for awhile and then I got very fed up and came home early.

By the way, when I was talking to Joe he began kidding me about you, he said, "You may be sitting at home keeping true to Ray, but I guarantee he's not, he's Italian and Italians are hot-blooded, I should know, I'm Italian myself." Ray, why do people talk that way, aren't there any decent people left in this world. Everybody I meet talks that way—they all say that no matter who the boy is he'll go around with other girls even when he's in love. That reminds me of what you said once while you were here on your first leave. You told me if I didn't do something which isn't right because we're not married, you would go back to England and you know the rest. I know you didn't mean what you were saying and I know you love me and will always be true. You're different to all the other fellows, Ray, and I'm trusting you with all my heart. It hurts a little when people talk the way they do but I always keep saying to myself, "They don't know just how much we love each other, they think ours is only a war time engagement, we'll prove them wrong someday." —*Forever yours, Muriel*

Sunday, October 10th

My Dearest Ray,

This morning I got up early and went to the Harvest Thanksgiving service with Daddy, Audrey, Olive, also Betty and Raymond. The service was very long and we didn't get home until one o'clock. I noticed quite a few American nurses, officers and technicians in the church.

Hazel called about ten minutes ago—I guess I'll finish now as there isn't anything new to tell you. —*I adore you as always, Muriel*

Monday, October 11th

My Dearest Ray,

Another day and still no letters, what can be wrong, the last letter I received was written on the 13th & 14th of September and it's almost four weeks since then. It's very hard to be bright and cheerful when I'm not hearing from you. I'd love to write to your mother again but as yet I have not received an answer to the letter I sent her. Do you know if she has written yet?

Today in the office things weren't so bad. In the morning I heard Yvonne asking Maureen to go to Mr. Johnston (the boss) and ask him for more ink as there wasn't any in her inkwell. Maureen said she didn't want to go near him and Yvonne said she didn't want to go as he had seen her coming in ten minutes late this morning and he might say something to her about it. Anyhow, they argued for awhile and at last I swallowed my pride and told Yvonne if she wanted ink I would go to Mr. Johnston. I was late in getting to the office too but I wasn't caring whether Mr. Johnston would say anything or not about it. Yvonne seemed surprised but she said alright and thanked me. After that she spoke to me about work now and again but that was all. This afternoon Maureen didn't come back. I heard her complaining to

Yvonne all morning about not feeling well. Yvonne and I had to do Maureen's work between us as well as our own and that meant we had to speak to each other. At 5 o'clock I walked home with Rita, another girl in the office. Yvonne passed on the way and smiled at me so I guess everything isn't so bad now.

Everything is all right at home once again. Mommy is herself again and I talk sometimes although I don't say much as I still feel hurt about what she said last week.

Tonight I have to go for a theory lesson so I'll have to stop writing. I wish I knew how you were getting along. —*I adore you, Muriel*

Tuesday, October 12th

My Dearest Muriel,

So much is happening here since I last wrote to you. I'm at college now, North Carolina State in Raleigh, North Carolina—yes, that's the town we visited on our three day pass and the place where we were stationed before. We were hoping to be sent to New York State, close to home. It's very nice here but we were wishing we would go to someplace we hadn't been before.

If you knew what was going on here you'd probably have a fit. Maybe they do the same thing at colleges back there—the upper classmen have us doing all sorts of crazy things, it's our initiation and boy they are really giving it to us. Friday, Saturday and Sunday we were restricted in camp at Greensboro, left Monday and arrived in Raleigh at 10 p.m. The minute we got off the train things really started to happen. Now don't get me wrong—it is all in the training for a cadet. One minute you're so mad you could cry and the next minute you laugh yourself sick....I had to stop as they just ran us in for ice-cold showers and then made us put on our clothing without drying ourselves. This is what happens all night until twelve o'clock and at about three o'clock they awaken us again.

Today is Wednesday, last night I had to stop writing as they raised h--- with us all night long. We had a lot of fun but very little sleep. As I understand it our course is from three to five months. For two weeks we can't go out at all and after that we will get off Saturday night until 12 o'clock (if we pass everything and don't get any marks against us such as dirty rooms or shoes not shined). As to what we are going to study, I'm not sure yet but the last month we're here we will do a lot of flying so I can hardly wait until the last month does come.

We are in very new and beautiful four story brick buildings. Our rooms are swell, four men to a room, soft beds and everything that

59TH
COLLEGE TRAINING DETACHMENT

NORTH CAROLINA STATE
RALEIGH, N. C.

goes with it. The food is very good also with a quart of milk a day for every aviation student. I'm not in the same room with Bill and Howard but when they change us around, which will be soon, I hope to be with them.

I have a lot more to say but won't have time for maybe a week or so but will write at every opportunity. When things settle down here I will be able to write every night. I have sent one box and I'm sending another later. *—I love you, Raymond*

Tuesday, October 12th

My Dearest Ray,

This morning two cards arrived from you and I was very glad to receive them but disappointed because they weren't letters. They were postmarked August 30th & 31st. You say you'll send more cards later on, if you're so busy you can't write I'll be glad of the cards but try and write letters instead. Cards are too unsatisfactory and you can't say much on them. Please try and understand what I mean. Right now I shouldn't be writing to you, instead I should be practicing as I have to go for a lesson at 7:15. After that I have to go to Cheltenham Park. I haven't much time to explain why but I'll give you a rough idea and write more about it later. Florence McCullough who used to work in Inglis is having a party tomorrow night and she has invited 35 or 40 boys and girls in our office, me included. Ivy Frazer is going to sing at the party, Maureen is going to recite, Victor is going to play swing music on the piano and a few others are going to entertain in some way. Edna Buchannan made out a programme today and she put my name on it. I have to play several duets with Jean Story. Jean lives in Cheltenham Park and tonight I have to go there and practice the duets with her. It should be good fun, Ray, because we are all leaving the office together and going straight to Florence's house. A few don't work at Inglis but we are meeting them on the way. I may not have time to write tomorrow but if not I'll tell you all about the party on Thursday. —*Yours forever, Muriel*

Saturday, October 16th

My Dearest Ray,

Yesterday I received 3 letters from you, they are dated the 30th of August and the 8th & 29th of September. The one dated the 30th of August took 6 weeks & 3 days to reach here.

I didn't write on Wednesday or Thursday because on Wednesday night I went to the party I was telling you about and on Thursday I had to practice extra long. Last night after my music lesson I started to write to you, I got seven pages written, but I'm not mailing it as it's all jumbled up. I don't know what's wrong with me, Ray, but lately I can't settle to do anything. I can't even put my mind in my music.

Last week I received an invitation card to a dance in the Red Cross, also a letter telling me if wasn't going I was to call and let Miss Laverack know before Wednesday night. The dance was held on Thursday night by the American baseball players stationed in Northern Ireland. As I was going to the party on Wednesday night and had to practice extra long on Thursday I called at the Red Cross during the lunch hour on Wednesday and told Miss Laverack I wasn't going. She said she was sorry I couldn't go, also that the dance was going to be very good. On the back of my invitation card was written table 22. I asked why that was and she told me that every girl who went had to sit at whatever table was written on her card. The boys also had cards and had to do the same. That meant if their table numbers were alike they had to dance together all night. She told me she had arranged for me to be Captain DiDaggio's partner. She said, "Would you not come, Muriel, Captain DiDaggio is very nice, he's Spanish and there's going to be a stage show." I said no, I couldn't go and she said she was very sorry as she had arranged for the nicest girls to be the officers' partners, and she thought I would be a very suitable partner for the Captain. That didn't tempt me one bit Ray—I wasn't the least bit anxious to meet Captain DiDaggio. By the way, I'm not sure if I spelt the Captain's name correctly. All Thursday night while I was practicing I felt awful, Ray. I hadn't received any letters from you and to tell the truth I began thinking I should have gone to the dance and tried to enjoy myself.

The party on Wednesday night was a great success. We had entertainment and at intervals we played games such as forfeits, etc. You remember we played forfeits at Kathleen Bailey's house. I put my locket in the hat and each time it was picked out the crowd sang "Yankee Doodle Dandy" so that the Dreamer would know whose turn it was to do something, and make me do something extra silly. I won't tell you all I had to do but once I had to stand in the centre of the room and show everybody how far my suntan went. I told them it didn't go any further than my knees but they wouldn't believe me, and it all ended up with me running out of the room amid their laughter.

The party was held at a house in Moreland Avenue at Cliftonville and as that is a good distance past Bellevue we all had to leave in time to get the last tram home. There were about 40 of us so we all went upstairs in the tram and all the way home we sang at the top of our voices. A few strangers got in the tram, amongst them an American officer. For awhile they smiled at us and then they joined in the singing. It was really fun, Ray, and to make it even more so Edna borrowed a hat and everyone put a penny in it for the Red Cross. Yesterday a letter arrived at Inglis from Florence to say that the people next door overheard Ivy singing and the piano playing, they enjoyed it very much and wished it had lasted longer. Ivy sings for the E.N.S.A. (Entertainments National Service Association) she has a trained voice and it's really beautiful.

Now that I've told you all I've been doing I'll start answering your letter of 30th August. In it you say you hope I forgive you for not writing. I'm very sorry you didn't find time to write even a short letter to me, but so long as you were out having a good time with your cousin it doesn't matter. I'm very disappointed you didn't write for so long. I thought when you started training you wouldn't have time to go anywhere, but that's only one of the many things I don't understand about your letters. Maybe after your special leave you will write to me every day, I sincerely hope so.

I guess I'll have to end now as my tea is almost ready. After tea I have to practice and learn theory. I have your two other letters to answer but I'll have to wait until tomorrow.   —*Yours as always, Muriel*

Sunday, October 17th

My Dearest Muriel,

I haven't received any letters since I was in Greensboro but since I've been moved here a lot has happened. First, now don't get excited, but I'm writing this letter from the hospital, I'm here for a cold. I didn't want to go in but the doctor said it will only be for a few days, so here I am. I came in yesterday morning. I've had this cold and couldn't get rid of it so a few days here should fix me up OK. It's a good rest as they have been keeping us on the go since I've been here, honest, Muriel, I have not had a minute to myself, I haven't even written home. Here's a brief outline of what we do—up at 6:20, 7 to 8 breakfast, 8 to 12 classes, 12 to 1 lunch, 1 to 4 drill, 4 to 7 parade & retreat, 7 to 10 study and then to bed. We will get off Saturdays from 5 to 12 and Sundays from 4 to 11 if we have good marks and pass our inspections. Sundays we also have a big parade. For two weeks we can't leave the building at all. We will have about 1 hour to ourselves after dinner but after that have to be in to study. If I'm lucky I may get out once a week for a few hours. So you see, my love, I won't be going out much. We have 12 books and how we are going to keep up on our studies is beyond me. They call us Dodos and have been making it very hard for us from 7 to 12 every night. The other night at 12 o'clock we all had to fall out with just our shorts on, no shoes—some kids didn't have anything on, and stand in the cold for 15 minutes. I think that's why I have this cold. We had to polish the floors on our hands and knees and our clothing has to be just so. We have two inspections everyday and a million other things. From this letter you may think that I hate it but I really don't. I'm having lots of fun and besides after our two weeks are up we're not Dodos anymore and life will be normal and no more kidding around. As to the time I will be here I think about three or four month. After that we will probably go to Nashville for classification as pilot, navigator, or bombardier, and then I'm not sure how long it will be, but not too long, I hope.

Muriel, I sent you two packages, when you receive them please let me know. Mother also sent you one and I hope you like them. If there is anything you want let me know and I'll try my best to get it for you.

I miss you more than ever—I've been thinking of you quite a bit, of all the good times we had and I keep wondering how long before we will be having them again. You should have put your foot down and not let me leave, not that I don't like being in the Air Corps, but I miss you so much more. But someday I'll have what I've always wanted (to be a pilot) and you also so maybe I shouldn't be so blue about the whole thing.

I hope I receive some of your letters soon as they will cheer me up quite a bit. —*Forever yours, Raymond*

Sunday, October 17th

My Dearest Ray,

Yesterday I answered your letter of the 30th August and now I'm going to answer the ones of the 8th & 9th September. So you're going to be moved to school and will be there for 5 or 6 months. That's bad news, Ray, I was hoping you would be back here at Christmas or shortly after, but now it doesn't seem like you'll be back until the summer or autumn of next year. There are a lot of things I don't understand, if you are going to be an instructor you'll have to stay in America (I found that out) and yet you say you'll be back soon. Please try and tell me more about it, Ray, I'm all confused.

I agree with you about the censors, they are a pain in the neck, some of your letters have been censored 2 and 3 times, but I did receive one which wasn't censored at all. Fancy your letter of the 30th August taking 6 weeks & 3 days to reach here. By the way, have you received the disc yet? I hope it reaches you safely and isn't lost on the way. The girl in the Post Office said I was taking a chance mailing it while the war is on.

So your mother and father celebrated their 32nd wedding anniversary, boy, I wish I could see into the future and know all that's going to happen before we are celebrating our 32nd anniversary.

I haven't seen Hazel since last Sunday, she may call this afternoon but I'm not sure. As regards when she and Louis are getting married, I don't know. Louis is coming over in November and they'll probably settle it then.

As I wasn't out last night and don't feel like staying home now, I think I'll call for Marie Neill at about 3:15 and go down to the Red Cross with her. Tonight I have to stay home and learn theory so I may as well go out this afternoon.   —*Forever yours, Muriel*

Monday, October 18th

My Dearest Ray,

Yesterday afternoon I called for Marie Neill and we went to the Red Cross. There was a very big crowd there and about twice as many boys as girls. The dance was quite good but as usual I was missing you and couldn't enjoy myself. The Red Cross is beginning to have lots of dances through the week now and if you were here we could be having a wonderful time.

After my theory lesson tonight I have to practice scales as I'm going for a music lesson tomorrow night. Honest, Ray, I've so much to learn and practice I don't know how I'm going to do it. Sometimes I almost decide to wait and try for the diploma next June instead of Christmas.   —*Forever yours, Muriel*

Tuesday, October 19th

My Dearest Muriel,

Today I'm very happy as I received three of your letters dated September 15th 19th & 20th. Before I start I want to tell you I'm out of the hospital. They let me out yesterday afternoon and as I don't have to drill for two days I have the afternoon off. We started classes this morning and boy are they hard. We go to school six days a week from 8 until 12. In the afternoons we drill until about four, then supper and retreat. When it's all over it's about 6:30 and at 7:30 we have to be in our rooms to study. On Saturday if our marks are passing and our inspections for the week are good we will be allowed out from 5 o'clock until 12. Sunday morning there is an inspection, at 2:30 a big parade and then dinner. If everything is OK we can go out until eleven, that word IF means a lot.

Muriel, the mail, as you know, is something I have no control over. I'm sorry to hear it's been so long since you've had a letter and I know how you must feel but it's just one of those things we can't do anything about.

About the music, you know how much I want you to continue your lessons but I don't want you to kill yourself staying in every night and forcing yourself to get through it. If you see it's too hard for you, don't do it.

Muriel, I understand how you feel about going out but I think if you did go out once in awhile it would be better for you and keep your mind a little off me. Now don't take me wrong, it's just that you're young and should have a good time and you can and still not have dates. If there is a dance now and then I don't mind if you do go.

In some of your letters you make me realize how much I have hurt you since I left you, if I had known it was going to be this bad for both of us I never would have left. I could kick myself sometimes, but then if I didn't join the Air Corps, all my life I would have wished that I had.

I tried to stop myself many times but just couldn't. I hope you understand how I feel, maybe someday you will. I will do everything in my power to make you stop worrying, so please take it easy on me, after all there's a war on and I have to take what's coming just like the rest of the boys. I only hope I can make up for all the unhappiness I have caused you.

I see where there must be more troops in Ireland by the sound of your letters. Remember how few soldiers there were before I left? My sister Jo's husband is in England, somewhere around Bristol I think. When they hear from him I'll let you know.

I'm sorry to hear about Lily's brother but I really wish you wouldn't go over too often. I know I shouldn't say this but it's dangerous for you so please try not to.

I see that at the dances they're still bothering you for dates, can't they see that big ring and know enough not to ask you? I can't blame them but if I was there I would really get mad, but then it wouldn't be happening if I were with you.

As I have to get ready for a parade I'll stop writing now. Please don't worry because it worries me. Give my regards to everyone. — *Forever yours, Raymond*

Tuesday, October 19th

My Dearest Ray,

Today has been a typical winter's day, very cold and wet. Nothing worth talking about and I didn't even receive a letter from you. I sincerely hope that now you are settled you're writing every day. I just arrived back from my music lesson, it's now about 8:30 p.m. and when I finish writing I'm going to wash my hair and then do some practice. What a dull time I'm having.

The crowd in the office still kid me and keep asking how you are. They ask in such a nice way now I hate to tell them to mind their own business. Once I told one of the boys that and he said, "What's wrong? I only asked you a civil question, has he left you after all?" You see it gave him the impression something was wrong to make me talk like that. All the girls say they are going to be at the church to see us getting married and they tease me a great deal. Now I think they are beginning to realize you are coming back to marry me. —*Yours forever, Muriel*

Wednesday, October 20th

My Dearest Muriel,

Tonight I have been studying since seven o'clock—it's now 9:30 so I'll write as much as possible until the lights go out.

Boy, with all the work I've had I haven't had a minute to myself. These are some of the subjects I have....Basic Mathematics for Pilots, College English, European History, College Geography, Physics, First Aid, Speech, Civil Air Regulations, Trigonometry, and Logistics. We haven't much time to study but I'll do my best.

I received a letter from Mother today and she said she sent you another package, I hope you receive it. I'm sorry to hear that you haven't received all my other letters—I hope they haven't been lost.

I'm sorry to hear that Louis is in the hospital and hope he's much better. As to the hospital moving, it may be true but I doubt it. From Luke's letter he said there's no such chance.

I'm sorry to hear that John died but maybe it's for the best, after all he was very sick and really there wasn't any chance of him ever being well even if he did live. Give Lily my regards and tell her I'm very sorry.

I have to stop for now as the lights are going out. —*Loving you more each day, Raymond*

Wednesday, October 20th

My Dearest Ray,

It's about 10:45 p.m. Mommy and Daddy have just gone to bed, before they went they told me to hurry and come to bed too, but I wanted to write a few lines to you before I do so.

All night I've been busy practicing theory and honestly, I'm going crazy. I didn't receive any letters from you today again and there's no need to tell you how disappointed I am. Tonight when I was in the sitting room learning some theory I overheard "As Time Goes By" on the wireless and honestly, Ray, I felt so awful I cried. If only your letters would come more often I wouldn't feel so bad. I'm sorry this letter is so short but there isn't anything to tell you and I must get to bed. —*Forever yours, Muriel*

Thursday, October 21st

My Dearest Muriel,

It's just about 8 o'clock now and after drills and the parade we received some more clothing and just got back. We now have two hours to do our homework and clean up for tomorrow's inspection. I'm so tired right now I can hardly keep awake, I think I'll take a nice cold shower, maybe that will help. My body is sore as h--- every muscle in my body hurts. They're either going to make a real man out of me or kill me trying (just kidding). Tomorrow I have to get my hair cut down to ½ inch, I hate to do that but it's orders and I have to. I'm throwing my comb away as I won't need it.

I'm sending you a drawing of the layout of the school so you can see all the walking I have to do. Our barracks are really swell, the food is very good—a quart of milk and ice cream every day, but with all the marching and drills we need it.

There's not much more to say so I think I better close now and start my studies. —*Always loving you, Raymond*

Thursday, October 21st

My Dearest Ray,

I'm just after having tea and want to write to you now because I have to practice for 4 to 5 hours tonight and won't have time later. Adeline coaxed me to go to the Red Cross with her tonight but I had to say no and told her to go by herself. She said she wouldn't like to go alone so I have promised to meet her after my music lesson tomorrow night and go with her then.

It's about 6:20 p.m. now and it's almost dark already, the nights certainly are getting longer. Today again I was very disappointed, no letters came. Right now there isn't anything to tell you, all is quiet at home and in the office. —*Forever yours, Muriel*

Saturday, October 23rd

My Dearest Muriel,

It's Saturday afternoon and I have a few minutes to do a little writing. Last night I didn't write as I had too much work, I had to write two English compositions and do some math problems. At 9:30 to

10:00 we had to polish all the brass here for this morning's inspection, which as far as I know we passed. I hear they have a dance in town tonight but I'm not sure if Bill, Howard and I are going.

I told you I had to get my hair cut to ½ inch, boy what a haircut—you wouldn't know me.

Everything is just about the same here only they have stopped treating us like Dodos and we don't have to put up with the horseplay, thank goodness. There's going to be a mail call in a few minutes so I'll stop now and continue this later.

At mail call there was no mail from you but as I have a few minutes I'll continue this letter. Tonight I have quite a few things to buy in town. I also have to take my shoes in (civilian) and have them fixed. I have to buy stamps and leave some clothing off at the tailors, so until about eight or nine I will be shopping for myself.

They say we first have to learn how to be gentlemen before we become officers but I think I'll be a sissy before they get through with me, if they keep this up. We have to start wearing garters, those things that hold up your socks. I never have worn them in all my life but it's an order so I'll have to wear them. I'm buying them tonight in town.

I was going to mail this now but just found out I haven't any stamps so I'll keep it until tomorrow and then mail it. (*Stop*)

Sunday, October 24ᵗʰ

My Dearest Muriel,

I had to stop short yesterday as we had to fall out in the hall for an announcement and I was unable to finish this letter. Last night Bill, Howard and I went to town. I tried to buy some garters and went to over a dozen stores and none of them had any. Orders are we have to start wearing them by Monday and here I am without them.

At about nine o'clock we didn't know what to do as the shows in town were not so good. We finally went to a dance, it was as all the dances go and I couldn't enjoy myself as I was thinking of you and wishing I were there with you. Anyway, I had two dances and at about 10:30 Bill and I left, Howard stayed till the dance was over at 11:30. The girls came in buses and had chaperones with them. After the dance they got back on the buses and were taken home so you see there's not even a chance for anyone to get a date. I'm telling you this just so you won't get any ideas and if and when I do go again you won't have to worry.

This morning we had an inspection and after it was over Bill, Howard and I went to church. As I walked in the first thing I thought of was you and of how wonderful it would be if we were walking in together. It's getting so that now I start laughing to myself and sometimes talk to myself when I'm thinking of you. —*I love you, Raymond*

PS I'm sending you this patch we wear on our right arm 4" above the cuff. It's for Aviation Cadets—I hope you like it.

Saturday, October 23rd

My Dearest Ray,

As I begin writing this letter I am in the house alone, Mommy and Daddy have gone to the plot and Audrey and Olive are at the pictures. All this week I didn't receive a letter from you and you'll never know how disappointed I am. Last night when I came home from the office I was feeling so blue with not hearing from you I didn't write and instead I wrote an application to a firm in Lisburn. It's a government firm and I heard they were needing office staff. Anyhow, I wrote giving details of my experience so I'll probably hear from them sometime next week. Right now I'm wondering if I did the right thing, you see if my application is successful I'll have to get up very early in the morning to catch the 7:45 or 8:00 train, besides I won't get home again until 6 o'clock. I may have to work late several nights in the week and perhaps on Sundays. However, I heard the pay is very good and if I take the job it will enable me to save quite a lot of money for my trousseau, also for our home when we are married. Perhaps when the time comes Mommy and Daddy won't see me stuck but the way things are I want to buy everything myself. You know what I mean (with Mommy being against us getting married). She hasn't said anything lately and I think when you come back she'll change her mind. Mommy is like that, several times she has tried to stop me from doing something and in the end she has let me go and please myself. For example, when I first started going to dances she was mad and promised all kinds of punishment if she found I went again. However, I insisted on going and now she even encourages me to go.

After I wrote the application and was getting ready to meet Adeline in town to go to the Red Cross, I noticed Daddy trying to fix his cigarette lighter. I asked him if he wanted some fluid as I had some. He said he didn't need any fluid, the lighter wasn't working properly and he wished he had one he could depend on. Then he said, "Muriel, is your cigarette lighter still working?" I said, "Yes," and he said, "I wish I had it, you might give it to me, I never can find a decent one." For about 10 minutes after that I didn't speak, Ray, I didn't want to part with the lighter because you gave it to me and I'd had it and cherished it since before you went away at Christmas. Some of the boys at the office coaxed me to sell it to them and I told them I wouldn't part with it for all the money in the world. Anyhow, I thought and I thought and then I took the lighter out of my handbag, put some fluid in it and gave it to Daddy. When I gave it to him he was delighted and I told him never to lose or part with it as you had given it to me and I'd had it a long time. I hope you don't mind, Ray, you see I just thought of how good and understanding Daddy is about us and that's why I gave it to him. I never would have let anyone else have it. He is really pleased about it, today at dinnertime he said to me, "That's a great wee lighter, Muriel." I was really sorry to part with it, Ray, but now I'm glad I gave it to Daddy and I hope you don't mind, I'm sure you don't.

After that Marie Neill called and we both went into town to meet Adeline. When we arrived at the Red Cross it was absolutely crowded, most of the boys were absolute strangers and I heard that --------------------
-------------------------------------*censored*--
----------- The band was an American Naval band and it was really good, the best I've heard since the Ambassadors of Swing went away. Joe and his pals were there and one of them (Benny is his name) danced and talked to me all evening. I introduced him to Adeline and she was very amused at him. Between the dances he sat and talked to us and honestly, Ray, we almost died laughing at the funny things he said. Deep down I was miserable because you weren't with me but in a way I enjoyed myself. At 10:30 I noticed Joe and Marie leaving so I said "Cheerio" to Benny and went home with them. All the way home Joe lectured me, he said I should have let Benny leave me home. I asked him why, and also told him I never let anyone walk home with me and this is what he said. "Benny is a good clean decent fellow, he may kid a lot

in the dances but he's a pal of mine and I know if he walked you home or took you to a show he'd say goodnight like a gentleman and wouldn't try to kiss you. I told Benny you were engaged and unlike most women you are keeping true to the boy you're engaged to. He said he knew as you had refused several times to walk home or go out with him, also he knew you were a good, intelligent and very nice girl and he couldn't see what harm there would be in you going out with him on friendly terms. After all, Marie and I go out and there's nothing to it, we're just pals, that's all." Joe also accused me of being afraid of Benny. I told him I wasn't afraid of anybody, that I had my own ideas and was sticking to them. Also, if Benny wanted to dance with me anytime I was at the Red Cross I wouldn't refuse, but that was all, I didn't want to go out with him or with anyone else who would ask me. Joe didn't seem too pleased and his reply was, "I never could understand you Irish girls."

That's how it is with me, Ray, I love and think so much of you I can't and never will go out, even on friendly terms with anyone else. Besides, I know how I would feel if you took a girl out, if you did I doubt you would tell me but don't ever go out with girls, Ray. Some people here try to make me believe you will and it hurts, but I'm trusting you with all my heart.   —*Forever yours, Muriel*

Sunday, October 24th

My Dearest Ray,

Last night I practiced until 8:45, then I got fed up and went down to the Red Cross. When I got there I met Marie Neill in the cloakroom. She had had a row with Joe and was getting ready to go home with him. When I arrived in the dance I was immediately sorry I had gone because the place was absolutely packed, there wasn't room to walk let alone dance. Thousands of new boys have landed here and the town is full of them. A girl can hardly walk or go to a dance in peace anymore. Such a pack of wolves this new crowd is, they aren't half as nice or decent looking as the first Americans to arrive here. Anyhow, when I pushed my way through the mob and reached the place where I usually sit I met Lily. She told me she was absolutely fed up and the Red Cross wasn't anything like it used to be. It isn't really, Ray, some of the boys are quite nice but the majority of them don't look or speak like gentlemen. It's considered rude over here to refuse to dance when someone asks you—at that rate I must be very rude because I have refused a lot of dances. I only stayed in the dance about half an hour. I had two dances and then told Lily I was going home. She had the same notion so we left together. Coming up Chichester Street and round by the City Hall it was awful, Ray, fellows tried to stop us and walked up beside us and was I mad. When two fellows tried to get us to talk I turned to Lily and said, "This town is becoming worse, now decent girls can't walk in peace because of the scum on the streets." After that they left us alone and we called in the Blue Bird Café for supper. You remember the day we were walking along the Lagan Banks and we met Mr. Graham, the man who works in the Time Office in Inglis and who used to hear me talking to you on the phone—well, he was in the café and he stopped to talk to me on his way out. He was quite ill for awhile and hasn't been working for weeks. He asked about you, also where you were. I told him you were in America undergoing training and he said, "No wonder you are looking so forlorn, can't you find a good substitute while he's away?" "No," I said, "No one will ever substitute for Ray." "I don't blame you," he said, "Ray seems a nice fellow and you looked very well together the day I saw you along the Lagan." He left then saying he was starting work again on Monday and would see me at the office.

That's how it is, Ray, everybody asks me about my boyfriend, even girls I hardly know in the Red Cross. Sometimes when I'm combing my hair in the cloakroom a girl standing beside me will turn around and say, "You've been coming here a long time now. I see you are engaged, are you engaged to the dark haired boy I used to see you with all the time?" Then they ask how you are and when we're getting married, also they want to know if you've been sent away and why they never see us together now. It really surprises me why so many people are interested in us. I guess they noticed us going about together so long and now I'm always alone.

Today I called to see Hazel and stayed and talked about an hour. Louis is coming on leave the 3rd November. I hope I don't see him because it would probably make me miss you all the more.

I must stop writing now, have supper and get to bed.   —*Forever yours, Muriel*

PS Have you heard the songs "You'll Never Know How Much I Miss You" also "Silver Wings in the Moonlight?" They are very popular here.

Monday, October 25th

My Dearest Muriel,

It's Monday night and all is well, there's not much to say as I haven't received a letter from you in the past few days.

Last night our outfit put on a show in town. We all went to see it and I never laughed so much in all my life. The boys dressed up as girls and they put on a dance, love scene and a play. After the show we stopped in and had something to eat (steak) and then came back to camp.

This afternoon we had drill and exercise for four hours and honest, my love, I'm so sore and tired I can hardly write this letter.

Next Saturday I'm on guard duty for 24 hours so if I get out Sunday night I'll be lucky.

Just about now I would love a Coke but we can't leave our rooms after 7:30. After dinner and retreat (parade) it's 6:30 or 7 o'clock and all we have is ½ hour to do as we please, but we can't leave the grounds. Bill and Howard are on the same floor as I am and it goes for 2 or 3 days sometimes before I see them or have a minute to talk to them.

Today has been very damp and raining and all I can think of is you and all the times we got caught in the rain and how I would kick about it. I have to stop now, Muriel, as the lights are going out, I will continue with this tomorrow. —*I love you forever, Raymond*

Monday, October 25th

My Dearest Ray,

I just got home about half an hour ago thinking there would be some letters from you but there weren't any. What can be wrong, Ray, surely all your letters aren't going to take 5 or 6 weeks to reach here.

When I left the office and came home for lunch today there was a letter awaiting me. You remember I told you I had applied for a job in a government firm outside Lisburn, well, the letter I received was asking me to go for an interview at 3:30 this afternoon. I didn't know what to do Ray, you see as this is stock-taking week in Inglis we are very busy and I knew if I took the afternoon off I'd get into trouble and maybe be dismissed. Besides, I began wondering if my interview would be successful, also if I'd like working there. I asked Mommy what I should do and she said, "Please yourself, Muriel, if you do get the job and are prepared to get up early in the mornings to catch the train, by all means go for the interview. On the other hand if you don't get the job and are dismissed from Inglis for staying off you won't have any job to go to." Anyhow, I sat and thought for so long I discovered it was 2:15 and too late to go back to Inglis so instead I got ready and went to the station to catch a train to Lisburn. I got to the station about 2:45 and as the train wasn't due to pull out until 3:15 I had to sit in the carriage for quite awhile. The station was full of new

American troops and the train along side of the one I was in was packed with them. They were all eating cookies and drinking what must have been coffee. In the carriage opposite the one I was in they must have had a gramophone because I could hear swing music being played. It was really funny, Ray, the fellows began waving and shouting at me and a lady and gentleman in my carriage were very amused at them. At first I took no notice and didn't even smile, then they began shouting, "What's your telephone number," and I couldn't help being amused at them. When my train pulled out they were still shouting and I had to laugh. I hope you don't shout at strange girls in railway stations, or anyplace else for that matter. If I thought you did I would *murder* you.

Anyhow, when I arrived at Lisburn I couldn't get a bus to the place I was going. (I can't tell you the name of the firm because of the censors. You see it's a government firm which has been moved from Belfast for safety in case of raids.) They have special buses to take the workers there in the mornings but none throughout the day. I had to inquire which direction to go, and boy, what a walk uphill, I thought I'd never reach there. Walking quickly it took me about 25 minutes and I didn't reach my destination until about 4:15 p.m.

To cut a long story short I was interviewed by two men, they asked me all kinds of questions and I answered them all. It's very difficult to explain the rest, it seems there will be several vacancies in a few weeks time and they will let me know when to start working there. At the end of the interview I asked them point blank if they were satisfied with me and they told me to rest assured I would be notified as soon as a vacancy occurred and that would be in 2 to 4 weeks time. Now I'm wondering if I'll take a job there, the work may be more difficult than what I'm doing at present and what is more I'll have to work overtime quite often. However, I have a few weeks to decide if I'll take it. Maybe I should, there's a war on and lots of people are working extra hard and earning more money. *—Forever yours, Muriel*

Tuesday, October 26th

My Dearest Muriel,

Here it is Tuesday night with not much to say or anything new. I was expecting a letter from home and hoping for a letter from you but I didn't get either.

Boy, do I wish I'd stayed where I was, with you. I know when I'm through I'll have what I've always wanted but it's a lot of hard work and sometimes I wonder if it's all worth it. I know I feel like this now but when it's all over I'll be glad, if it wasn't that I miss you so much it would be OK. My studies are coming along fine—it's not too hard if you study every night as I do. They are teaching us quite fast but it has to be done as there isn't much time. I expect to start flying right after Christmas. I found out today we don't get any furlough so I guess I'll be here and not at home again this Christmas. Take care of yourself and give my regards to all at home. —*I adore you, Raymond*

Wednesday, October 27th

My Dearest Ray,

Yesterday and today again I have been greatly disappointed as well as worried, no letters. It's now over 6 weeks since you wrote the last one I received and I can't understand why. ---
--------------------------------*censored*--

-- from them
and this is what it says.

Dear Madam,

With reference to our interview on Monday we wish to confirm your appointment on the staff of this company and should be glad if you will report to Mr. McConkey, Cost Office, Altona, on Monday 8th November at 8:45 a.m.

Please bring your Identity Card with you. This letter will gain you admittance to the works.

What do you think of that, Ray, I received word from them much sooner than I expected. I haven't given my notice in Inglis yet, but I'm going to take the job. I'll have to work overtime several nights in the week and perhaps Sundays now and then, but it's worth it. The wages are much better than I receive in Inglis and I'll be able to save quite a lot of money.

Peggy and another girl from Inglis are already there and they like it. When I went in the office this morning and told the girls I was leaving they could hardly believe it. Some of them have decided to apply for a job in the firm I am going to. They say when I go all the fun will be gone too, also, I haven't to forget to let them know when you and I are getting married, they don't want to miss seeing the wedding. By the way, last night Daddy asked me how you are and he sends his regards. He really likes you, Ray, and I know he's all for us. Mommy may sound like she's against us now, but I think when the time comes she'll be all right.

And now to tell you something which I hate to tell you, but I'm hoping you don't mind too much. When I went to music last night I told Mae Brown all about my new job, also I wouldn't have time to practice so much. I expected she would get mad but she didn't, she just said it would be a pity not to accept the job seeing it was much better than the one I had. She said the next Diploma Examination would be in April and I could practice gradually and go for it then.

I really hope you don't mind, Ray, it just can't be helped and you know how much I want to get away from Inglis. Fred and Maureen are ill and haven't been to the office for 2 days now. Yvonne and I have been doing their work along with our own and we're so busy we haven't time to lift our heads. Mr. Johnston came over today and told us we may have to work Saturday afternoon.

We wouldn't mind so much, Ray, if they would pay us, but Inglis never pay when the office staff works overtime. They tell us we can have a half day off sometime, but when we take a half day off we have to work extra hard the day before and after to keep the books up to date.

I almost forgot to tell you, I went to the Apollo last night after my music lesson to see a picture named "You Can't Escape Forever."
—*Forever yours, Muriel*

Thursday, October 28th

My Dearest Muriel,

I received a letter from Mother today but no mail in it from you—she said it has been quite awhile since she last received any.

Last night I didn't write as I had too much work to do and really there's nothing to say, everything here is the same—classes in the morning and drill in the afternoon. We did go swimming this afternoon for an hour but that's about the only thing different here.

Mother didn't have much to say, only that my cousin Kenneth and his wife had a baby boy. Kenneth is a Marine, he just arrived in Hawaii a month ago and wasn't there to see the baby. My Uncle Ed, a captain in the Armored Division, is still in Sicily and having a hard time. I guess the living conditions there are not so good. Remember my cousin that was in Greensboro with me, well he's in Maryland now, only 7 hours from home. Stan, my sister Jo's husband, is in England stationed near where I was.

My studies are coming along very well—I'm surprising myself with the high marks I'm receiving. I'm liking this place better as each day goes by. I don't like staying in every night but I'll get used to that.

How is everything with you, Muriel, I wish you would have some pictures taken and send them to me. Have you seen Marie yet, and when are she and Luke getting married? How about Hazel and Louis, is everything OK?   *—I adore you, Raymond*

Friday, October 29th

My Dearest Ray,

This morning I was glad to receive a letter-card which you bought in NC and has *Greetings from down in Dixie* printed on the front, it was postmarked September 16th. It took over 6 weeks to reach here and if my letters are taking that length of time before reaching you now that I'm sending them ordinary mail, please let me know and I will send them by airmail again. For quite awhile now I have been mailing my letters to you at your Greensboro address and I'm sure you are not there now. However, I'll just keep mailing them there until I receive your permanent address.

In the office yesterday afternoon Yvonne invited me to her house, so about 7:30 I left our house and went to visit her. Most of the evening she made me play the piano, she had some nice pieces and I tried sight-reading them. About 10:55 I left Yvonne's house and got a tram home.

As we have to give a week's notice before leaving Inglis I had to tell Mr. Johnston today and boy, did the crowd in the office make fun of me. I told them I wasn't going to tell Mr. Johnston until they left to go home at 5 o'clock and would you believe it, Ray, they wouldn't go home. They said they were going to stay in the cloakroom and watch me talking to him—also they wanted to know what he would say. Anyhow, when 5 o'clock came they all congregated in the cloakroom and started teasing me. Every time I went to go in the office they began laughing and made me laugh and I had to turn back. Then they promised they wouldn't laugh and I walked into the office and down the room. Once I looked back and I was sorry afterwards because I took another fit of laughing. The cloakroom door was open and all their faces were peering after me. Anyway, to cut a long story short, I told Mr. Johnston I was leaving and wanted to stop working there next Friday. He said he was very sorry to lose me, asked me when I was starting my new job and when I told him Monday 8th of November he asked me not to leave until Saturday. By the way, Ray, the other job I've got is only a wartime job whereas Inglis is permanent. Mr. Johnston remarked that, then he added, "In a way I don't blame you for taking this other job, it's only for the duration but you're getting married after the war so it doesn't matter, and the wages will be better than they pay here."

After I left Mr. Johnston the girls were all eager to hear what he said. I told them he said he was sorry I was leaving and they all kidded me by saying, "I bet it was the greatest relief of the man's life and he was just being polite." In a way I'm really sorry to leave Inglis, Ray. I've been working there about 2 years and in that time I've had a lot of fun with the crowd. If I don't like this place I'm going to maybe I'll go to Lockheed Overseas or someplace else. —*Forever yours, Muriel*

Saturday, October 30th

My Dearest Muriel,

It's about 7:30 and I have just gotten off guard duty, I have to go back at eleven o'clock tonight. Today I called Mother up as on Sunday the telephone lines are very busy and sometimes you have to wait hours before the call gets through. She told me she has just mailed me some letters of yours so I hope I receive them tomorrow. She asked me how you were and sends her regards.

She'd like me to call every week but I told her I don't have the time. It's almost impossible to get to the phones after supper and during the day we can't make phone calls, so there you are.

Dad was working so I couldn't talk to him.

Last night I didn't write as I had a lot of work to do. I was going to write after I got through with my studies but it ended up I didn't even get through.

It's getting so I'm always writing fast and always in a hurry. All day long we're on the move and in class you have to write down all your notes as fast as possible, then when I start writing letters I do the same. It's a wonder you can make out what I say with this awful writing. —*I love you, Raymond*

HEADQUARTERS
59TH COLLEGE TRAINING DETACHMENT
(AIRCREW)

North Carolina State College

P. O. Box 5366, Raleigh, N. C.

October 25, 1943.

Aviation Students,
59th College Training Detachment,
N. C. State College of Agriculture and Engineering,
Raleigh, North Carolina.

Gentlemen:

May I take this opportunity to welcome you to the Army Air Forces 59th College Training Detachment and to the campus of North Carolina State College of Agriculture and Engineering, Raleigh, North Carolina. Upon your arrival you have attained the status of Aviation Students. The Army Air Forces have chosen you gentlemen for your ability and interest in flying. You have arrived upon the threshold of becoming a pilot, bombardier, or navigator in the best Army Air Force in the world.

We of the 59th are very proud of our organization. We will endeavor to instill in you the same belief that we now have. We trust when you depart from the 59th that your conduct, your attitude, and your appearance will be so superior that you will be marked at once in any training or at any task that you will undertake as a man who has received his training at the Army Air Forces 59th College Training Detachment.

I trust that each of you will receive the classification that you so desire. I am confident that each of you will be the best in whatever you choose. Take every opportunity that is afforded you to learn, and continue to learn your jobs, because it's upon men like you that the speedy conclusion of the present conflict to preserve the American way of life depends.

Good luck to all of you.

Carl M. Adams

Major, Air Corps,
Commanding.

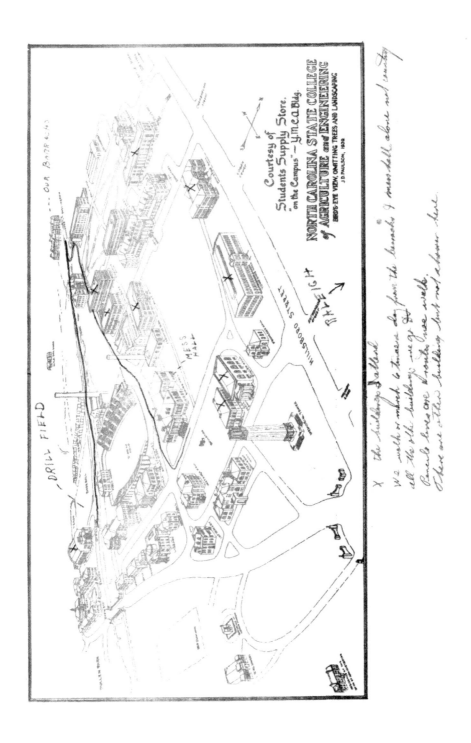

Five months of college training was the standard requirement for aviation students.

November 1943

Monday, November 1st

My Dearest Muriel,

I received three letters (24-28 Sept.) from you yesterday and was very glad to hear from you.

I will start with your first letter. As to your music, I told you long ago that if it was going to be too hard for you to drop it. I don't want you staying in every night going crazy with it so drop it if you can't do it, and go out and enjoy yourself. As to the dance at the Red Cross and the boy who wanted to leave you at the tram, well, if I say you should have let him you would say I didn't love you, but really, Muriel, as he said there's nothing wrong and it would be better to go with someone you know. If you want to let him walk you home I know I can trust you and never have to worry, so don't feel guilty or in the wrong. Maybe if you did go out a little more you wouldn't be so cross and blue, and write more cheerful letters to me. I'm longing for you also, Muriel, it's unbearable for me too. It's not roses living here, it's hard and a lot of work and sweat so if you think I'm having a picnic you're wrong. I know how much you want me back but have a heart, my love, I won't know until I arrive in Nashville, Tennessee in January or February if it will be a month or a year. At one time I wasn't happy where I was and when I joined the Air Corps I was, but I overlooked the most important thing in my life, and that was you. It was a mistake to leave you because I'm not happy now but try and help me along. I came home to be a pilot so I have to go through with it no matter how much it hurts me, there's a war on, Muriel, and I have to do my part. If I'm accepted I know you will be as proud of me as I will be of myself. I'm doing this because it's my job, Muriel, not everyone can be a pilot and they need them, so if I can help to bring this war to an end, I will.

My letters were written at home when I was on furlough, I put my camp address on them because I had to. As I told you after we got off the boat we were given ten days home, went to camp for eight days, then given another fifteen days because everyone coming from overseas is allowed fifteen to thirty days furlough. Why I want you to send the letters home is because I may move at any time without notice and with moving around your mail will get lost or be months late. Mother can send them to me, she doesn't mind at all.

The lights are going out so I will have to stop and continue tomorrow.

Tuesday, November 2nd

My Dearest Muriel,

It's about seven o'clock and we just got back from parade, tonight we won first prize, the first time since we've been here and boy, we all feel good.

So you finally got "As Time Goes By." I wish I was there to hear you play it.

Muriel, about Gloria, please go to Bangor and see her as soon as possible. Tell her to give you all the information she can as to how she got back—who, what and where, etc. so you'll know what to do in case I want you to come over here. Now don't get excited, it doesn't mean I'm not coming back, but just to be on the safe side in case I can't come back we'll know what to do.

Muriel, this music business has me worried. I don't want you staying in every darn night, it's not worth it. I didn't realize at the time it was so hard so please, if you can't go on with it I won't mind a bit.

I must stop now as I have some work to do. Give my regards to all at home and don't forget to see Gloria. See what she thinks of America and you can get an idea of how you're going to like it here. *—Forever yours, Raymond*

Monday, November 1st

My Dearest Ray,

Today I received your letter of the 26th September and Friday received the one you wrote September 16th. Before I answer your letters I want to tell you why I didn't write Sat. and Sun. On Saturday morning in the office I didn't feel well and at 12 o'clock I got permission to go home. I felt like I was taking the flu so I came home, took some Aspros and a hot drink and went to bed. About 7:45 Marie Neill called for me thinking I would go to the Red Cross with her. She told me the "Sad Sacks" band was celebrating their 1st anniversary and the dance should be good. I was in bed when she called and going to a dance was the last thing I wanted to do. After Marie left I fell asleep again and the next thing I knew it was about 10:30 p.m. and Mommy was coaxing me to take some supper she had brought up. I drank some tea but didn't eat anything. I lay awake until the early hours of the morning, then I did fall asleep and when I awakened it was about 12:30 Sunday. I felt much better, my headache was almost gone but nevertheless I stayed in bed. I was going to write to you but thought if I wrote while I was sick and not able to tell you I was quite better, you would worry needlessly. At 7:30 p.m. Marie called again to see if I was going to the Halloween Party at the Red Cross. She said Joe, her boyfriend, was waiting at the corner and he had insisted she should call and see if I was well enough to go. When Marie called I was still in bed and although I felt better I didn't feel quite well enough to go out. Even if I had wanted to go I couldn't have got up and started getting ready. It would have meant bringing Joe up to the house and then Mommy would have got suspicious and known where I was going, and you know how much she objects to me going to the Red Cross on Sundays. When Marie went away again I went downstairs for a few hours and sat before the fire listening to the wireless.

At 10:45 I went back to bed again and this morning I awakened feeling more like myself. I didn't arrive at the office until 9:30 but the boss didn't say a word, he knew I had been sick and besides I'm leaving next Saturday. All day I have felt wonderfully well and if you were here right now I'd make you take me to an all night dance.

That reminds me of one night in the Red Cross a few weeks ago. Joe and Marie were there and Benny, one of Joe's pals, began annoying me. He put his arm around me and began singing "You'd Be So Nice to Go Home With" instead of "You'd Be So Nice to Come Home With." He's real crazy, Ray, and sometimes I feel like killing him. Anyhow, I pushed him away and told him to go take a powder or drown himself. He still wouldn't go away and tried to kiss me on the cheek, that made me real mad and I hit him as hard as I could. "Boy, he said, "I heard the Irish could fight, what are you fed on you little Irish spitfire." I said, "Get down on your knees and say you are more sorry than you ever were in your whole life."

Would you believe it, Ray, the silly big fool got down on his knees in the dance and said it. It was really funny, Ray. Marie, Joe and a few of his other pals almost laughed their heads off. Maybe you will meet Benny when you come over, and when you do you'll have to laugh. He's almost 6'6" tall and is really nuts. I hate when he asks me to dance because I feel like a dwarf beside him. Once he asked me if I had any sisters who weren't engaged, I said, certainly, I have two and one is a very tall blond and she'd suit you nicely. I said that so seriously he really believed me and wanted to know where I lived. I said, "Never mind, she's joining the Red Cross very soon and when she does I'll introduce you." "Is she anything like you?" he said. "Not at all," said I, "When she's around no one notices me."

I'm very sorry to hear that you were sick again, Ray, darling, please look after yourself.

I'm sure I would love to see a football game on a field all lighted up and I'm holding you to your promise of taking me there when we are married.

I really must stop and practice as I have to go for a lesson tomorrow night.   —*Forever yours, Muriel*

Tuesday, November 2nd

My Dearest Ray,

Tonight I've got so much to write about I hardly know where to begin. This morning before I left for the office I received four letters from you and could hardly believe it. I need hardly tell you how wonderful I've felt since receiving them. All day long in the office I've laughed and been so happy that the girls began saying, "I bet she has had some letters from Ray, it must be wonderful to be in love like she is." I certainly did have fun and they're all saying they are going to miss me a great deal when I leave on Saturday. I'm almost beginning to regret taking this new job, I hope the girls in this other place are nice and friendly, I hate being with people who aren't.

Right now it is about 8:45 p.m., it's not long since I got home from my music lesson and Mommy is insisting I go to bed early since being sick at the weekend.

So you had to pile hay in the barn for Dot's horse, I wish I had been there to help. When I was in the country a few years ago I piled hay in the barn of the house I was staying at and I really had fun. I stood on the top of the hay and Victor, the farmer's son, forked it up to me and I piled it in place. While doing this the ladder I had climbed up on got lost under the hay and I couldn't get down. What a laugh— there I was away up high. Victor told me to slide down and he would catch me but I wouldn't. Instead I went over to the side and slid down into a pigsty and almost broke my neck. Gosh, but the pigs were surprised and was I dirty. I had to go and take a bath.

From your letter of September 24th, I see you are having to do a lot of drilling, etc. I'm glad to hear that as it will do you a world of good and with perseverance will take all your aches and pains away. (*Stop*)

Last night I didn't have time to finish this letter as Mommy called me for supper. It's about 5:30 p.m. Wednesday and I want to finish it now. Before I answer your other letters I want to tell you that yesterday I had one of mine returned. The censor sent it back with a slip enclosed telling me I wrote something I shouldn't have written. At lunchtime I inked part of the letter out and mailed it to you again, hoping you receive it this time.

So it was raining in Greensboro, just like in Ireland. It hasn't rained here today—in fact it has been quite nice and warm. I see you have been going around with your cousin Bob, is he wanting to be a pilot too?

I said hello to Yvonne for you, Ray, she is fine and we are just as friendly as ever. Only yesterday we got talking about the row we had and she told me the reason she was mad was because I came into the office and didn't talk to her as usual. Then after we had the row I began singing as if I didn't care, another thing, she threw sweets at me and I didn't eat them. I asked her why she didn't offer them to me the right way and she said she would have only she was afraid I would think she was trying to get friendly again. Also, she couldn't very well sit and eat them without offering me some, even though we weren't speaking.

Anyhow, she and I are pals again and she said she hoped I didn't write and tell you we had a row. When she said that I asked her what made her think I would tell you and she said, "Well, you write to him very often and if you didn't tell him everything that happens, you wouldn't have much to write about." Now I have her guessing because I didn't tell her whether I had told you.

You want to know if your letters to me are cut out by the censors—I think the only one cut out was the one you wrote on your way to America. Whenever I do receive any which are cut out by the censors, I'll let you know. Some of them aren't even opened at all.

Yesterday I received an invitation card to a dance in the Red Cross tonight and I think I'll go. Marie Neill just called at the door and now I'll have her for company. —*Forever yours, Muriel*

Thursday, November 4th

My Dearest Muriel,

I was very happy today as I received a letter from you, this one being the real Muriel I always knew. It's not blue and sad as some of your letters, especially the last one.

I didn't write last night as I was too busy with my work. Tonight I won't be able to answer your letter as we had a parade and after the parade had to see an army picture. We just got back and it is 9:30, at ten o'clock the lights go out so you can see I haven't much time. I'll have to stop now, Muriel, as I have a few things to do so I'll be ready in the morning. —*I love you, Raymond*

Thursday, November 4th

My Dearest Ray,

Tonight I have so much to write about I hardly know where to begin, but I'll try and begin where I left off last night. In your letter dated October 4th you say you're ashamed of yourself because you haven't written for a whole week, so well you may be ashamed, I'll try and forgive you this time but don't ever let it happen again. If you do I'll stop writing for a month and get my own back.

Fancy getting a three day pass and going with Bill and Howard to Raleigh to see some girls and pay your respects. What would you feel like if I told you I hadn't written to you because another two girls and I went to Dublin to see some boys we once knew? However, Ray, I'm not mad, I trust you and I'm very glad you told me the truth. If you had told me lies and I found out later I never could have trusted you again. By the way, remember the girl you went out with before you came over here, was she one of the girls you went to see? If not have you seen her since you went back? Please tell me, Ray, I'm just curious and I promise you I won't get mad. If you really love me you won't take other girls out or kiss them, so I'm loving and trusting you enough to believe you won't.

So Luke may be getting married this month, that's wonderful, Ray. Tonight on my way home from the office I phoned Marie but she wasn't home. Her mother told me that Luke is coming over on the 17th. I'll phone again tomorrow or Saturday.

Ray, darling, please don't feel so bad about leaving me to join the Air Corps. You can help me to feel better by writing everyday. Before long Christmas will be here and after that it shouldn't be so long until we are together again. I'm very happy to hear that you came through your tests way above average. Keep going like that and you'll be a great success.

Today for the first time in weeks I was talking to Hazel and this is how it came about. At lunch time today when Yvonne and I were walking home from the office Hazel was waiting at the corner of her street and could you guess why, it was a great surprise to me. She had a package for me and she said that Luke had sent it over. Louis arrived here yesterday on furlough and brought it with him. Hazel looked worried and not at all happy and I asked her if anything was wrong. She told me that Louis wasn't feeling well and she was worried about him. So far they haven't told her mother about his religion and I think she is worried about that too. Gosh, but I feel sorry for her. If and when I do find when they are getting married I'll write and tell you.

After I left Hazel and was walking home, all I did was wonder about the package—why would Luke send me a package, I kept saying to myself. When I got in the house and opened it I knew immediately that your mother had sent it to Luke to give to me. It really was very thoughtful of her to do what she did, such a lovely package. Tonight or Saturday I'm going to write and thank her and very soon I'll buy something to send her. I'm really delighted with all the things she bought me and I'll be even more so when I receive her letter, which I hope comes soon. —*Forever yours, Muriel*

Friday, November 5th

My Dearest Muriel,

When I got back to my room (I was at Camp Butner today getting my teeth fixed, it's about 30 miles from here) a letter was waiting for me from Mother. She told me she received a package from you but wouldn't tell me what was in it. She said they (the censors) had sent her a letter from New York City asking her if they could open it up for inspection, if not, they wouldn't send it to her, she said, yes. I guess she took a look to see what it was when it arrived, but she won't tell me. I think it is the disc, she said it was very nice and I didn't deserve it...how do you like that! I'm going to have your name and address put on the other side just as soon as I receive it.

I explained in my other letter why I was sent home again. After arriving from overseas everyone is allowed a 15 to 30 days leave. I had only ten days so they gave me and the others another fifteen after we arrived in Greensboro.

Muriel, about sending you anything, well, if you won't tell me I'll send you what I think you will like, so you can't get out of that one. —*Loving you forever, Raymond*

Friday, November 5th

My Dearest Ray,

When I came home from the office I practiced until 7 o'clock and then went for a music lesson. I'll have to hurry and get this letter written as I have to wash my hair and sew some hooks on a new dress I got.

Nothing much has happened today except that I had my fortune told for fun. The woman who told it to me said I had a very bright and happy future ahead of me, also I was getting another ring very soon and would have my greatest wish fulfilled inside a nine, probably nine months. She also said that I would be working at a new job inside a four.

Isn't that funny, Ray, I'm starting work at this other firm on Monday and that's inside four days. She also told me a lot of other things which are quite true and surprised me very much, however, I don't believe in fortune tellers, I'm superstitious, but not that much.

Lots of Americans have been getting married here lately. Only to-day I heard that a girl I knew got married to a technician recently.

As yet I haven't had time to write to your mother and thank her for the lovely package she sent, but I'll write tomorrow afternoon. She's really a darling, Ray, she sent me make-up and a lovely pair of silk stockings. Since the war it's impossible to get them here and I really appreciate her sending them to me. —*Forever yours, Muriel*

Sunday, November 7th

My Dearest Muriel,

They just had mail call and I received your letters of the 3rd and 7th of October. I just finished reading them and I don't know how to answer them. First, about the mail, I only wish I knew what has happened to all of my letters that I have sent you. If there was something I could do I would, but I can't. All I know is that I mail the letters—they are getting lost or going down on the boats. Keep the date of every letter I write and the day you receive it.

Last night Bill and I went to the show as Howard had a date, after the show we went over to see Howard as he was at a dance here. It's the same dance I told you about before. The girls come in and leave on buses.

I'll have to stop writing now, Muriel, it's almost parade time. After the parade I'm going into town with Bill and Howard for awhile and see "Sweet Rosie O'Grady." —*Forever yours, Raymond.*

Sunday, November 7th

My Dearest Ray,

Such a lot has happened since I last wrote to you I hardly know where to begin.

Yesterday at 12:45 I stopped working in Inglis. It was sad saying goodbye to the crowd there but I'm not to be separated from them altogether, I've arranged to go to the show with some of them now and then.

At 2:30 p.m., I called at Marie Neill's house and asked her to come into town with me as I wanted to buy a skirt. She came with me and after hunting around in the shops for awhile I found a lovely little green and black skirt, then I saw a very pretty little blouse which matched the skirt perfectly, so I bought it too. It meant using precious clothing coupons but I couldn't resist buying it. While we were in town Marie asked me if I was going to the Red Cross and I said I didn't think so as Adeline wasn't going and I would be alone. Then she said, "Why not come to the Air Corps dance in the country tonight, Joe told me I could bring you along too."

To cut a long story short, Ray, I went to the dance. Marie called at 6:15 and at 6:30 we left our house and went down to the Red Cross to meet Joe. The trucks and buses were supposed to leave Belfast at 6:45 but we stood until 7:00 and there weren't any sign of them. At last Joe went in the Red Cross and made inquires and they told him that they were leaving from High Street. When we got round to High Street all the transport except one truck had gone. Joe spoke to an officer and the officer told us to climb in the truck and we could go alone. As it was an icy cold night, and you know what those trucks are like, Joe wrapped blankets around Marie and me. Still they didn't keep out the cold and Marie and I were shivering when we reached the dance. Never will I forget that dance, Ray, and never again will I travel over 20 miles to go to an American dance. The dance itself was quite good, they had a good band and there was plenty of ice cream but something happened and I hate having to tell you. You remember I told you about the lovely fur coat I got, well I put it on because it was a cold night and now I've lost it. Yes, I've lost my coat and I just can't realize it. If I had bought it myself I wouldn't have minded so much but Mommy spent a great deal of money buying it, as well as 18 clothing coupons. Honest, Ray, I don't know what I'm going to do. I haven't told Mommy because I'm afraid and I know when she finds out it's lost there'll be no end of trouble. I really loved that coat and everyone admired it. What on earth am I going to do, if I could get another one exactly like it I would but the girl in the shop where I got it said it was a pre-war coat, also it was the only one they had and there wasn't another one like it in Belfast. Now I'm sure you're wondering how I lost it, well I'll tell you. When Marie and I arrived at the dance and inquired if there was a cloakroom we were told no, but there was a powder room and we could leave our coats there or hang them in the dance hall. As the powder room was only a hut about 100 yards from the dance hall, we decided to bring our coats and hang them in the dance hall. Lots of other coats were hanging from hooks on the wall so Marie and I hung ours up too. Well, Ray, I noticed my coat still hanging there at 10:30 but at 11:00 when I went to get it, it wasn't there. Honest, I almost went crazy. Marie went and told Joe and he and some other boys searched around thinking they might find it, but no, it had just disappeared. Joe went up to the band leader and told him to announce that a coat was lost. The band leader described what it looked like and asked if anyone had seen it. When the announcement was made crowds of fellows brought coats over to me but none of them was mine. Some of the girls got mad because some of the coats the fellows were bringing to me belonged to them. Ray, we hunted everyplace for that coat, I even went to the powder room to see if it was there although I knew it was most unlikely. You see, I distinctly remember the place I put it because I had to climb on a chair to reach the hook and besides Marie was with me when I did it. Although the dance wasn't ending until 12:30 Joe had arranged for a truck to bring himself, Marie, another two couples and me home at 11:00 as Marie had to be home before 12:00.

Anyhow, when we discovered my coat was missing Joe told an officer and the officer said the best thing to do was to wait until the end of the dance, and search all the trucks before they left. What a night, Ray, and what an ending to what might have been a quite pleasant evening. When 12:30 came and we went out to search the trucks it was raining heavily and very cold. There I was standing in a thin dress almost perishing with cold. Big Benny was there so he made me put his overcoat on, I didn't want to and leave him without, but he went and put on his half jacket lined with fur. Anyhow, a few sergeants, Benny, Joe, Marie and I searched all the trucks and buses. They were crowded with girls and a few fellows who were going into town with some of the girls, but none of the girls had my coat, we even looked under the seats. Lots of girls from the Red Cross were at the dance but quite a few lived in small nearby towns, close to the camp. Probably some country girl noticed my coat, liked it, then stole it and walked home with it instead of waiting for a truck.

I had to leave without my coat, before I got on the truck I took Benny's off and handed it to him and he got really mad. He wouldn't take his coat and insisted on coming up to town with me. What could I do, Ray, I had to let him ride in the truck with me, besides I wasn't in the mood to argue, I was heartbroken about losing the coat and still am. Manning, another pal of Joe and Benny, came too. He sat on one side of me and Benny on the other and Manning put his half coat around my shoulders so I wouldn't be too cold. Honest, I was miserable. Joe, Benny and Manning were very much annoyed and said they would try and get me enough coupons to buy another coat, they even said they would give me money but I told them on no account would I accept either coupons or money. You see, Ray, all the money and coupons in the world wouldn't buy me a coat like the one I lost. No doubt it was good of the boys to make that offer to me, but I made it quite clear that I wouldn't accept it, and thanked them. They keep telling me there was still a chance the coat would show up, they are going to keep a sharp lookout, and maybe they'll see some local girl wearing it.

Ray, it's now Monday night, yesterday at 5 o'clock while I was writing Marie Neill called to see me and she was feeling very miserable. It seems her mother lectured her for coming home so late on Saturday night. You see, it was almost 1 o'clock when we had searched all the trucks and 2 o'clock when we reached Belfast. Lately Marie's mother has been trying to prevent Marie from going out with Joe because of his religion. She has been going out with him since January and now she says she's in love with him. Her mother lectured her an awful lot and told her she wasn't going to allow Joe in the house again and if Marie still had dates with him she could go and live somewhere else. Isn't that awful, Ray, I know Marie's mother well and believe me she isn't like mine, she'll carry out her threats. I told Marie I couldn't advise her as to what to do. Marie is 22 years of age and if Joe really loves her and is serious about marrying her she is over age and can please herself. Such a mix up, Marie isn't sure if Joe really is serious, it seems his people own some property in Italy and he is going to live there after the war. I told her that if she truly loved Joe to have a talk with him and if she finds out he really doesn't love her to give him up before she finds it impossible.

After Marie Neill left I went out and phoned Marie Roberts. She and Luke are getting married on the 18th of this month, Ray, and I can hardly believe it. They are being married in a Registry Office and when they go back to America they are going to have a real wedding. In the meantime Marie is going to wear a wedding ring and they aren't going to live like they are married. Marie said that she went down to the American Consul and they told her that unless she was married she couldn't travel to America immediately after the war and would have to wait for years, whereas, if she were married she could go inside a few months. It's all very complicated, Ray, and I don't know what to do. I guess it's up to you, Ray, to inquire over there.

Marie mentioned that Luke had sent your package over and she also wanted to know if your mother had written to me yet. It hurt to have to tell her no. You see, Ray, it's months since I wrote to your mother and I really was looking forward to receiving a letter from her.

Ray, please try and find out when you're coming back—I'm missing you so. *—Forever yours, Muriel*

Monday, November 8th

My Dearest Muriel,

As I'm starting this letter it's starting to rain, and I mean rain. It's about seven o'clock now and we're off for the night. I have quite a bit of work to do but I'll leave it until I'm through with your letters. All day yesterday Howard and Bill wanted to know what was wrong with me. I told them I didn't feel good and I wasn't kidding. I was mad, Muriel, not at you, but at the girls in the office and your mother. I don't know what to say or how to stop all this. There's only one thing to do and that's for you to come over here when you're 21 years old. If I'm going to be here for a long time come over and we'll get married and you can stay with me here at camp.

I'm glad you took off and went to the show, if they don't like it well, maybe they will keep their big mouths shut. Don't be afraid to take off when you feel like it, Muriel, it might do them good.

As to what your mother said, it really hurts me to see she's still that way, from now on never mention my name to her.

Muriel, as to changing your job, all well and good but don't take a job out of town, there are lots of jobs in Belfast that you could do. As to Lockheed, if you think you want it OK because I love you and I can trust you, but if possible get a job in town.

Hoping you will be a little happier in your next letter—don't forget you can let me know everything.

Last night we went to see "Sweet Rosie O'Grady" and it was swell. Don't forget to see it when it comes there. *—I adore you, Raymond*

Tuesday, November 9th

My Dearest Muriel,

Today I received the surprise of my life, yes, I received your identity disc and I can't express in words how happy I am. It's really beautiful and I love it. I don't know how to thank you, Muriel, I've always wanted one.

I showed Bill and Howard the disc and they think it's very nice, I think it's wonderful. I'm going to take it into town as soon as possible and have a few links taken out and have your name and address put on the other side.

In one of your letters you asked me to tell you all about myself. Honest my love, there's nothing much to tell, it's the same thing every day, classes all day and study at night. I can't get use to being in bed every night at ten o'clock. I lie awake for a few hours every night thinking about you and wondering what you are doing.

Before I forget, I received a letter from Luke the other day. He didn't have much to say—only that he misses me quite a bit. He told me he is getting married next month (no date) and wished I was there (as if I didn't). He says he's very homesick, especially since I left. I really miss Luke too. If you see him before or after they're married tell him I send my regards and wish him and Marie all the happiness in the world.

Tomorrow I have to go to Camp Butner to the dentist again, after that I'll be back here to do my homework, a lot of work since we have two tests on Thursday. I heard today that instead of five months here we will be flying at the end of three. That's good news to me and I'm sure to you. —*I love you, Raymond*

Tuesday, November 9th

My Dearest Ray,

It's about six o'clock and I've just arrived home from the new office I'm working in, yes, I've started in another firm and now I'll tell you all about it. In the mornings I have to rise at 6:45 and at 7:40 I leave the house to get a train at 7:55 and the train arrives in Lisburn at 8:15 or 8:20. Then I get on a bus outside the railway station and it arrives at the firm where I work at about 8:30. By the time I leave my coat off at the cloakroom and reach the office it's 8:45 and that is the time I have to begin working. At 1 p.m. we stop for dinner and at 1:55 we commence working until 5 p.m. Then we get on the bus again, reach the railway station and if we are lucky get a train for Belfast right away, you see, sometimes it's overdue and doesn't reach Lisburn until 5:30. Anyhow, I arrive home between 5:55 and 6:15. (I had to stop writing and have tea, it's now 7 o'clock.) Tonight and last night I could have worked until 7:00 but the girls told me it didn't matter as I was new in the firm. You see when I get used to the work I'll know exactly how much I have to do each day, and if I don't get through it all before 5:00 I'll have to work until 7 o'clock. Some of the girls work until 7 every night, but others please themselves and work late two or three nights a week.

I'm working in the Bonus Office of the Cost Office and so far I like the work all right, although it is much more complicated than the work I did in Inglis. The girls are quite friendly and nice but I miss the crowd in Inglis and know I'll never have the fun I had there. Yesterday some of the girls noticed I was engaged and immediately began asking who I was engaged to and when was I getting married. I avoided answering their questions as best I could, you see, I don't want them knowing any of my business and I'm sure you know why. (Have to stop again as Marie has called.) Marie has just left and it is now 9:30. She called to tell me she was out with Joe last night and he told her that he and a few others got the addresses of all the girls who went to the dance on Saturday night and sent letters asking whoever took my coat to return it. If that doesn't work he said he and the boys are going to insist on me accepting money for another one.

Mommy knows I lost my coat, she asked me where it was when I got home tonight and I had to tell her all about losing it. However, she didn't take it as badly as I thought she would, no doubt she noticed I haven't been myself lately and didn't want to make me more miserable. —*Forever yours, Muriel*

PS If my coat isn't returned to me I'm not letting Joe and his pals buy me one.

Wednesday, November 10th

My Dearest Muriel,

It's about seven o'clock, I got back from Camp Butner (the dentist) at about five and then took your disc into the jewelers and had three links taken out. I had to leave it there and will pick it up Saturday as he's going to put your name on it. (With love from Muriel / Belfast, Ireland) I want to tell you again how much I love the disc—I keep looking at it and think of you.

I didn't receive any mail today, not even from home. I'll have to stop now as I have a lot of work to do as I missed class today and have to make up for it now. —*Forever yours, Raymond*

Wednesday, November 10th

My Dearest Ray,

It's just about 1:35, I'm just after having lunch at the canteen here and now I want to write a short letter before I begin working again. Tonight Yvonne is calling at the house and most likely we'll go to a show, that's the reason I'm writing to you now. If you could only see me now, Ray, I'm sitting here at my desk and the other girls are sitting about in groups either knitting or talking. When I began writing they started kidding me by saying, "I bet that's a very important letter when you're in such a hurry to get started to it." I didn't tell them who I was writing to but I'm sure they have a good idea.   —*Forever yours, Muriel*

Thursday, November 11th

My Dearest Muriel,

Today they really made us work—three times around the field, one hour of drill, half an hour of exercise and then a three mile hike (half we had to run), I just about made it back to camp I was so tired. After that I took a hot shower and went to dinner. Somehow I'm liking this place more and more, they work us hard but I'm starting to like it.

Last week one of the fellows had his wife come down and she is going to stay here with him. They will only see each other about two hours a day but I bet they're happy. I know if I could see you two hours a day I'd be very happy. Married men can get weekend passes, they're the only ones. Boy, do I wish I was married to you with you here. Muriel, what do you think of you coming over here after you're 21? I know you're not going to like the idea, but I may be training here for a month or maybe a year. I won't know until after Christmas. I can't stand being away from you for so long and maybe you think I'm nuts, but it's either I'm coming back soon or you're coming over here. Please write and let me know what you think of the idea. I know your mother will say no but I think if you talk to your dad he will understand. If you want me to write him a letter maybe it would help. —*Forever yours, Raymond*

Friday, November 12th

My Dearest Muriel,

I received you letter of October 9th and was very pleased to hear from you. I see from your letter it's the second one you wrote that day, as yet I haven't received the first. This Joe you talk about in your letter, I think I remember him but please don't pay any attention to him, just because he's no good doesn't mean everyone is like that. It really burns me up that fellows talk to you that way and yes, you are "One in a million" and that's why I love you so much.

Today has been the same as always. Tomorrow I'm Sergeant of the Guards so won't be out, and Sunday it's the same. (I hear we can't go out.) I'll have to stop now as I have to study.   —*With all my love, Raymond*

Sunday, November 14th

My Dearest Muriel,

It's one o'clock now and I just got back from lunch. I didn't write yesterday as I was very busy. I went to the dentist in the morning, came back at two and at four had to go on guard. The boys had a parade in town last night. After the parade they were given open post, and here I was on guard, it happens every time, it's open post and my turn to pull guard duty.

At the dentist yesterday I had *eleven* fillings—most of them were old fillings so he took them out and put new fillings in. I have to go Wednesday again for the last time, I hope, I hate the dentist.

On the way back I stopped in town and picked up the disc. I have it on now and I'm very happy, he engraved it just as I said. I'm going to leave it on at all times. Many of the boys wanted to know where I got the pretty disc. I showed them the other side and they started asking a million questions. I told them it was from my wife and then they wondered how my wife was in Ireland.

Finally I broke down and told them that I was there, and you know the rest. —*I love you, Raymond*

Monday, November 15th

My Dearest Muriel,

Last night Bill, Howard and I went and saw "Destroyer" staring E.G Robinson and after the show we went and had supper, walked around awhile and then came back as we have to be in by eleven. It takes half an hour to get back to camp, we always leave early to make sure we are not late. For every minute late you spend one hour drilling so you see why we're always early.

This afternoon we moved again, to the second floor. Tonight we had to sign the payroll, we started at 6:30 and it's about 8 o'clock now and I just signed it. After this I have to study (physics and civil air regulations). I'll write a longer letter tomorrow. —*I love you, Raymond*

Tuesday, November 16th

My Dearest Muriel,

Last night we had two fire drills, one at 12:30 and another at 1:00. The first time I only had time to put on my shoes and almost froze outside, but the second time I had my overcoat ready. I hear we may have another one tonight, if so I'll be ready—they're not going to catch me off guard this time. You may think it's crazy but that's part of our training, the same as our haircuts and wearing garters. My marks in school are very good so far and I'm proud of them. It's a lot of work but it's worth it.

I enquired about the mail and was told that 9 times out of 10 the regular mail would reach you as soon as airmail, so I'm going to mail your letters regular mail. If you find they take much longer let me know and I'll send them airmail again. If it takes too long send a telegram—say (mail too long) I'll understand, don't use more words because it's awfully expensive.

I still have your disc on—I look at it and keep thinking of you. I think of all the swell times we had and wish I was back there. Yes, I think of Bangor, the Red Cross, the walks we had and how I always would be tired, how I would grumble about the rain all the time. If I didn't love you as I do I wouldn't think of Ireland but with you on my mind it's always Ireland. The other day we were outside and the boys got together and started singing. All of a sudden they started with "My Wild Irish Rose." Honest, I didn't know what to do—it hit me so I had to leave, I felt like crying.

I hope you haven't had any more trouble at home or at the office. Take good care of yourself.   —*I love you, Raymond*

Wednesday, November 17th

My Dearest Muriel,

There's nothing new to tell, no mail today. I hope by now you have received some of the packages I have sent. If there is anything else you want be sure to let me know.

I just happened to think, Luke is getting married sometime this month—I wish I knew the date. If you see the wedding let me know how it was and all about it, will you, Muriel?   —*Forever yours, Raymond*

Thursday, November 18th

My Dearest Muriel,

It's just about 8 o'clock and we just got back from parade, yes, we had a parade tonight

Today I waited for some mail from you but no luck, so there is not much to talk about. Oh, yes, the other day a lieutenant told me to do something and I wouldn't, you know how stubborn I am at times. Well, he turned me in and they gave me 10 gigs, as they call them here, so this weekend I won't be able to go out. I'll have to walk, or run I should say, for five hours. They only give us 10 minutes rest every hour. I guess I asked for it so I can't complain.

I was just thinking by the time you receive this letter it will be Christmas or maybe after. I hope by then you have received my Christmas packages and I hope you like them. Boy, did I feel silly going into a women's store and buying stockings, powder and lipstick, etc. I didn't know what color, shade or size or things like that when they asked me and I didn't know what to say. I told the lady just how you looked—in fact I showed her your picture and described your hair, eyes and complexion. So from that she picked out powder and lipstick, I hope she was right.

Christmas is going to be one day off, that's all—I'm in the U.S. and can't be home for Christmas, it sounds funny doesn't it? I'll never forget how awful last Christmas was.

I forgot to tell you in tonight's parade we came in first in our squad, it doesn't do us much good, only to know we looked the best at parade. I heard in today's room inspection we came out the highest also, so you can see we are on the ball, as they say here. *—I love you, Raymond*

Thursday, November 18th

My Dearest Ray,

I hardly know how to begin this letter and I know that when you receive it you will get a very unpleasant surprise, because I haven't written since Wednesday 10th. No doubt you will hardly believe that, Ray, but now I'll try and tell you why I didn't and couldn't. The letter I wrote on the 10th was written at lunchtime in the office because I thought I was going to the show with Yvonne that night. Yvonne called but we didn't go to a show, we got talking about the latest happenings at Inglis and I began telling her all about my new job and before we knew it, it was 8:30 and too late to go to a show so we stayed home instead.

On Thursday we were very busy at the office, two of the girls were already out ill and another one got sick in the morning and had to go home. I don't wonder at this, the weather is cold and frosty here and the office I'm working in is so big that it can't be kept properly heated. Some days we have to keep woolen jackets and our overcoats on. We have complained to the manager several times but he says nothing can be done about it. Anyhow, with these girls being out ill the other girls, including myself, had to work late on Thursday and Friday night, also Saturday afternoon. When I got home Thursday night I tried writing to you but before I got a page written Mommy called me for supper and after that I had to wash stockings (I'm wearing them now because I'm travelling and it's so cold) and get something ready to wear the next day. After that I was so tired I had to go to bed. You see, I have to get up before seven o'clock every morning and if I didn't go to bed before 11 p.m. or 11:30 at the latest, I wouldn't be able to get up. On Saturday I didn't arrive home until 6 p.m. and I was mad. You see I had intended going into town to buy Christmas cards, etc. but it was too late to do that. Anyhow, when I got home I was very disappointed, there weren't any letters from you. All the time I was worrying because I hadn't written you, but then I began thinking I was silly because you often missed lots of days in writing to me. Yes, Ray, I began thinking things like that. I don't know what came over me, I'm a self-centered thing and you'll never know how sorry I am. Honest, Ray, I'm sorry for missing so many days in writing to you, but I've been punished by myself and I promise never to let it happen again. After tea (Saturday) Marie Neill called, we went to the Red Cross but as usual I didn't enjoy myself. The dance was very crowded and without a word of lie there were about three times as many boys as girls there. I left the dance at 10:45 and got a tram home. I came home alone as Marie met Joe there and I didn't want to walk home with them.

On Sunday about 3 p.m. Yvonne called. She has joined the Red Cross now and as she goes out with her boyfriend on Saturday nights the only times she can go to the dances are on Sunday afternoons. Anyhow, she called and I went with her. I didn't feel like going because I was worrying about you but she coaxed me and said she wouldn't care to go alone. After the dance Yvonne invited me to her house for tea. Yvonne, her sister Alice and I sat around the fire talking and before I knew it, it was 9:45 p.m. I hurried home and tried to write to you but it was so late and I had so much to tell you I stopped writing and decided to wait until Monday night. On Monday, Tuesday and Wednesday I had to work late and each night when I arrived home I was disappointed because there weren't any letters from you. Tonight I hadn't to work late and was home before six o'clock. When I got home there was a note from Yvonne awaiting me. There was a dance in the Red Cross last night and she called for me but I wasn't in so she went by herself. The note reads, "Sorry you were working late and couldn't come to the dance. I met Lily there and introduced myself. You had better go around and see Lily—she has a message for you from Luke." As soon as I had tea I went around to Lily's house and she told me that Luke was at the dance looking for me and he told her to tell me to be sure and come on Saturday night as he wanted to see me about something. Marie and Luke were married today, can you realize that? God bless them and may they always be very happy.

Mommy is calling me for supper so I must stop writing. I think I've to work tomorrow night again but I'll write to you. It will probably be a short letter as I will have to wash my hair and do countless other things, so please forgive me—I really have very little time to spare these days. *—Forever yours, Muriel*

Friday, November 19th

My Dearest Muriel,

No letter today from you, I don't know why I haven't received any letters from you, it may be on account of the regular mail being so slow, but whatever it is I hope I do hear from you soon. I have been worrying about you so much lately. I never missed any person in all my life as I do you. Boy, wouldn't I be happy if this war was over and I was back with you. There I go dreaming again.

I'm loving, missing and thinking of you every minute of the day. Please don't lose faith in me as I love you too much. *—I adore you, Raymond*

Friday, November 19th

My Dearest Ray,

It's nine p.m. and I only got home from the office about half an hour ago. Right now I hardly know what to say or how to thank you. Luke called at the house about 10 this morning and left a beautiful birthday present for me. Ray, I can't put on paper the way I feel— when I opened that package I can't explain the way I felt. I want to kiss and hug you but I can't, you're too far away.

The make-up set is beautiful, the stockings are just the kind I like and the pin is what I've been waiting for since you went in the Air Corps. As soon as possible I'll have some pictures taken with the films you sent. You're a darling, Ray, and I won't be able to thank you the way I want to until you come back. The make-up set is so lovely that I'm not going to use it until we are together again.

Tomorrow I have to work overtime again and I'm not at all pleased. I was intending to go into town and do some Christmas shopping and now I can't. Ray, I'm wondering what to buy you—I want to get you something really nice but can't think of anything you may need. I have thought of knitting you a pullover (or sweater as you call it) but they do not have any good wool here, all they have in the shops is more like cotton and it isn't nice and warm.

Although I want to write much more I haven't time so I'll end now and add a few more lines tomorrow before I go to the Red Cross. Marie and Luke will be there and I promised Marie I would see them there.

It's about 7 p.m. *Saturday* and very soon I'll have to get ready to go to the Red Cross. Somehow, lately I haven't had time to tell you much about the new job I have but I want you to know that I like it very much even though I have to work harder and longer. The girls are all very nice and I've made friends of them all. A good many of the girls live in Belfast so I have company when I'm traveling.

As it's getting late I must end now and get ready. I wish you were going with me—it would be like old times if you, Luke, Marie and I were together again, but someday soon we will be. —*I'll always be yours alone, Muriel*

Saturday, November 20th

My Dearest Muriel,

It's about 8:30 now and I just got off from marching my "tours" as they call them. I had to walk two hours tonight and I can't leave the post until I have the other three walked off.

Today again I didn't receive any letters from you, I'm getting worried. I received a letter from Mother today and she wanted to know if you received the packages as yet—I hope you have. She asked me about Christmas and I wrote and told her I didn't think I'd be home as we only get one day off. As long as we are here there are no passes or leaves, what do you think of that? Boy, don't I wish this war was over, not only for me but for everyone.

With me there is nothing new, everything is still the same. I'm going to try and be good from now on, I hope.

Happy Birthday to you, my love! —*Forever yours, Raymond*

Sunday, November 21st

My Dearest Ray,

The time is about 9:30 p.m. and I've just got back from Yvonne's house. Last night I went to the Red Cross and just as I was leaving my coat in the cloakroom someone caught me by the arm and who was it but Marie or should I say Mrs. Piccarreto. Yes, Ray, Luke and Marie are married and they are so happy it is written all over them. Luke danced one dance with me and all the time we talked of old times and both wished you could have been with us—we even had an argument as to which of us missed you the most. He is absolutely crazy about

Marie and said he was so happy he was in a fog and couldn't think straight. Marie's eyes were shining like stars and they were hugging and kissing in the crowded dance hall and didn't care who saw them.

Supper is ready so I must stop now, I'll finish this letter at lunchtime in the office tomorrow.

My Dearest Ray,

It's 24 minutes to two and I'm just after having dinner in the canteen. Tonight I have to work late so I want to finish this letter now.

Ray, I wish I had your new address and for your sake I hope you are stationed close to home.

It's almost time to begin working so I must end. Give my regards to all at home.   *—Forever yours, Muriel*

PS I haven't seen Hazel for a long time.

Monday, November 22nd

My Dearest Muriel,

I just got in and was hoping to find a letter from you but was disappointed. Today I went to the dentist again and I just got back. I'm all through now, I may have to go in a few weeks for a checkup—but that's all.

Sunday from 9-12 I marched the rest of my tours off and honest, I was really tired—I guess I'll be good from now on. After the parade Howard, Bill and I played around with a football outside until six o'clock and then we had to go up to our rooms—that's when the fun began. All the boys were mad as we have to be in at six now, so they started making horseplay, as we call it here, you know, throwing water, putting a fellow in a cold shower with his clothes on, fighting, etc. I wanted to write to you but it was impossible with all that was going on. I had to make up my bed and look around for my blankets before I could go to bed and some of my clothing was tied up in knots. This morning when we got up we really had to do a lot of cleaning up.

We were told today that we had to have passing marks in all our subjects or we will be "washed out" as we call it, so I'm going to have to study more to make sure I have passing marks.   *—I love you, Raymond*

Monday, November 22nd

My Dearest Ray,

Although I finished writing a letter to you in the office at lunchtime, I feel I must write to you again. It's 9:15 and I just arrived home from the office about half an hour ago. Yes, I was working late again but somehow I don't mind it as it helps to pass the time and the girls are so jolly and friendly. We are very busy but nevertheless, at times we have fun.

These past few weeks I haven't seen much of Belfast because when I leave to get a train in the mornings it's blackout and it's blackout when I arrive home in the evenings.

On the 24th of next month we will have been separated for exactly one year. It's a long time since I heard your voice and yet it's as fresh in my memory as ever.   —*Forever yours, Muriel*

Tuesday, November 23rd

My Dearest Muriel,

I received a great surprise today—I heard from Luke (two V-mail letters dated November 12th & 13th). He said you received two packages, is that right? If so you still have two more coming. He told me he was getting married the 18th, did you see the wedding, I hope so. Please write and tell me all about it as I know Luke will forget. Where is Marie going, with Luke or staying home?

Muriel, I still haven't received a letter from you, I'm afraid regular mail is going to take a bit longer than airmail. I'm getting impatient.

Today we were told we would have Thanksgiving off, tonight they read a special order saying it was canceled and the only day off this year is Christmas. Everyone here is mad about it but I guess it doesn't do any good. Everything here is work and more work...

I hope you like the presents I sent you.   —*Forever yours, Raymond*

Tuesday, November 23rd

My Dearest Ray,

I'm starting this letter in the office and probably won't be able to finish it until tomorrow night. I'm going to rush as much as possible and get my work up to date so I can go to a show tonight. "White Cargo" is showing at the Curzon and I heard it is a good picture. As it's been a long time since I've seen Hazel perhaps I'll call and see her before I go to the show. She borrowed my toffee coupons six or seven weeks ago and I've only seen her once since then, and that was the day she gave me the package from your mother.

Ray, I haven't had a letter from you for two or three weeks and I can't understand why. I'm sorry I can't write anymore just now—it's 1:50 and I'll get into trouble if I'm caught writing when I should be working. (*Stop*)

Wednesday, 24th

My Dearest Ray,

Right now I'm in an awful hurry as it's 6:30 and I have to be ready when Yvonne calls at 7:30. Last night I called to get my toffee coupons from Hazel. The first question she asked me was how I liked my new job, and then she admired my Air Corps pin and said, "I suppose Ray sent it to you." She didn't mention Louis so I asked her if everything was alright with them. Hazel gave me the opinion she didn't want to talk about him and to tell the truth, Ray, I think Louis may have backed out. On the way to the Curzon (Hazel came to the show with me) all she said was she still wrote to him but he mightn't get back here as the hospital was likely to be transferred someplace else. Then she began talking about the dates she was having with other boys and said she had got "fed up keeping time" and was going to enjoy herself. If I thought Hazel really loved Louis I would feel very sorry for her. I never did think much of Louis, but now I hate him for going so far in handing her a line. I must end now.   —*Forever yours, Muriel*

Wednesday, November 24th

My Dearest Muriel,

No letter today again. ...

This weekend on Saturday I have to pull guard duty again and boy, I'm mad. I would like to get away from this place once in awhile. I had a fight with the 1st Sergeant about it last night—I told him this is the last time—there are some fellows here that have never pulled guard duty on a Saturday. Oh, well, there I go again...

Tomorrow is Thanksgiving and we go to school, it's just another day. Boy, do I wish I was at home. I hear we are going to have quite a meal here for Thanksgiving—turkey, ice cream, etc. The men who have their wives here are allowed to bring them for dinner, I wish you were here with me, honest, it would be wonderful.   —*I adore you, Raymond*

Thursday, November 25th

My Dearest Muriel,

This morning we went to our classes as usual and then we had a big turkey dinner which was really good. After dinner they told us we had off until six o'clock so I went into town with the boys. My main reason being to buy you a Christmas card and a few other things, but all of the stores were closed. I don't know what I am going to do, I want to buy the family a few presents but any time I get in town they are closed. On Saturday they close at six o'clock. Anyway, we walked around for awhile and I had one beer before we got a bus back at 5:15. After supper we came back to our barracks and were told we had to move again so from six, and it's now after eight, we have been moving across to the next building, don't ask me why.

I heard some good news today—after February I should know just how long I will be in training and where I will go when I'm through, etc. —*I adore you, Raymond*

Thursday, November 25th

My Dearest Ray,

The time is about 9:30 p.m. and this is the first opportunity I've had to write. When I got home at 6:00 I had to go on a message for Daddy, after that I washed my hair.

Last night Yvonne, Adeline and I went to the Red Cross. Dorothy and a few other girls I know were there and it would have been perfect if only you had been with me. To my surprise Marie and Luke were there and I was talking to them. Poor Luke, he tried to get permission to stay in Belfast a few days longer but they wouldn't give it. Marie says she doesn't know how I can stand being parted from you for so long and I told her she didn't realize how lucky she was that Luke was stationed in England and could phone her every week. Wouldn't it be wonderful if you could be here the next time Luke comes over? —*Forever yours, Muriel*

PS I've put on a little weight and everyone tells me I look lots better since I started working in the country.

Friday, November 26th

My Dearest Muriel,

I received a letter from Mother today, but none from you. She said to cheer up and learn to take it and that she has no pity for me because I asked for it. It's not that I can't take it or don't like it here, Muriel, because I do. At times they do things so crazy here I think they do it on purpose. I don't like it and neither does anyone else, but I want to be a pilot so I'll go through anything just to be one. If you were here it would be OK but I keep worried over you. I know I shouldn't but I think of you every minute, wondering how you are getting along and how you are doing.

What do you think about coming over here? Let me know as soon as possible. —*I adore you, Raymond*

Friday, November 26th

My Dearest Ray,

This is a very short letter as I'm only after having lunch in the canteen. Tonight I want to see a picture named "Waterloo Bridge," it's showing at the Regal. Maureen Harris, one of the girls in the office, is going with me. We are very busy here at the office and I'm dreading in case the boss asks me to work late tonight. Such a busy office, Ray, the work is endless but I like it and I'm not the least bit sorry I left Inglis. I admit I haven't the spare time I used to have, but I feel a little better and not so easily depressed.

I still haven't received any letters.   —*Forever yours, Muriel*

Saturday, November 27th

My Dearest Muriel,

Today I received the greatest surprise of my life, yes—I received 12 letters, all of October. First they went to Greensboro and they must have held them awhile before sending them here. I really don't know how to express my happiness. I received your letters at 5 o'clock mail call and from then until seven, the time I went on guard duty, I read them. I keep wishing I had never left you, honest, my love, I never thought I could love a girl as I love you.

I have to go back on guard duty at eleven o'clock—I just got off for a few hours. It's 9:30 now so I'm going to make this letter short so I can mail it. I'm going to send it airmail hoping it arrives faster than regular mail.

I won't be able to answer your letters all at once so I'll answer a few at a time. I don't understand why you aren't receiving more of my mail, my love, honest, I can imagine how you feel—I wish there was something I could do so the mail would arrive there faster.

Muriel, about the job in Lisburn, I wish you don't accept it as it will be quite hard on you, but if you think you will like it better, OK. Are you sure they won't send you to England, I hope not.

As long as you were at Inglis I felt you were safe. I should think you can get a job in Belfast, there's lots of work there.

Well, my love, it's time for me to go on guard again. I'll start tomorrow answering your letters. —*I adore you, Raymond*

PS The fellows told me today, "We hope you're more pleasant now that you got some mail from your wife." Yes, they call you my wife, I can hardly wait until the day we are married.

Sunday, November 28th

My Dearest Muriel,

Today I had another lovely surprise, yes I received five more of your letters, honest, I hardly know what to say. What has me bothered is how I'm going to answer them all. I've had 17 letters in two days so the only thing I can do is answer as many as possible.

Last night I got in bed about 1:30, after guard duty, and boy it was cold. The days are warm but the nights here are very cold. This morning I had to get up at seven o'clock reveille, yes, even on Sundays, but went back to bed. I was just about to get up at eleven when one of the boys walked in with your letters and boy, was I happy. I read them in bed and as it was 12 o'clock before I got through I had to hurry and get dressed for lunch. After lunch Howard and I went to the show in town and saw "Princess O'Rourke." Muriel, if it ever comes there don't forget to go and see it. We saw it twice so it was 5:30 before we got out and we didn't have time to get a bite to eat as we have to be back here at 6:00. I'm hungry now but the picture was worth it.

Muriel, as to my training, well it's hard to explain because I don't know much about it. We should get out of here by February and go to a classification center for one month. There they will tell us what we will be—pilot, navigator, bombardier, etc. Then and only then will I know how long it will take. Also, I may wash out and if so I am through with the Air Corps. I heard they are washing out a lot of boys so until then I won't know anything more. Things change so much here I can't keep up with them. If I am made an instructor would you come over here and marry me? If I wash out I'll be back as soon as possible. I can't stand being away from you much longer. I have your lovely disc and I haven't taken it off since the day I received it back from the jeweler. (The boys here want to know if I'm writing a book.) When I got all that mail yesterday boy did they ask questions, and this morning when they brought the others in I told them we were married and they believe me.

I see that the Red Cross is having a lot of dances. I don't mind if you go once in awhile, but please don't go too often.

Don't work too hard at your new job—I hope you like it.   *—I adore you, Raymond*

Monday, November 29th

My Dearest Muriel,

Today has been very cold, just like your Irish weather, can't make up its mind whether to rain or shine. This afternoon, on the field drilling, I almost froze. Tonight we got h--- again, not me alone, everyone here—they're making changes all the time. They make me sick at times—the way they want things done would take a book to explain. A few examples: all clothing buttoned on the hanger and set in a uniform way, beds made up in a certain way, and articles in drawers and toiletries set in a certain way. Oh, well, as I said before, I asked for it so I guess I'll have to take it. When I was with you I didn't know enough to stay there, I guess I didn't realize how lucky I was, but you know me, I never listen to anyone.

I see that the crowd in the office is still kidding you but if you take that new job as you said, that will be over with. As far as inviting everyone from Inglis to our wedding, well, it's up to you but I wouldn't invite them. Maybe I'm wrong but I can't forget all the times they made you feel miserable.

You wrote and told me that you put in an application for a job in Lisburn and that you have been accepted, I only hope that you like it there.

I think it was sweet of you to give the lighter to Dad, no, I don't mind. I know he will take good care of it. I'm glad he thinks it's a "great wee lighter." When I read that it sounded like your dad was saying it, I'll never forget how he would put "wee" in his sentences—I used to like hearing him talk.

You were talking about the boys at the Red Cross, "I heard that ----
--------censored---------." A sentence was cut out by the censors. (Letter of Oct. 23) I see this Benny is quite a boy. As to Joe, he may be OK but don't let him tell you what to do. I know I'll never have to worry because I trust you. I'd hate to see you stay home and not enjoy yourself but again, I don't want you to go out with other fellows. Yes, people are going to tell you things about me, but in the first place I couldn't go out if I wanted to, in the second I have no desire to. If you don't have any dates and stay true to me, I can do the same, which I am. I see you are having quite a time at the Red Cross, that's why I wish you wouldn't go so often, especially on the weekends. I know it's not fair but you see all the trouble the fellows cause. As to Christmas and New Year's, I hope you stay away from there, I know I shouldn't say this but I wish you would. *—I love you, Raymond*

Monday, November 29th

My Dearest Ray,

Once again I am writing to you in the office as I am working late tonight and won't have much time when I get home. What can be wrong, Ray, it's ages since I've had a letter and don't even know if you are still stationed in Greensboro or if you have been transferred someplace else. By now I expect you are flying and it worries me. Please be very careful, take plenty of rest between times and write to me every day. If you don't I'll have your life when you come back. —*Forever yours, Muriel*

Tuesday, November 30th

My Dearest Muriel,

I hope by now you have my new address. If you didn't have it before Luke came over I hope you got it from him as he has it. I'm still wondering how Luke's wedding came off.

Our new canteen opened up here today, it's very nice. They have quite a few articles—gum cigarettes, Coke, candy, etc. I wish you were here to enjoy all these things.

I can't understand why you haven't received my letters. I sent you a lot of pictures I took when home, I hope you receive them.

As I said in last night's letter about the Red Cross dances, well, it's up to you, Muriel, but I think if you went to the show you would be much better off seeing they're so crowded. Don't be afraid to refuse a dance, it isn't rude so don't worry about it. In fact I want you to dance with only the decent looking fellows, stay away from the others. I wish you would keep off the streets after dark, especially around City Hall, as you know why. I'm sorry Mr. Graham was sick, if you see him say hello to him for me.

About Hazel, she's expecting to marry Louis very soon and still she's going out with other boys, I don't get it. I'm glad you're not like her—if you were I wouldn't love you.

Every time you write you talk about all the Americans there (boy am I jealous). I'm glad you enjoyed yourself at the train station (but keep your distance). I hope you like your new job.

I'll have to stop now as there is a lot of homework I still have to do. Take good care of yourself. —*Forever yours, Raymond*

Tuesday, November 30th

My Dearest Ray,

It's about 5:40 p.m. and I've just arrived home from the office. At the moment Mommy is getting my tea ready and I want to write this short letter to you while I'm waiting. Tonight I should have worked late but I just didn't feel like it. Another thing, I wanted to hurry home because I was almost certain there would be a letter from you, but there wasn't and honestly, Ray, I was more disappointed than I can describe, what can be wrong? Honest, Ray, I don't know how I'm going to live through the long months until you come back. If only your letters would come more often I wouldn't feel so bad, but as it is I don't know how you are or exactly where you are stationed.

Tea is ready so I'll end now and after tea I'll go to the Regal and see a picture named "Slightly Dangerous," because tomorrow night I have to work late and won't be able to go then.   —*Forever yours, Muriel*

Aviation students.

Ray with good friends Howard Merkel and Bill Hammond.

Ray and Bill.

Howard and Bill.

December 1943

Wednesday, December 1ˢᵗ

My Dearest Muriel,

I'll have to make this letter short tonight as I have a million and one things to do.

I wish there was something I could tell you about myself but there's really not much to say. It's the same thing everyday, classes in the morning, drill in the afternoons, study at night—same thing day in and day out. The boys just walked in, we are going to study physics as we have a test tomorrow but I'll finish this letter first. Every time we have a test we all get together and tell each other what we know, which isn't much.

In your letter of November 1ˢᵗ you said you didn't write Saturday and Sunday because you were sick. That worries me very much. I get sick quite often but it's my stomach, as you know, some days I can eat a certain food and then again other days it will make me sick, but that has been the trouble with me ever since I was born. But you, I don't like hearing this, please take good care of yourself. I'm glad you didn't go to the dance, being sick. Again, I wish you wouldn't go to so many dances—I know it's OK but I'd rather not have you go to so many. That Benny again, is he always hanging around you? ... So he put his arm around you, tell him to take it easy or when I come back there will be trouble. Then trying to kiss you ... this better stop, Muriel. I don't mean to be jealous, but I am, so don't let him try anymore of that. I'm glad you do have fun because I want you to, but be sure that's all it is and nothing more. *—I adore you, Raymond*

Wednesday, December 1ˢᵗ

My Dearest Ray,

I'm writing this letter in the office as I'm working late tonight. Evelyn Morris didn't come in yesterday or today and I have to help do her work as well as my own.

Honest, Ray, if there isn't a letter from you when I go home tonight I'll go crazy. It's over 7 weeks since you wrote the last one I received and I can't think what is wrong.

Ray, I can hardly realize I'll be 21 years of age on the 21st of this month. I'd like to stay 21 all my life and not get any older but I guess I'll have to grow old like everyone else. —*Forever yours, Muriel*

Thursday, December 2nd

My Dearest Muriel,

I finally got you a Christmas card—they had them at the PX (canteen), they came in today. I know it's going to be a little late in reaching you, but I hope you like it.

Today we had four tests and my head is still spinning. I'm telling you, Muriel, I haven't had a minute to myself. If it wasn't that I wanted to fly so much I would drop out but as I said before, I asked for it so I'm going to stick it out. It's a lot of work but I'm proud to be in as a cadet.

I think I better get to answering your letters..... The one you wrote the 27th of October, you start again as usual, no letters...then the censors cut out what you said before you continued on about your new appointment. So the girls in Inglis are going to miss you, well, they surely didn't show it by the way they carried on.

As to your music lessons, no, I'm not mad—I did want you to get that diploma but in a way I'm glad you did stop as it was too much for you.

Boy, I'm glad to hear how happy you are receiving my letters (November 2nd), only 4, you should have received more than that. (The censors cut out what you said you inked out in the letter they sent back.)

My cousin Bob is not going to be a pilot, he's going to be a ground mechanic.

I'm glad to hear that you and Yvonne are on good terms again, I'm glad you didn't tell her you wrote and told me about it.

You went to the dance with Marie Neill on Tuesday but never said anything about it in Thursday's letter. What happened, did you forget? I would like to know. —*I adore you, Raymond*

Thursday, December 2nd

My Dearest Ray,

Today again I hurried home from the office feeling sure there would be some word from you but there wasn't. It's about eight weeks since you wrote the last letter I received and I can't understand why I haven't received any since then. If I only knew you were safe and well it wouldn't be so bad but for two weeks now I've been thinking that perhaps you've been sick, too sick even to write. If I don't hear from you within the next few days I'm going to send a cable to your mother to find out if you are all right.

Last night I was working late and didn't arrive home until 8:30 p.m. Mommy had supper ready and after supper I went straight to bed and lay awake for the longest time thinking about you. Then I went to sleep and had the strangest dreams.

I dreamt that you came back and lived in Aunt Vi's house. Aunt Vi came and told me you were in her house but I didn't go to see you—instead I waited until you would come to our house to see me, but you didn't come. This seemed to be on a Friday, all day Friday I stayed in the house waiting for you to come to the door but you didn't. On Saturday night I went to Aunt Vi's house to find out what was wrong and see if you were still there, but you weren't, and Aunt Vi told me that you had gone to the Red Cross by yourself. I started to run down to the Red Cross and the next thing I knew Mommy was shaking me and saying, "Muriel, get up it's 7:45 a.m. and you'll miss the train if you don't hurry." Wasn't that a queer dream, Ray, I wonder what would have happened if Mommy hadn't wakened me and spoilt it.

I'll end now, Ray, as I want to wash my hair, also a blouse before I go to bed. —*Forever yours, Muriel*

Friday, December 3rd

My Dearest Muriel,

I wish you would make up your mind and come over here, if you want to I can have it fixed up so you can come here and we can get married. Of course this will have to wait until January or February when I go to Nashville. When we go there they will tell us what we will be and how long it will take, but if I don't make it then I'm sure I'll be on my way back as they won't hold me anymore. So think about it my love—either I'm coming over there or you're coming here.

Please, Muriel, don't ever stop writing because I live for your letters. I know I didn't write for a week (Greensboro) but if you were ever in an army camp you'd probably realize why. Now that I'm settled it's OK.

Now listen, my love, I didn't get the pass to go and see the girls as you put it. True, I knew some girls but I wanted to see their parents also as they were very nice to me before, so the least I could do was pay them a visit. The girls I did know are either married or away so don't start thinking I was there to go out with them.

I'm glad you liked the package, if Luke gave you that one you have two more coming, another from me and one from Mother. (Christmas and birthday presents.)

Muriel, just because Mother sends you a box doesn't mean you have to run out and buy her something. Now be a good girl and forget about it. Mother loves to send you anything you want.   —*I adore you, Raymond*

Friday, December 3rd

My Dearest Ray,

As I begin writing this letter the time is about 10 p.m. Tonight I arrived home from the office at about 6 o'clock hoping and praying there would be a letter from you, but once again I was very disappointed as well as worried. Ray, if you could only know how I feel, I could hardly eat my tea. After tea I went upstairs and lay across my bed for over an hour trying to figure out what can be wrong. After that I went into Aunt Vi's house to see her about a blouse she is making for me and we sat talking until 9:15 p.m. She told me not to worry, that you were all right and probably the Christmas mail was the cause of your letters taking so long in coming.

Today all the girls in my department had a heated argument with the boss because he came to us and told us we have to work until 5 p.m. Saturday (tomorrow) and all day Sunday. Personally, I don't care but the others are very mad because they had other plans made for the weekend. I don't mind working over the weekend because I like the type of work I'm doing now and not only that, the girls are very jolly and I'd rather be with them than sitting at home.

As it's getting late I'll stop writing now and continue this letter tomorrow night before I go to the Red Cross. I promised Adeline I would go with her then, she coaxed me to go and said if I didn't go she wouldn't go alone. What a girl, she won't even walk through the door of the Red Cross unless I am with her. I've often asked her why and her answer is, "I wouldn't take a pension and walk past all those fellows by myself, they stare and make me feel embarrassed."

Adeline is a sweet kid but very self-conscious and she often says to me, "Muriel, I wish I could be like you, you walk into the Red Cross as if you owned the place, you hold your head in the air and if any of the fellows bother you, you give them a look that's enough to wither them."

I could write lots more but it's getting late and I must get to bed.

Saturday, December 4th

My Dearest Ray,

Tonight I was working until 5 o'clock, missed the 5:10 p.m. train leaving Lisburn and had to wait in the station until the next train came along at 5:35 p.m. Right now the time is 7 p.m. and I have to hurry and finish this letter, get cleaned and meet Adeline in town at 7:45 p.m. What a life, all I seem to be doing is rushing all the time.

Ray, I didn't get any letters from you today again and I'm very, very worried, however, perhaps it is the Christmas rush with the mail that's holding them back. *—Forever yours, Muriel*

Sunday, December 5th

My Dearest Muriel,

It's just about seven o'clock now as I'm writing this letter. (I didn't write yesterday.) I'll tell you all about my weekend starting with yesterday morning. We had classes from 8 to 12, at 2 p.m. we fell out for P.T. (Physical Training) and ran about a mile back to our barracks. Then we cleaned up in a hurry, and I mean in a hurry, for inspection. After inspection we had a parade which lasted until five o'clock, then dinner and back to our rooms at six. I hurried as fast as I could to get clean as I wanted to do some Christmas shopping, but not much luck as most of the stores were closed. Howard, Miller and Parker, fellows here that I know, came with me. Before we did anything after we found the stores were closed, we went and had a steak dinner. Then we went to a show and saw "Thank Your Lucky Stars," it wasn't bad, but not as good as I'd expected. After the show, which ended at about 11:00 o'clock, we stopped at the USO. The dance was just about over when we got there. After the dance we stopped at a restaurant again on the way back to camp and had more to eat, yes, I know, I'm eating like a pig. We got in just about 12:00 o'clock and as I just was getting into bed one of my roommates came in drunk as a fish, honest, Muriel, we had an awful time trying to keep him quiet and the best part of it all, we are still wondering where he got the liquor as North Carolina is a dry state and you can hardly find it here. If they had caught him he would have been expelled, boy, was I scared. Anyhow, we put him under a cold shower and then to bed, everything ended up OK. Gosh, all I've had since I've left home is one glass of beer—believe it or not, we are not allowed to drink.

This morning I was up at 7:30, showered and dressed, as we had to go to church at 9:00—all 200 boys from the 59th training detachment had to be there. After church they had a breakfast for us all, it was quite good. All morning I've been sick (eating too much I guess) and after our breakfast we came right back and I went to bed and slept until 4:00. I felt a little better after that. I then went a few blocks over to a fruit store and bought some oranges, grapes and apples and came back to camp. This was my dinner. I'm eating an orange now and keep thinking of you and wishing you had this orange instead of me.

Before I started writing this letter I stopped at the PX and listened to the radio (wireless) for a good hour. It's the first music I've heard over the radio since I left home, we can't have a radio here and boy, do I miss it.

I miss you so much, I try not to think of you during the day so I can study, but even that doesn't stop me. All day long I wonder what you are doing, when it's 12 o'clock here it's 5 o'clock in Belfast, then I think, well, it's just about time for Muriel to get out of work, and so on through the day, all day and every day. After this schooling I'm going to do all in my power to get back to you as soon as possible, I promise.   —*I adore you, Raymond*

Lockport, New York
Sunday, December 5th

Dear Muriel,

I heard through Raymond that you hadn't received my last letter, but this being war times I suppose one is to expect such things. I hope that this letter reaches you as I wouldn't want you to think I wouldn't care to write to you.

My dear, you have me worried about you because you feel so badly about Raymond's entrance into the Air Corps. Naturally I worry very much too because he is my one and only son, but remember, if anything is going to happen to him it will, no matter where he is or what he does.

We ourselves don't govern such things, there is a greater power than ourselves. I don't like the Air Force any more than you do but Raymond has a mind of his own and he knows what he wants. Please my dear, take care of yourself so you will be there for Raymond to come back to—we mustn't let ourselves go for his sake. As far as I'm concerned, if my son chose you for himself I know you are a nice and very sweet young girl. I like the things he likes and I know he has good judgment. If he cares for you there is no doubt in my mind that I will care for you a great deal myself.

Please don't worry about my son not being true or going out with other girls because I know he doesn't, and won't. Just be brave and pray that this war is soon over and the two of you can be together. I want him home more than I can express.

You seem quite worried about religion, but my dear, I am broad minded enough to understand that there are other beliefs as good as the Catholics. Religion doesn't make you good or bad, it's the person themselves. No matter what you believe, we all worship a God which is all that is necessary.

I have taken it upon myself to send you several boxes. I don't know if their contents will please you, but I hope so. If there is anything you would like, please let me know and I will gladly send it to you.

I want to assure you that Ray is fine and well, he writes to me once a week and he enjoys his work. Muriel, if you want to come over and there is anything in my power that I can do I assure you I will with all my heart.

Well, my dear, it's a pleasure to write to you and I hope you will write to me more often.   —*Sincerely, Mrs. B. Friscia*

Monday, December 6th

My Dearest Muriel,

Nothing new, my love, only I think Wednesday they are going to rearrange our schedule, more classes and less drill, I'm glad of that.

The weather is still fine here, nice and warm—how is it there, raining as always? Boy, I wish I was there, even with all the rain.

I hope my mail is coming to you more often—it's been about a week since I heard from you. How's your new job? How's the family? I wish you would tell me more about yourself.

This letter will reach you after Christmas, I hope you had a merry one, well, as merry as I can expect. I'll be thinking of you all day. Last year was bad enough, I'll never forget that.   —*I adore you, Raymond*

Monday, December 6th

My Dearest Ray,

For long dreary weeks I've been waiting for your letters and none have come. Ray, I have hundreds of questions I want to ask you, such as, have you found out yet when you will get back? Do you like being where you are now? Do you still think the war will be ended when your training is completed? What type of plane are you learning to pilot or are you going to be an instructor? Do you think you will be sent near the Pacific, some people tell me you may be sent there and not get back here until after the war. Right now I'm determined to stop worrying, although it's very hard not to, but I'm trying, Ray. I keep saying to myself, Ray will get back here early in the Spring, the war will be over then and in years far ahead I'll be sitting with my grandchildren around me, telling them of how I met their grandfather and advising them not to go out with the same boy twice unless he lives within a reasonable distance and there isn't a war on. I'm only joking, Ray, all the time we did have together is worth all this and the day you come back to me will more than compensate. In other words, I'm glad we met and I wouldn't change places with anyone else in the world.

I guess I better tell you what I did yesterday. I had to work all day and arrived back in Belfast at about 4:55 p.m. After tea I washed my hair for the second time this week and then I listened to a good pro-gramme on the wireless. About 9 o'clock I went upstairs and reread all of the letters I received since you went to America—rereading them made me feel better.

Tonight I didn't work late and arrived home about 6 p.m. — *Forever yours, Muriel*

Tuesday, December 7th

My Dearest Muriel,

Well, it's two years today that Japan attacked Pearl Harbor. Two years ago today I was in Raleigh, NC. I had just come out of a show and I heard about it. Two years, and a lot has happened since then. I wonder what I'll be doing two years from today. I often think about things like that, how about you?

I just came back from seeing Howard and Bill for a few minutes, it's the first chance I've had all day. You see, from 6 until 7:30 we can do as we please, walk the halls, etc., but after 7:30 we can't leave our rooms.

No mail again today... *—I adore you, Raymond*

Tuesday, December 7th

My Dearest Ray,

This is just a short letter as I'm writing in the office as I have to work late tonight and won't have much time when I get home. Right now there isn't much to tell you, everything is just the same. Today is another dull, misty day.

If I was receiving your letters I would have more to write about, but somehow, it's very hard to write when I'm not hearing from you. *—I love you, Muriel*

Wednesday, December 8th

My Dearest Muriel,

Another day has passed and still no mail, it's now 9 days since I've heard from you. I wish there was something new I could tell you, but really there isn't.

Today I heard that they are washing out (failing) a lot of the boys that went to Nashville last month, as much as 60% of the class. You see, Muriel, after 5 or 6 months we are sent to Nashville, Tennessee. This is the classification center where we will be told if we are going to be a pilot or what have you. If you are washed out, and very high percentages are, well, then you are through. If that happens to me I'll put in for Foreign Service to Ireland or England. They may want to send me to school for mechanic or something with the ground crew, but as that would take another 5 or 6 months I'll turn it down and try to get back as soon as possible.

It's about 7:30 so I have to start with my studies. —*I adore you, Raymond*

Thursday, December 9th

My Dearest Muriel,

It's the tenth day and still no letter, I'm a little worried. Today I received a letter from Mother. She told me she was very glad to hear you have received our packages. She wrote you a letter and a Christmas card, have you received them?

Take care of yourself and remember me to everyone.   —*I adore you, Raymond*

Thursday, December 9th

My Dearest Ray,

For 6 or 7 weeks the world seemed dismal and full of troubles because I hadn't heard from you and was very worried. Now I'm feeling wonderful and the world is a beautiful place. I'm nuts, Ray, but what can be expected when I received seven letters from you today and another package from your mother. Honest, Ray, you've no idea how much better I feel. Tonight I came home from the office telling myself there wouldn't be any letters from you so that I wouldn't be disappointed. I guess I'd better start from the beginning.

Last night I worked overtime at the office and when I arrived home at 8:30 p.m. and discovered there were no letters from you, words can't describe just how awful I felt. I've had a head cold these last few days so I took a hot drink and some aspirin and went straight to bed. Everybody, or nearly everybody I know has a cold or flu, I guess it is the cold damp weather which is causing it. It is very misty and very dark, even during the day time. Anyhow, my cold was a little better today. Tonight I didn't think I would have to work late, but at the last minute the boss asked me if I would work until 6:30. Betty, one of the girls, couldn't get her analysis to balance and he wanted me to help her find out what was wrong. I arrived home at about 7:35 p.m. and just as I was walking up the street I got a very big surprise. I walked right into Joe and Fay—they had just been after leaving the package from your mother at our house. They are living at Balmoral now and they told me to call and see them anytime I wanted to. By the way, Joe has written to you and I sincerely hope you manage to find a little time to write to him. I asked how the baby was and they said he was very well and growing big. When I left them and got home another very delightful surprise was awaiting me—your seven letters. Your mother is a darling, Ray, she sent me soap, bath perfume, nail varnish, oh, all kinds of toilet articles, and a lovely silk underskirt. She also sent a Christmas card and wrote a little note on the back of it. One sentence of it is, "I asked Ray ---------- and being a boy he didn't know." (*Stop*)

Sunday, December 12th

My Dearest Ray,

I've finally got back to writing this letter and I have so much to say I don't know where to begin. Yesterday I wrote and told you about the bundle of letters I received. I mailed the letter last night so you should receive it before you receive this one. Now I'll start telling you why I couldn't finish this one on Thursday night and why I couldn't write on Friday. Thursday night I didn't arrive home until about 8 o'clock as I stood talking to Joe and Fay for quite a while, they both send their regards and hope you are well. When I got in the house Mommy had supper ready and with taking supper, reading all your lovely letters and looking at all the very nice presents your mother sent, it was almost bedtime before I knew. I started this letter but didn't have time to finish it. On Friday night I worked until 7 p.m. and didn't get home until 8:15 p.m. When I got in the house I almost went crazy with joy as there were another 7 letters awaiting me. Mommy and Daddy were invited into Aunt Vi's house to play cards so Mommy asked me to bath Audrey and Olive and put them to bed and you know how hard it is to coax them to bed. By the time I finally did make them go and got to reading your letters, it was too late to start writing to you.

On Saturday we stopped working at 12:15 and I arrived in Belfast at about 1 o'clock. I didn't come home, instead I went into town to buy a pair of shoes. Mommy gave me the money and coupons for a birthday present. The town is as crowded as ever these days with people doing their Christmas shopping and I had to wait in the shop for ages before it was my turn to be served. Anyhow, I was lucky, I got a very nice pair of black suede shoes—almost the last pair they had in the shop. You see they have stopped making that kind now and very soon they won't be selling anything but wooden clogs. Have you ever seen them, Ray, I guess not, but lots of girls are wearing them and you'd hear them a mile away.

When I arrived home at 3:30 I can't express how very happy and delighted I was to find another 7 letters from you. While I was reading your letters Mommy said to me, "Muriel, I want to do some shopping so will you come into town with me and I'll buy you a new dress for Christmas." Although I didn't feel like pushing through the crowds in town again, I couldn't refuse Mommy so we did go and I got a very nice woolen dress. While I was in the shop I tried on some coats. One of them (cream colour) looked so very nice on me I couldn't resist buying it, but I couldn't bring it home because neither Mommy nor I had any coupons left. Anyhow, I paid for it and the girl in the shop is keeping it until I give her the coupons. We don't get anymore until February but maybe Aunt Vi will have some to lend me.

So you are at college now, Ray, I'm so glad to hear that only I'm so sorry that you're so far from home. I'm also very glad to have your new address. So they called you Dodos and made you do all sorts of crazy things the first two weeks you were there. Fancy making you all fall out with just your shorts on and no shoes, and some of the boys with nothing at all on. Were they not embarrassed standing in their birthday suits?

No, Marie hasn't gone to England—she is living at home and still working.

Thanks for the snaps and the Air Corps patch, I wish I could write much more but it's almost 8 o'clock and I have to visit my Aunt Margaret's house. —*Forever yours, Muriel*

Friday, December 10th

My Dearest Muriel,

It's 9:15 so I'll have to write this in a hurry. We just got back from a Graduation Exercise, 160 boys graduated today and tomorrow they are leaving for Nashville, Tennessee.

I didn't receive any letters from you today. This is the 11th day, or is it the 12th, anyway it's a long time. Now I know how you feel when you don't get any letters from me.

Tomorrow is going to be a rough day as we have inspections and a parade—I wish I could miss it all. I'll have to stop now as the lights go out at 10 and there are still a lot of things I have to do. —*I adore you, Raymond*

Saturday, December 11th

My Dearest Ray,

I'm so happy now I'm going nuts, honest, I can hardly realize it. I've received 21 letters from you, 7 on Thursday, 7 on Friday and 7 today! What a break, after waiting for weeks. I'm really sorry I wrote so many blue letters to you and caused you to worry so much about me, but your letters have acted like a wonderful tonic to me and I'll never have cause to get so depressed again. Right now I have so many things to do I can't write anymore, but will explain why tomorrow. I just had to write this short letter now and tell you how wonderful I feel and make you feel better too. —*I adore you, Muriel*

Sunday, December 12th

My Dearest Muriel,

Here it is 13 days from Christmas and I can hardly believe it. I didn't write yesterday as they let us out at 4 o'clock so we could go into town and do some Christmas shopping. I got myself some Christmas cards and a few odds and ends. Howard had to buy his girl a Christmas present and I'm still laughing about it. He went in a women's store to buy his girl a bathrobe (I waited outside) and it was funny. His face was red when he walked in and when he came out. A sales girl put the robe on to let Howard see how it would fit and they asked him questions such as, are you married, if not, how soon will you? When he came out he was sweating.

After supper we went to a show and saw "For Whom the Bell Tolls." Honest, my love, you really have to see that picture. Gary Cooper and Ingrid Bergman played in it. She reminded me so much of you in the way she loved him, and he her. His last words to her were, "You're part of me now so carry on." Honest, Muriel, if anything did happen to me I would want you to carry on as Gary told her. Remember when I left and you came running around the corner to say good-bye again? You'll never know how hard it was for me to say "Cheerio" to you. If I didn't love you as I do, I never would have been able to tell you to go back. (That's me in the picture.) Honest, my insides felt as if they had been dragged out of me. Gosh, I love you, Muriel.

This morning I got up at 11 o'clock and after dinner (about 1:30) six of us went into town and saw the show "Government Girl" with Olivia de Havilland and Sonny Tufts. It was silly but very good—it took me out of the awful mood I was in. At five we left to come back to camp and before coming to the barracks we stopped and had supper.

I still haven't heard from you, it's now 13 days ...   —*I adore you, Raymond*

Monday, December 13th

My Dearest Muriel,

This is the 14th day that I haven't heard from you, gosh, I really wish I would soon.

I just got off guard duty—I went in at 6 and got off at 8:30. I go back again at 12:00 and stay until 2:00. Looks like I won't get much sleep tonight.

Today we started our new schedule and Muriel, it's awful. Before we were always rushed but now it's even more so. We don't get through supper now until 7:15 and we have to be in our rooms by eight. We don't even have time to read our mail. Everyone is mad— our work has just about doubled.

Only eight more days till your birthday and you'll be 21. Now you'll be able to do as you please. Yes, a young lady and darn it, I would have to be here.   —*Forever yours, Raymond*

Monday, December 13th

My Dearest Ray,

As I start writing this letter the time is 9:55 p.m. and I just got back from the office and had supper. Honest, Ray, I never worked so many hours each day in all my life. As you know I work in the Bonus Section of the Cost Office and such an office, Ray, the work is endless and we have to work a great deal more because of the Christmas holidays.

When I got home a short while ago it was to find that Daddy is sick with the flu and wasn't at work today. He wasn't too well last night and I had an idea he was taking the flu, as nearly everyone is sick with it here.

Ray, although I haven't much time to write anymore I want to say something about the letter you wrote telling me if you don't get back in March or April it may mean you may not get back for another year and you want me to come over to you. I don't think I'll mention anything to Daddy until I know definitely that you can't get back. To tell you the truth I'm worried about what he might say and I know Mommy will go crazy. Ray, please don't ever think badly of her, you know your mother would feel the same way if you were coming here to live.   —*Forever yours, Muriel*

Tuesday, December 14th

My Dearest Muriel,

Another day has passed and still no mail, I hope I hear from you soon, I'm getting very restless. It's just about 7:30 and I just came back from supper, it's awful, Muriel, we're on the go from 6:00 in the morning till 7:30 at night. Believe it or not, everyone here is fed up. I just saw Bill for a few minutes and he was saying how he wishes he were back also, so you see, I'm not the only one. Bill got a letter from a lady there that used to invite him and a bunch of the boys over, and she was telling Bill how many Americans were over there. I hope you are careful and take care of yourself. Please don't go out too often, and don't stay out too late as it's dangerous. Maybe you think I'm crazy, but I do worry about it very much.

I have quite a cold today—I got some medicine for it tonight. (Nose drops) Last night on guard duty I almost froze.

Well, my love, I better stop now as I have a lot of homework to do.   —*I adore you, Raymond*

Wednesday, December 15th

My Dearest Ray,

Yesterday I had to work until 8:30 p.m. and the train leaving Lisburn was late. I didn't arrive in the house until about 9:30 and boy was I tired and sleepy. When I got home a very happy surprise was awaiting me, yes, another 3 letters from you. I read your letters while I was having supper. No, I'm not mad at you for saying I can allow someone I know to leave me to the tram or walk home with me. It just goes to show that you really love me and trust me a lot. You are very understanding, Ray, but I want you to know that I prefer to come home alone. Perhaps I'm silly but I can't help it. Somehow I keep thinking of the nights we walked home together and I know I wouldn't feel right walking with anyone else.

Right now Mommy is calling me down for supper and telling me I'll have to get to bed early as I missed the train this morning and had to get a later one. Mommy finds it hard to awaken me in the mornings and now she won't go to bed unless I go too.

As yet I haven't written to your Mother but honest, Ray, I never have time and feel awful for not doing so. Take care of yourself. — *Forever yours, Muriel*

Thursday, December 16th

My Dearest Muriel,

I didn't write yesterday as I will explain. I told you Monday I had a cold, well, it kept getting worse and Wednesday morning I reported to the doctor. To make a long story short I had a fever, so here I am in the hospital at Camp Butner. I came up with six other boys. I was quite sick last night but feel much better today. I don't know how long I'll be here, I hope to leave by Saturday—if I get too far behind in my classes I'll never catch up.

We have been on a liquid diet and boy, I'm hungry, juice is all they'll give us. Maybe tomorrow we can go on a regular diet, I hope so.

I'll be out of here in a few days so don't worry about me, Muriel. —*I love you, Raymond*

Thursday, December 16th

My Dearest Ray,

It's about 9:20 and I just arrived home from the office about an hour ago. Honest, Ray, I have never been so busy in all my life as I am now since starting in my new job. As yet I haven't been able to answer all your letters. Ray, please don't be mad at me for taking the job in *censored*. I like it and feel better since taking it. Another thing, don't worry, they'll never send me to England and I'm just as safe, if not safer, than I was in Inglis. The place where I'm working is an aircraft factory and now I feel that I am doing my part in helping to end the war. It's a small part, not like the big share you'll be doing soon, but nevertheless it has to be done and I want to do it. Now you are in the Air Corps and I'm in an aircraft factory—what more can we do. Sometimes I see the planes being made and feel like getting into one and flying over to you. Such a crazy idea, even if I could take one I wouldn't know the first thing about flying it.

Olive is just after telling me that supper is ready so once again I'll have to end this letter in a hurry wishing that I could have more time to write. God bless and keep you safe. —*Forever yours, Muriel*

PS I'm glad you received the disc and like it. So the fellows call me your wife, tell them from me, I'll never be anyone else's.

Saturday, December 18th

My Dearest Muriel,

It's about six o'clock and I just finished my supper, if you want to call it that. I had a slice of bread and a few potatoes. The other three days I lived on juices. Last night I was sick again but today I feel much better. I asked the doctor when I was getting out of here and he said maybe Monday or Tuesday, I sure hope so.

Last night I had a woman from the Red Cross come up here to send you a cable, it's for your birthday. She told me I couldn't send any greeting such as Happy Birthday or Merry Christmas, so we made up what I did send you, hoping it would make it through. I said "No letters for two weeks." (Actually, it's almost 3.) "Thinking of you on the 21st and always, love, Raymond." I hope it got there on time.

One of my roommates came here yesterday to have his teeth worked on and after he was through he stopped in to see me. He brought a letter from Mother and the newspaper, yes—I get a hometown newspaper here at camp. He didn't have much to say as he'd had a tooth pulled and couldn't talk.

One thing I can say about this place is that I'm getting enough sleep, boy, it's good to lay in bed and not worry about getting up. Nice, quiet and peaceful, not bad at all, I'm just a little restless, but not much.

Take good care of yourself and don't worry about me, I'm coming along fine and will be out of here in a few days.   *—I adore you, Raymond*

Saturday, December 18th

My Dearest Ray,

Here I am again writing to you, and not being able to find the words to thank you enough for the beautiful presents you have sent. Last night when I got home from the office there was another package awaiting me and honest, Ray, I'm delighted with what it contains. Although it said on the lids of the two boxes inside, "Do not open till Xmas," I didn't notice that until it was too late. All I know is that I put one of the lids on the cabinet and Daddy lifted it and said, "Muriel, it says here do not open till Xmas, is this Christmas?" Ray, you should have written that outside the package in big writing, but I'm glad you didn't because I doubt I could have waited until then.

The manicure set is beautiful and except yourself you couldn't have sent anything I'd appreciate more. The little vanity powder bag is beautiful too, Ray, I'll be able to put my lipstick in it and always carry it while I'm dancing. Thanks a million too, for the good old Phillip Morris cigarettes, boy, do they bring back happy memories of the times when you took them off me and threw them in the fire. Remember, sometimes when I wanted to smoke you told me I smoked too much and then we would start fighting.

Ray, I think I've stopped a dozen times since I started this letter. Once Yvonne called and I had to talk to her for awhile, now I'm just back from having tea. While I was having tea I listened to the 6 o'clock news on the wireless. One thing I didn't like hearing the announcer say was that there was a flu epidemic in America and thousands of people have died from it in Washington. Is Washington far from where you are, Ray, I hope so. Please take care of yourself and watch you don't take it because it is a very dangerous sickness. Every time I read the newspapers I see reports of train and launch disasters in America, and so many soldiers being killed in them. I wish you were back here where nothing like that happens. By the way, Daddy had the flu but he is better now, thank goodness. I was thinking the flu epidemic was caused by the bad weather we're having here, but it mustn't be that because it's in England and Germany too.

Last night Aunt Vi, Uncle Harold and another couple came in and they along with Mommy and Daddy had a kind of party in the sitting room. I wanted very much to write you but I had to put Audrey and Olive to bed, wash my hair and help Mommy make supper. Uncle Harold wanted me to play the piano but I was so busy I hadn't even time to do that.

I'll have to stop writing now as I have to get ready to meet Adeline at 7:40. As I haven't been out since last Sunday I think I'll go with her to the Red Cross tonight.

I know you are being good, Ray, but please take very good care of yourself for somehow I worry in case you get sick.   —*Forever yours,* *Muriel*

Sunday, December 19ᵗʰ

My Dearest Ray,

As I start writing this letter I can hear Christmas carols being played over the wireless, (radio) and can't help feeling sad. Remember about this time last year you were here and the carol singers stood singing outside the door.

Just think, on Tuesday I'll be 21 years of age and no one on earth will be able to keep me from marrying you. The girls and boys in the office are wanting me to have a party, but I said, no, I was going to celebrate later on. Remember the party you planned for me at Dot's house last year, I'll never, never forget that night, Ray. You gave me the locket then, everybody admires it, and when they ask where I got the lovely little heart shaped locket I tell them you gave it to me on my 20th birthday. My ring is often admired too and I'll never, never, take it off.

Last night I met Adeline and we went to the dance in the Red Cross. What a place, Ray, it was so crowded I could hardly even get moving. The band was very good and the crowd quite jolly. In a way I had fun but as usual I couldn't really be happy because you weren't with me. Yes, Ray, the boys can see the big ring I'm wearing but they just ignore it. One in particular never gives me a moment's peace. He follows me around always coaxing me to go out with him and no matter how much I refuse he keeps insisting. Honest, Ray, he's impossible and I never met anyone so determined in all my life. (*except you*) Last night he must have gotten wise to me slipping past him because when I got out of the cloakroom he was standing right beside the door and caught my arm before I could get away. In a way it was very funny, Ray, I said to him, "How many more times have I got to impress upon you that you are not leaving me home," and all he did was stand there and say, "I am." The look on his face was so funny I had to laugh and said, "Oh, you are," then I pushed him, rushed through the crowds, and ran into the street. When I was running up Chichester Street in the blackout, I could hear him shouting after me—"Merle, will you be at the dance tomorrow afternoon." He kept on shouting but I didn't answer him. He always calls me Merle, why I don't know because I've told him dozens of times that my name is Muriel, not Merle. I guess he can't say Muriel.

Anyhow, today, just as I was about to begin writing to you, Yvonne called wanting me to go with her to the dance this afternoon. I told Yvonne I wanted to write to you and your mother and didn't feel like going to the dance so she went on alone.

Just as she was leaving Greta came to the door so I had to let her in. Greta was in the mood for talking so I lit the fire in the sitting room and all afternoon we talked about nothing in particular. I showed her the lovely presents you and your mother sent and she says I'm the luckiest girl she ever knew. I know I am, Ray—I have you—that's the main reason, besides I don't believe there's another girl in Belfast who's got so much lovely makeup and nail varnish. Lots of girls would give anything to have the lovely presents I have. I love them even more because you sent them.

Greta stayed all afternoon and had tea with me and she didn't leave until after 7 p.m. That is why I'm in a hurry to finish this letter and want to write to your mother, I know I won't have time next week. Please don't worry about me, I'm safe and well. —*Forever yours, Muriel*

Monday, December 20ᵗʰ

My Dearest Muriel,

I'm writing this letter from the hospital, I'm being let out tomorrow, thank goodness.

Today I received 4 of your letters. Muriel, maybe I shouldn't say this, but when I read your letter about going 20 miles to a dance, losing your coat, and of Joe and Benny (every letter has Joe and Benny in it) my blood just boiled. I want you to promise, no more out of town dances. I know it's OK for you to go to the Red Cross dances but I'm jealous, I can't help it. Once in a while is OK but not 2 or 3 times a week. It was very nice of Joe and Benny to go through all the trouble of looking for your coat and I know they feel bad, but as to them buying you a coat, don't take money or coupons from them. I'll buy you a coat when I come back. I know Benny is a swell fellow and maybe he hasn't tried to kiss you, but sometimes I think he has and you didn't write and tell me. Please tell me more about yourself, it's you I love and I want to know everything you do, how you feel, and what you think.

Tomorrow is your birthday and you will be 21 years old, now you can do as you please, but remember, Muriel, don't do anything you will regret later. I hope you received the telegram I sent you. My heart aches for you and words can't describe how much I love and miss you. —*I adore you, Raymond*

Monday, December 20ᵗʰ

My Dearest Ray,

I just arrived home 10 minutes ago to find a cable awaiting me and I don't need to tell you how happy I am to receive it. I'm very sorry to hear you haven't received any letters from me for two weeks, I understand how you must feel.

I had to stop and have tea, Greta is supposed to call at 7:30 and I'm to go with her to Albert Whites. Well, I'm not going, Ray, that is where I met you and I know if I saw the place again it would make me feel worse than ever. I think I'll stop writing now and hurry out to the Majestic before Greta calls. I forgot the name of the picture that is showing but I heard it was quite good. —*Forever yours, Muriel*

Monday, December 20th
Lockport, NY

Dear Muriel,

This is just a note to tell you that we are all still alive and fairly well, as we have been ill with the flu.

I am Josephine, Ray's oldest sister, writing these few lines to you. Ray is fine but won't be able to be home for Christmas with us. We will all miss him so, and do hope and pray that next Christmas we will all be together again.

Muriel, don't be surprised if you receive callers. My uncle and husband are both in England and you can never tell what they are apt to do.

We often think of you and wish you could be over here with us. Maybe that day will be sooner than we think. Let us hope so. I will write you again soon, I promise. We all send you our love, and regards to your fine parents. —*Love, "Jo"*

Tuesday, December 21st

My Dearest Muriel,

All day long I have been thinking of you more than ever, wishing I was there with you. I hope you had a nice birthday and received my present and telegram.

Tonight I am back at camp—yes, I was discharged this afternoon, thank goodness. I still ache all over but I have 3 days where I only have to go to classes, no drill or exercises, so I'll be able to rest up a little. I still have to write home and tell Mother about myself at the hospital, as yet I haven't told her a thing.

We don't get much time off for Christmas, just Friday afternoon and all day Saturday and Sunday. It seems funny, I'm in the States and can't go home—I'm so far away. Honest, my love, I'm so homesick (mostly for you) I'll have to spend Christmas here alone. Many of the boys are having their wives or girlfriends come down, but us, I guess we'll have to do like last year, cry. —*Happy Birthday, my love, I adore you, Raymond*

PS I had the flu but I'm over it now.

Tuesday, December 21st

My Dearest Ray,

All day long I've hardly been able to concentrate in the office with thinking that I'm 21 now and can marry you if you come back tomorrow. I keep thinking of this time last year. You were here and we had a party which was the most wonderful party of my life. Remember you planned it as a surprise for me at Dot's house and gave me the locket which I love and am wearing now. Just about everybody in the office yelled "Happy Birthday" the moment I arrived this morning.

At the moment I'm chewing a piece of the gum that you sent. I gave the kids some and ever since they've been saying, "Muriel, I'll do anything for you if only you'll give me a piece of your gum." They love it and I'm keeping some to put in their stockings on Christmas Eve.

Tonight I arrived home about 6 p.m. and received a lot of birthday cards from different people I know. Miss Laverack from the Red Cross sent me a card saying there's going to be a party there on Boxing Day and she wants me to go down tomorrow night for square dancing practice. She said she is only inviting a few couples tomorrow night to practice so that they can teach the others during the party on Boxing Day. As regards to that party, Mommy and Daddy saw the card and told me I wasn't even to think of going to a party on a Sunday. There is a dance on Thursday, Friday and Saturday at the Red Cross and I'd be the happiest girl in the world if you were here to go with me. To tell the truth I wish Christmas was over because I'm going to feel more lonely than ever. If I stay in the house all through the holidays I'll go crazy missing you and if I go to the dances it will be the same, the only difference being that if I go to the dances I'll see some of the girls I know there, and have someone to talk to.

Mommy has just sent my cousin Betty to the door to tell me to make supper for Audrey, Olive and myself and put them to bed. Mommy and Daddy have gone into Aunt Vi's house. Aunt Vi has some friends from England living with her and I think they are having some sort of party. —*Forever yours, Muriel*

PS After writing to you last night I went to the Majestic by myself to see "Three Hearts for Julia." It was quite a good picture. When I got home I asked Mommy if Greta had called and she said, "No." It didn't surprise me because Greta never could stick to her promises.

Wednesday, December 22nd

My Dearest Muriel,

It's about 8:30 now and I just got through writing all my Christmas cards, I'm late with many of them but it couldn't be helped.

Today I have felt much better. I have missed so much work I don't think I'll ever catch up. After class I went to bed until 6 o'clock. (I'm excused from drill for three days.)

I have been thinking all day as to what you will be doing Christmas. I suppose you'll be at the Red Cross—on New Year's Eve also. I wish you wouldn't go but by the time you receive this it will be over and forgotten. This Christmas is going to be as bad as last year, but it's all my fault so I shouldn't cry.   —*Forever yours, Raymond*

Thursday, December 23rd

My Dearest Ray,

As I begin writing to you the time is about 8 p.m. There is a dance at the Red Cross tonight but I'm not going because I want to write to you, wash my hair and countless other things.

Last night Yvonne called and I lit a fire in the sitting room and we sat talking. She told me the latest happenings at Inglis and I told her all about my new job and how much I like it. When Yvonne came last night I got a surprise, she has got engaged to a civilian boy. I can't believe that she really loves her boyfriend because she goes out with others behind his back. She says she thinks she loves her boyfriend and might as well be engaged and in the fashion, but nevertheless, she said, "I'm going to have a good time before I get married, because once I do I'll be tied down." Can you believe that? When you were here I dreaded the nights I wasn't seeing you and could hardly wait until the nights I was going out with you. Often I think of the first night we met and believe that I must have fallen in love with you right from the beginning.

Today Evelyn Agnew (she sits beside me) told me something that quite surprised me. She said, "Before you started working here the word got around the office that a new girl was coming and she was engaged to an American." I asked her how she discovered that but she said she didn't know who told it first, she just happened to overhear some girls talking in the cloakroom. I think it must have been Peggy, you see she left Inglis and started working in Short & Harland before I did, and when she heard I was coming most likely she told the others. Peggy works in an office way at the other end of the factory and I seldom see her.

When I got off the train tonight an American stopped me and asked me where the Red Cross was. I asked him if he hadn't been there before and he said he had only landed in Ireland a few weeks, was stationed in the country and been to the Red Cross a fortnight ago but had forgotten where it was. As I was going into town to send you a cable I said to him, "I am going in the direction of the Red Cross, so if you care to walk with me I'll show you where it is." On the way there he told me that so far he liked this country, but he was home last Christmas and was wishing he could spend Christmas home this year, too. Honest, Ray, I felt sorry for the poor soul and told him to cheer up, the war would be over soon and I felt sure he would be home next Christmas. When we arrived near the City Hall I directed him where to go, and then left him to send a cable to you.

Ray, I sincerely hope you will be spending Christmas with your family. In some of your letters you said you weren't sure if you would get home but as I wanted to be on the safe side, I sent the cable to your home address and hope you get it on the 25th.   *—Forever yours, Muriel*

Friday, December 24th

My Dearest Muriel,

Here it is one day before Christmas and to me it still doesn't seem like Christmas, I guess it never will until we are together, honest, my love, I miss you more than ever.

I didn't write last night as I was too miserable. It's hard for me, I haven't got you and I'm not at home, so I have two reasons to be so unhappy.

I'm glad you like the makeup set and stockings—that was the first pair of stockings I ever bought so I'm very proud you like them. Please use the makeup set and when we're together I'll get you a better one. I hope you received the Christmas present I sent from Greensboro, I think you will like it, I sure hope so. As to why you're not receiving my letters and you still haven't received any from Raleigh (your letter of November 18th) I really can't understand that.

Muriel, my love, I love you and you love me—that's the only present I want—keep loving me as always and I'll have everything so don't go and buy me anything, I don't need anything and what I want you can't buy.

I'm glad you like your work even though it's harder and longer hours, anyway, it will make the time go by faster, I find it's the same here, before I know it the week is over.   *—Forever yours, Raymond*

Friday, December 24th

My Dearest Ray,

Daddy bought a turkey and an aunt of Mommy's who lives in the country sent her a duck, so part of this afternoon I helped Mommy stuff the turkey and then I did some sewing. After that I began washing some stockings and undies and while I was doing that a knock came at the door and who was it but the man I love next to you—wouldn't you like to know who he is, well, I'll tell you, he's the postman and he gave me three lovely letters from you. (November 25, 26, 27) I stopped washing so I could read them—then I continued washing and after that went upstairs and took a bath. When I was finished bathing it was about 5:30 p.m. so I came downstairs. Mommy was resting on the couch so I made the tea and as Daddy is working all night tonight I got his lunch ready. There was a dance at the Red Cross tonight but I didn't want to go because I knew if I did I wouldn't have time to write to you.

So you had a big turkey dinner which was really good, well, I'm going to have one tomorrow. The turkey is cooking in the oven at this very moment and it smells good. So the boys were allowed to bring their wives to the Thanksgiving dinner you had, gosh, Ray, I wish I could have been there.

I haven't seen my cousin Gloria yet but someday soon I'll go to Bangor and get talking to her. Ray, if you didn't get back in the spring-time and I did go over there perhaps you would be sent someplace else. What then?? I would be in America and you someplace else and things would be as bad as ever.

Exactly this day last year you left Ireland to go to England. That reminds me of the row we had one Sunday night and I wouldn't go out with you again until the following Wednesday night, so you went out with Peter Rogers Wednesday afternoon and got tight. We went to the Classic that night and while we were waiting in line you showed me all the Christmas cards you bought. Then when we were coming home on the tram you kept telling me you loved me and kissed me right in front of everybody. Do you remember this, Ray, I can remember everything we did together, even the smallest little details.   —*Forever yours, Muriel*

Christmas Day, December 25th

My Dearest Muriel,

As you can see from the paper I'm writing this letter at the USO. It's about 5 o'clock and Bill, Howard and I just came out of the show. The picture we saw was "Lady Takes a Chance" with Jean Arthur and John Wayne. The picture was silly but good.

Muriel, my love, there is no need to tell you how much I'm loving and missing you, words can't describe how miserable I've been these past few days.

Last night Bill and I came to the USO—they had a dance and served food (I didn't dance). Three of the boys in my section had their wives down so we stayed with them until 11:30 and then we all went to midnight mass. It was a lovely mass and afterwards we went to get something to eat and then went back to camp. This morning I got up at eleven and went to dinner at 12:00, and I must say, Muriel, they really had a swell dinner for us, it cheered me up a little. Tonight looks like another miserable night. I'm going out to have supper and after that, I don't know. —*I love you, Raymond*

Saturday, December 25th

My Dearest Ray,

Right now the time is about 7:30 p.m. All day I tried to get writing to you but had so much to do I couldn't find the time. Yvonne is due to call for me and we're going to the Red Cross. We're going to meet Adeline in town at 8:00. To tell the truth I'm not keen on going, one reason being that you're not here to go with me (I won't enjoy myself without you) and the other I feel like I'm taking the cold because I've sneezed all day. However, I know you want me to be bright and cheerful so I'll do my best. —*Forever yours, Muriel*

Sunday, December 26th

My Dearest Muriel,

Well, this is the end of the Christmas holidays and they were anything but merry, as you know. This morning I got up at eleven o'clock and boy, it's good to sleep in late.

Last night after I wrote to you Bill, Howard and I went out to supper, then back to the USO as they were having a dance. It's a good thing they had a lot of magazines there, it's a good way to pass the time away. Honest, my love, I don't think I know how to dance anymore.

This room here is a mess, the boys haven't cleaned it since Friday so after I'm through with this letter I'm going to clean house, and it really needs it.

Everyone from home sends their regards to you. —*I love you, Raymond*

Monday, December 27th

My Dearest Muriel,

I got a Christmas package from Mother today, it was a little late in coming but I was glad to get it. I just had a phone call from Mother, I didn't tell you but I tried to call home Friday, Saturday and Sunday but I couldn't get through. Mother said she also tried to call me but couldn't get through. She told me you sent me a telegram for Christmas, Muriel my love, I really don't know what to say. I feel 1000% better. I would like to know how you can send Christmas greetings to me, but I can't to you, I tried and they wouldn't let me. Did you think I would be home for Christmas? Oh, Mother also told me that my sister Jo's husband is in England and was over to my old camp, so he may have seen Luke, I sure hope so. He has your address so he may come over to see you sometime. Remember I told you I had an uncle in Africa, in the armored division, well, he's in England now too.

I'm sending this drawing of myself I had made on Christmas Day. It doesn't look like me but I thought maybe you would like it. *—I adore you, Raymond*

Monday, December 27th

My Dearest Ray,

As I begin writing this letter the time is 3 p.m. and I have so much to tell you I don't know where to begin. On Christmas morning I got up around 9:30 and from then until about 2 p.m. I was kept very busy helping Mommy with the Christmas dinner. What a delicious dinner, Ray, turkey with all the trimmings.

After dinner I listened to the King's speech over the wireless (did you hear it), also the Christmas greetings from different countries all over the world. I had just started to write to you when Daddy asked me to go up to the Ormeau Road to Mr. & Mrs. Ellis's house and ask them to come down that night as they were going to have a party in Aunt Vi & Uncle Harold's house. I went to the Ellis house but didn't get home again until about six as I started talking to Lillian, their daughter, and she made me stay to have plum pudding cake and ginger wine. When I got home again and had tea and got dressed for the Red Cross, I only had time to write a short letter to you. Yvonne and I met Adeline in town and when we got to the Red Cross it was absolutely packed full of soldiers. Such a crowd, Ray, there wasn't room to walk never mind dance. It was just about impossible for a girl to get resting for 5 minutes because the fellows came over in droves asking for dances. Once when I was sitting talking to one of them, two others came over and tossed a coin to decide who was going to dance with me next. I used to think if the boys saw a girl talking to someone they wouldn't bother to come over, but they do. It really doesn't matter to me how many ask me to dance, but if you were here I wouldn't dance with anyone else in the room. I kept thinking of you and wondering how you were spending the day. The orchestra they had was very good, they played *Let's Get Lost, Silver Wings in the Moon Light, You'll Never Know Just How Much I Miss You, White Christmas, That Old Black Magic*, and countless other popular tunes including *If I Had My Way*. They are all underlined because I like them all, especially *Let's Get Lost*, do you know it? Anyway, I left the dance at 10:30 and came home alone. During the evening several fellows asked if they could walk home with me and if I would go out with them, but I refused and when some of them asked why not, I didn't bother to say or argue with them.

When I got home, Betty and Ray, along with a few other kids were in the house having a party with Audrey and Olive. I made them all supper and after they went home put Audrey and Olive to bed. Then I went to bed myself as I was tired and felt like I was taking the cold. When I awakened Sunday morning I felt awful and could hardly lift my head off the pillow. Mommy brought my breakfast up and told me to spend the day in bed. Anyhow, Ray, I stayed in bed most of the day and got up at seven for a few hours. I wanted to write to you but didn't because my eyes were heavy and I had a sore head. I went to bed again about 11 p.m. and this morning Audrey came up to awaken me and give me two letters. Honest, Ray, I could hardly believe my eyes. I got 3 letters on Friday, 3 on Saturday and now 2 more today. By the way, today I feel much better although I'm sure I've used up about a dozen handkerchiefs since I got up at dinnertime today.

So the only reason you think of Ireland is me. I like that but then I can't say anything because you never travelled around her to see all the beauty spots. Yes, it's a beautiful country and you should think of it as well as me.

Ray, I didn't see Luke and Marie's wedding, it was just a marriage of convenience in a Registry Office here, and they have invited us to the big wedding they're going to have back home in America.

Ray, I'm very glad it was you who chose the presents for me, they were just what I wanted and I love them. You keep asking me to let you know if I want anything, well, if I did want anything I can't let you know because the censors don't allow anyone to ask or express willingness to receive anything from America.

You say you're only having one day off for Christmas and not getting home, I'm very sorry to hear that, Ray. I sent a cable to your home address so most likely you'll get it sometime next week. As I haven't been outside the door since Christmas night and I am fed up being in the house, I think I'll go to a show tonight.   —*Forever yours, Muriel*

Tuesday, December 28th

My Dearest Muriel,

There's nothing new to tell you tonight, only that it's raining and we had to go to supper and coming back we got all wet. I just got back from seeing Bill and Howard. Bill will start flying January 3rd. I won't know until tomorrow if I start on January 3rd or February 3rd. After we are through here (March at the latest) we will be sent to Nashville to be classified or washed out.

It's raining very hard now and the rain is hitting the windows and gosh, does it bring back memories, the sweetest memories of all my life.   —*I love you, Raymond*

Wednesday, December 29th

My Dearest Muriel,

I found out today I'm not flying until February, we will start either the 3rd or the 9th of the month, then on March 9th I will move to Nashville, Tennessee. It looks like Bill will start flying this month and will be leaving Howard and me. It's going to be hard to see Bill go after we three have been together for so long—April 23rd 1944 will be three years.   —*I love you, Raymond*

Wednesday, December 29th

My Dearest Ray,

It's three o'clock and I'm writing this letter in bed and not feeling too good. The last letter I wrote was on Monday and I told you I had a cold, but was going to the pictures. Well, I did go and now I know I shouldn't have gone feeling the way that I did. Of all the colds I've had this has been the worst, but I feel lots better now and hope I'm quite better and able to go to work tomorrow. Somehow, when I'm at work it keeps my mind occupied, whereas while I'm at home, I keep worrying and thinking about us and get very depressed.   —*Forever yours, Muriel*

Thursday, December 30th

My Dearest Muriel,

I shouldn't be writing this letter to you tonight as I have four tests tomorrow and need all my time to study, but I received a letter today from Mother and inside it she had your telegram—it was wonderful to receive it. It seems the more I try to keep my mind off you during the day so I can study, the more I think about you. It's funny, every little thing that happens I think of you and all the little things we did when we were together. Like when it rains, or when I'm on a long walk or someone mentions Ireland, or even at a show. It seems that you're right beside me only I can't reach out and touch you. When I'm at the show with Bill or Howard I always look by my side to see if you are next to me, crazy things like that, but I can't help it. When I left Ireland I brought half of you with me it seems, now if I could only get the other half I would really be happy. I've gotten so I don't care if I make it in the Air Corps or not, all I want is to get back to you. I didn't think I would ever love a girl more than the Air Corps but I guess you win.

Yes, I made a great mistake when I left but maybe it's for the best because now I realize how much I do love you. Before I wasn't sure if it was the Air Corps or you, well, it's you and you forever. Of course I'm in the Air Corps now so can't drop out unless I'm washed out, but if I do wash out I'll stay out of it for good, I promise you, Muriel. When I leave here March 9th and go to Nashville, I'll know within a week if I made it or not. It's funny how a girl can change a man's life, but I love it so stay with me and don't ever, ever leave me. Honest, my love, I haven't been happy since the day I left you. Please wait for me.
—*I Love you, Raymond*

Thursday, December 30th

My Dearest Ray,

By now I expect you know that I haven't been feeling too well since Christmas and had to stay in bed for a few days. Last night after tea time I got up and went downstairs for a few hours then went back to bed again at 10:30. Mommy wanted me to stay off work today again, but I knew how busy they are at the office and not only that, I was feeling lots better and didn't want to stay in bed another day. Anyhow, Ray, I went to work today and I'm glad I did. I still have a head cold but otherwise I feel fine. Now I may as well tell you it was a touch of the flu I had, but I'm better now except for the cold so please don't worry. You know how common colds are here (you ought to) and they don't mean a thing. Remember we used to take colds in turn when you were here, we had fun then.

When I arrived home tonight I was delighted to receive another letter from you. Lately I've been receiving them more often and I'm very grateful for that.

It's funny, Ray, all the girls I know here are running around having "a wonderful time" as they put it and yet I wouldn't change places with any of them. I'd rather be me waiting for you even though it is dull and miserable while you're away. If I didn't love you so much, I too could be going out a lot but I never want to do that. There's one thing I'm thankful for, I'm decent and not like a great many of the other girls I can't help noticing. If you could only see them, Ray, it's disgraceful, they flirt with all the fellows they meet and make themselves as cheap as dirt. Sometimes I overhear scraps of conversations in the dance or down in the cloakroom and honestly, it isn't nice. I get so disgusted and mad I feel like asking the girls and fellows if they have no respect for themselves. This town is overrun with soldiers and rotten girls, most of them were decent in pre-war days, but now—you know the rest. (They've just gone to the dogs.)

Adeline and one of her girlfriends have called to see me and right now they're waiting in the sitting room while I finish this letter. I'm really glad they have called because I get lonely for someone to talk to.
—*Forever yours, Muriel*